Jill S. Gilbert

SAMS
Teach Yourself

TurboTax® Deluxe

in 24 Hours

SAMS

A Division of Macmillan Computer Publishing
201 West 103rd St., Indianapolis, Indiana, 46290 USA

Sams Teach Yourself TurboTax Deluxe in 24 Hours

Copyright © 1999 by Sams Publishing

International Standard Book Number: 0-672-31360-X

Library of Congress Catalog Card Number: 98-85305

Printed in the United States of America

First Printing: 1999

00 99   4   3   2   1

Trademarks

EXECUTIVE EDITOR
Angela Wethington

ACQUISITIONS EDITOR
Jamie Milazzo

DEVELOPMENT EDITOR
Brian Proffitt

MANAGING EDITOR
Thomas F. Hayes

PROJECT EDITOR
Lori A. Lyons

COPY EDITOR
Shanon Martin

TECHNICAL EDITORS
Patty Brooks
Jo Ann Schiller
Dan Welytok

INDEXER
Larry Sweazy

PROOFREADER
Tricia Sterling

LAYOUT TECHNICIAN
Christy M. Lemasters

COVER DESIGNER
Aren Howell

BOOK DESIGNER
Gary Adair

Overview

Contents

Dedication

To my husband, Dan, and my little writing buddies Tara, Julia, and Daniel.

Acknowledgments

I'd like to acknowledge my book-writing relatives, Stan and Jane Schatt. (Isn't this fun?)

Also New Horizons Computer Learning Center in Milwaukee for excellent training and support.

Tell Us What You Think!

As the reader of this book, *you* are our most important critic and commentator. We value your opinion and want to know what we're doing right, what we could do better, what areas you'd like to see us publish in, and any other words of wisdom you're willing to pass our way.

As the Executive Editor for the General Desktop Applications team at Macmillan Computer Publishing, I welcome your comments. You can fax, email, or write me directly to let me know what you did or didn't like about this book—as well as what we can do to make our books stronger.

Please note that I cannot help you with technical problems related to the topic of this book, and that due to the high volume of mail I receive, I might not be able to reply to every message.

When you write, please be sure to include this book's title and author as well as your name and phone or fax number. I will carefully review your comments and share them with the author and editors who worked on the book.

Fax:	317-581-4663
E-mail:	office@mcp.com
Mail:	Executive Editor
	General Desktop Applications
	Macmillan Computer Publishing
	201 West 103rd Street
	Indianapolis, IN 46290 USA

Introduction

TurboTax is perhaps the most popular individual income tax return preparation program on the market today—and justifiably so. The program makes the complicated task of complying each year with a new round of tax laws and regulations almost pleasant. Well, if not exactly pleasant, how about manageable?

What This Book Will Do for You

TurboTax not only consolidates all the tax code provisions, regulations, rulings, forms, and schedules that could possibly apply to *you* in a single desktop application, it does so in a way that enables you to access them all without even knowing you are doing so. The EasyStep interview walks you through a series of straightforward questions (for example, are you married or single?) and determines which forms you need to file and which rates apply to you. Similarly, it enables you to basically copy a lot of information off forms you don't really understand—like W-2s and 1099s—onto its user-friendly screens. Trusty TurboTax performs all the necessary calculations with no intellectual effort on your part, if that is how you want to do it. Of course, this is only one way!

The creators of TurboTax recognize that there are, scattered among the tax-paying population, people who actually *want* to gain a comprehensive understanding of the process. Accordingly, TurboTax comes with an impressive database rivaling many law firm tax libraries. It also provides a comprehensive overview of tax law changes that have occurred during the year. Accordingly, TurboTax is not only capable of preparing your taxes, it keeps you informed as to what is happening in Congress.

Sams Teach Yourself TurboTax Deluxe in 24 Hours is designed to acquaint you with all the amazing features of this multifaceted tax program. This book is designed to help you use the program in the way that best suits your needs and personal management style. You can endeavor to process an accurate return with a minimum of effort, or you can use the tools provided to analyze your tax liability, the impact of the latest changes in the law, and the planning opportunities available to you in subsequent years. Whether it is simply your goal to complete the task at hand by April 15, or to plan for the future, *Sams Teach Yourself TurboTax Deluxe in 24 Hours* will provide you with the knowledge of the necessary program features.

Conventions Used in This Book

Sams Teach Yourself TurboTax Deluxe in 24 Years uses a number of conventions that are consistent throughout this book:

- Every hour begins with an overview of what you will learn and the highlights of the hour.
- Step-by-step instructions are preceded by a To Do icon.
- Every hour ends with a series of commonly asked questions and answers; hopefully you'll find the answers to yours among them.

In addition to these conventions, each hour also includes the following elements:

Notes provide valuable supplemental information about the tax topic or program feature being discussed.

Tips offer alternative or time-saving ways to do things.

Cautions warn you about program pitfalls and tax traps, and counsel you to avoid them.

PART I

Getting Started with TurboTax

Hour

HOUR 1

Welcome to TurboTax

This hour introduces you to the popular and highly regarded TurboTax program. In this hour, you learn about the nuts and bolts of the TurboTax software, prior to contemplating the requirements of the Internal Revenue Code in all its glory.

By the end of this first hour, you will have installed the program and will be comfortably navigating the TurboTax menus. You will also learn about registering your software, and you will get tips on maintaining your tax files and the integrity of your TurboTax data.

Highlights of this hour include

- Installing TurboTax
- The advantages of registering your copy of the program
- Importing data from a prior year
- The Head Start and Final Edition of the program
- Setting program preferences
- Navigating the TurboTax menus

Installing TurboTax

Before you install TurboTax, make sure that you have enough free space on your hard drive. TurboTax requires 30 megabytes for the regular version or 35 megabytes for TurboTax Deluxe. You can check to see whether you have space available by doing the following:

1. Double-click the My Computer Icon on your desktop.

2. Select the desired drive by clicking once on its icon or name (generally the C: drive).

3. The amount of free space on your hard drive appears in a window as shown in Figure 1.1—if you are using the Large icon view in your Windows Explorer.

FIGURE 1.1.

Viewing this window quickly tells you whether you have enough space for TurboTax without deleting other files.

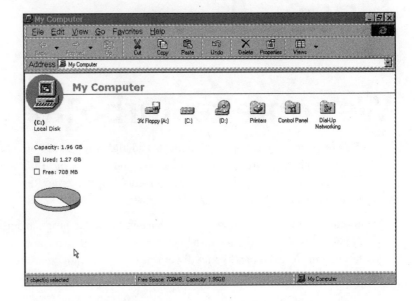

 This book assumes that you have Windows 95 or later and are working with a CD-ROM version of the software. If you are working with an earlier version of the software or installing off of disks, check the installation card included with your software.

To Do: Install TurboTax

1. Start your computer, or if it is already running, close out any applications that are open and running.

2. Insert the TurboTax CD in the CD-ROM drive. You receive a message indicating that the CD has been inserted and asking you whether you want to install the program.

3. Select Yes. The Welcome Screen appears.

4. Click Next to continue.

5. A copy of the software license agreement appears. Click Yes to accept the terms of the agreement; if you do not accept them, the installation is halted.

6. The next screen asks you to choose a directory for your file or to accept the default directory, which is C: \Tax98. Click Next to begin copying files.

   If you do not want to use the default directory and want to give the file a more descriptive moniker (or already have a file with that name), you can choose any directory name that you like. The choice of the directory name does not affect how the software runs.

7. After the files have been copied, you are given the option of subscribing to America Online. Click Don't Install.

8. A message appears that setup is complete. Click OK.

Registering TurboTax

The first time you run TurboTax, you are prompted to register. Why should you bother to register your TurboTax program? The answer is simple. You get more for your money: more services, more support, and more information.

As a registered TurboTax user, you are entitled to telephone the TurboTax technical support representatives with questions about running or operating the TurboTax software (but not tax questions). Technical support can be reached at (520) 901-3242. The first thing you are asked when you call is your registration number; they won't talk to you without it.

As a registered user, you're on the TurboTax mailing list. You receive periodic updates, coupons, and information about new Intuit products. You also receive special renewal and upgrade offers. If you bought the Head Start version of the software, discussed below, and want to receive the Final version free of charge, you *must* be on the mailing list.

Finally, and most important, you must register the software to activate your warranties. Intuit actually reimburses you for a software-caused error in preparing your tax return—but only if you register.

You may either register online or by completing and mailing the registration card included with your software.

To Do: Register TurboTax

When you first start the program, a dialog box appears offering the option of registering the software online. You can use this dialog box by clicking Yes, or register at any time by following these steps:

1. Go to the Help menu.

2. Choose Online Registration. A screen with fields for your name, address, and other relevant information appears as shown in Figure 1.2.

FIGURE 1.2.

You may register your program online using this screen.

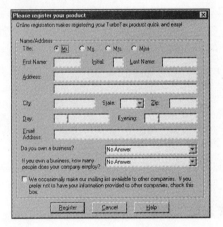

3. Enter the required information. Click Register. Your Internet connector starts, and your data is sent. Or, if you do not have an Internet connection, alternate instructions appear.

4. A message appears thanking you for registering. Click OK.

You cannot file a return unless you have the Final version. If you purchased the Head Start version of the software, you must register to receive the Final version.

You can also register by calling Intuit directly at (800) 757-3279.

Getting Started with TurboTax

After you have either registered the program or told TurboTax to skip the registration process for now, you are presented with the screen shown in Figure 1.3. You can click any controls or hyperlinks to get more information. Or, if you are anxious to get started, without such preliminaries, simply click the Let's Get Started button.

FIGURE 1.3.

You may opt to review program and tax law changes using this screen.

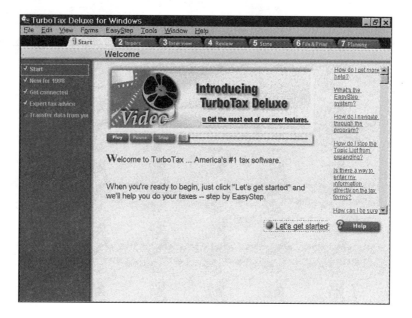

As you progress through the next two screens, you are confronted with more information and more options calculated to keep you current. TurboTax is serious about this! You can click any link to read more, or click Continue and then Skip Update to bypass it.

The next screen, shown in Figure 1.4, presents you with a veritable "wealth of expert tax advice." If you feel it is too early to hit the books offered on this screen, because you've yet to begin your return, click Continue. You are then offered the option of importing or transferring data, as discussed in the following section.

FIGURE 1.4.

*An impressive tax ref-
erence library may be
accessed from this
screen.*

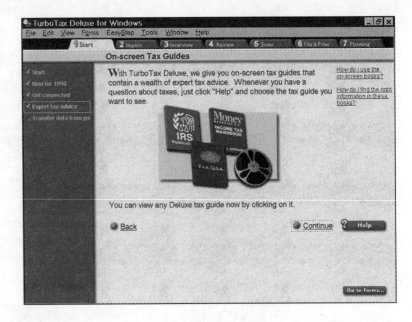

Importing Data

Importing data can save you considerable time if you have used a prior version of
TurboTax to prepare a previous year's return. Transferring data from a prior year's return
can save you time entering names, addresses, Social Security numbers, and certain numbers and calculations (such as your dependents). It can also be a helpful exercise if you
use Quicken, QuickBooks or a software package other than these programs that uses
TXF (tax exchange format) files.

> If you are going to import data from multiple program files—including a
> prior version of TurboTax—be sure to import from the TurboTax files first. If
> you use the EasyStep Interview, TurboTax makes sure that you import data
> in the correct order.

To Do: Import Data From Last Year's TurboTax

If you did not use TurboTax or compatible software to prepare a prior year's return, click
the Skip Transfer button, as shown in Figure 1.5.

FIGURE 1.5.

TurboTax carefully guides you through the process of importing data.

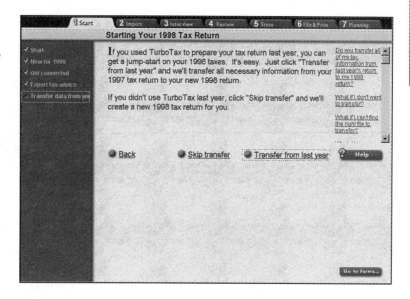

If you do want to transfer data from a prior year's TurboTax return:

1. Click the Transfer from Last Year option, as shown in Figure 1.5.

2. Select the file from which you want to transfer. It is probably in a folder called Tax 97.

3. Click Open.

4. A Transfer Report appears, indicating all forms that have been imported. Review it for accuracy and delete any unwanted forms.

5. Click Continue to continue with the preparation of your 1998 tax return.

Importing Data from Quicken or QuickBooks

After you have imported data from the prior year's TurboTax return, you are ready to import data from Quicken or QuickBooks using the screen shown in Figure 1.6. Both Quicken and QuickBooks use the term "TaxLink" to refer to data that is summarized online of a QuickBooks or Quicken report and then associated with a specific line of the Form 1040 when data is imported.

To Do: Import Data from QuickBooks and Quicken

1. Make sure the Import tab is selected.

2. Clik Import from Quicken or QuickBooks.

3. Click Quicken or QuickBooks, whichever you have (see Figure 1.6).

4. Click Import Now.

5. Confirm the file from which you want to import data using the dialog box that appears, as shown in Figure 1.7.

FIGURE 1.6.

Click the Import tab for a list of programs you can import from.

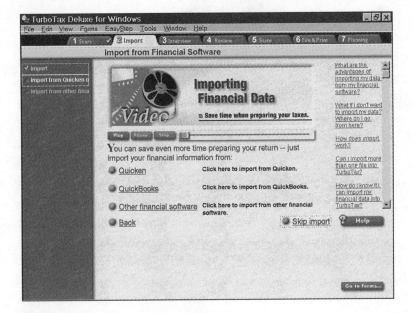

FIGURE 1.7.

Identify the file from which you want to import data using this screen.

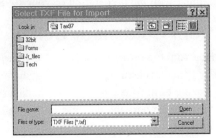

6. After you have verified that the correct file is open, click Continue.

7. Examine the links displayed in the TaxLink window to be sure that they are correct. Click the Change Links button to make any necessary modifications or click Import to import the data shown in the window.

▲

Importing Data from Other Financial Programs

What about importing data from programs other than TurboTax, Quicken, or QuickBooks? You can import data from any program that maintains TXF (tax exchange format) files.

To Do: Import Data From Other Financial Programs

To Do

1. Open the data file for the financial program from which you want to import data.

2. Create and save a TXF file to your hard drive (you need to consult the instructions for the program from which you are importing).

3. Close the program from which you are importing data.

4. Open TurboTax.

5. On the Import tab, click Import from Other Financial Software.

6. Click Import now.

7. In the select TXF File for Import dialog box, select the TXF file that you want to import, and then click Open.

8. After you have verified that the correct file is open, click Continue to complete the process.

Importing data is a useful function that you may find yourself using with surprising frequency. One instance occurs when you are updating from the Head Start to the Final version of the software, as discussed in the following section.

The Head Start and Final Versions of the Program

Many TurboTax users want to begin preparing their tax return prior to year end, using some of the powerful TurboTax research tools and data bases discussed in Hour 2 to help them with their year-end tax planning. But this can be a problem, because tax laws, forms, and regulations can change right up to the end of the year. Intuit resolves this dilemma by issuing two versions of the TurboTax software each year: the Head Start version and the Final version. You pay one price for both versions and get the best of both worlds, with a few caveats.

If you have purchased your software before the Final version was released, you will need to update your software. The IRS won't accept a return filed from the Head Start version of the software. TurboTax prints a "Do Not File" message on the form.

If you have registered your software, as discussed earlier in this hour, the Final version of the software is mailed to you at no extra charge. This version encompasses all the last minute changes.

> If you have not received your final version of the TurboTax program by the end of January, call the TurboTax customer service department at (800) 825-0089. Your registration card may have been lost or incorrectly processed.

Navigating the TurboTax Menus and Toolbars

The TurboTax menus are few in number and easy to navigate. Figure 1.8 points it out.

┌ Menu bar

FIGURE 1.8.

The standard TurboTax menu bar is shown here.

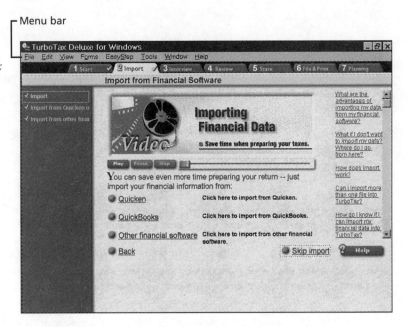

This section takes you through some basic tasks that shorten your learning curve considerably. A good one to start with is opening a tax return file:

1. Go to the File menu.
2. Select either New Tax Return or Open Tax Return.

The Open a Tax Return option takes you to an existing return, whereas the New Tax Return initiates the preparation process. If you attempt to open a new return while you already have another one open, you are prompted to save the changes to the current open file. The File menu is also the place to go if you want to electronically file a return, or import, print, or remove data.

Your Edit menu contains the standard cut/copy/paste options, with a few little bonuses. For example, you can mark numbers "estimated," add supporting details and information to your return and override numbers that are automatically calculated by TurboTax.

Not sure where to find a Tax Form or Schedule? Your Forms menu is a mini database and indexing system for this sort of information. Select the Open a Form option to view a listing of all forms available on the system.

The Tools menu contains some useful additions, such as the TurboTax Calculator shown in Figure 1.9. Click the buttons to perform mathematical operations onscreen just as you would with a regular calculator.

FIGURE 1.9.

The TurboTax calculator is a convenient feature accessed from the Tools menu.

The Tax Summary option on the Tools menu, shown in Figure 1.10, allows you to view a condensed summary. This analysis can be particularly useful in telling you how you got to your bottom line because it consolidates information from a number of different schedules.

FIGURE 1.10.

This condensed summary is useful for quickly pinpointing the sources of tax liability.

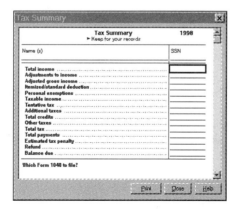

When all else fails, head to the Help menu. You find answers to tax questions, assistance in using the program, and a surprising array of reference sources to answer your questions.

Hour 2 covers the Help menu in detail and helps you to decide which approach works best for you in preparing your taxes.

Summary

This hour helped you get up and running. It discussed a number of preliminary matters to be addressed before you begin using the software. You learned how to install TurboTax, if you had not already done so, and how to perform some basic program tasks. This hour also provided you with some compelling reasons for registering your program and told you how to do it.

Importing data, another topic introduced this hour, gave you some added insight about how to increase your efficiency in using the program from year to year and how to combine the power of TurboTax with that of other financial programs you may have at your disposal.

Finally, this hour pointed out the differences between the Head Start and Final versions of the TurboTax software. The Head Start is used strictly for planning purposes. You must obtain the Final version of the software to file your return.

Hour 2 continues your introduction to TurboTax and covers its Help features and research tools in more depth.

Q&A

Q How do I know whether I have the Head Start or the Final version of the TurboTax software?

A The box that software comes in is labeled Head Start in the lower-left corner. Additionally, if you purchased your software prior to December 1, it is most likely a Head Start version because the Final version of the software was not officially released prior to that date. Finally, the HeadStart version does not allow you to print a final version of your return for filing. You receive the "Do Not File" error message on the printed form if you attempt to do so.

Q What warranties does TurboTax come with?

A Obviously, TurboTax cannot be held responsible for errors that you make in entering information data, such as adding an extra digit to the amount of federal income
tax withholding reported on your W-2 Form. Intuit does, however, warrant against
software-caused errors on the final version that end up costing you money. It pays
the amount of IRS and/or state penalties and the interest that you end up owing as
a result of its error.

Q How do I remove imported data?

A To remove the data that you have imported from QuickBooks, Quicken, or other
financial software, simply go to the File menu and choose Remove All Imported
Data.

**Q How do I change the TaxLinks when importing data from Quicken or
QuickBooks?**

A If you want to add, change, or remove a TaxLink, select File, Tax Link, Import,
and then Quicken TaxLink or QuickBooks TaxLink. Click the Change Links button
that appears in the TaxLink dialog box to access a dialog box offering several
options for changing the links.

Hour **2**

Preparation Options and Help Features

This hour expands your knowledge of TurboTax by acquainting you with two different options for preparing a return, and provides in-depth insight as to the type of help available to ensure successful completion of the process. TurboTax recognizes that not all program users approach the tax preparation process with the same level or familiarity (or patience). Some users know exactly which forms and schedules to file with their return and are comfortable entering information directly onto them for TurboTax to calculate. Other folks haven't a clue as to which forms to use or where the numbers belong. Not to worry in either case. TurboTax offers both a Forms-oriented approach and the EasyStep Interview.

Highlights of this hour include

- The difference between the EasyStep and Forms approaches to preparing returns
- How to get help on the TurboTax system

- How to keep up with new tax developments
- TurboTax Internet features

Two Ways to Get Your Taxes Done: The EasyStep Versus the Forms Approach

Although TurboTax offers two entirely different approaches to tax return preparation, both approaches yield the same end result. In other words, you come up with the same bottom line tax liability regardless of the method you select. It's strictly a matter of personal preference and your level of familiarity with preparing tax returns.

The EasyStep Interview

With this approach, you never have to worry about which forms to use or where to enter information. The EasyStep Interview prepares your income tax return based on your answers to a series of straightforward questions relevant to your tax situation. The program automatically decides which forms and schedules you need to file and what information should appear on them. For example, the screen shown in Figure 2.1 asks you about your marital status and dependent status. When you respond to these questions and some of the related questions on the screens that follow, TurboTax determines your filing status and applicable tax rates (for example, married, single, or head of household).

FIGURE 2.1.

Enter your response to the EasyStep Interview questions by clicking the appropriate option or entering requested information in a blank field, depending upon what is requested onscreen.

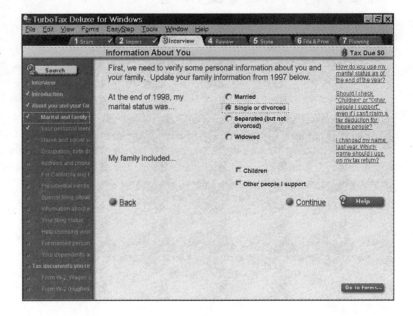

To begin preparing your return using the EasyStep Interview, use the following steps:

1. From the EasyStep menu, choose Start.

2. Progress through the interview screens, selecting the appropriate options or entering the information requested.

The interview questions are organized into topics that roughly follow the organization of the tax return forms and schedules. It is a good idea for the novice to follow the organization of the interview, but you can skip around from topic to topic by scrolling through the outline that appears on the left corner of the screen. A copy of the form on which you are currently working appears at the bottom of the screen.

You can search for a specific topic within the interview by clicking the Search icon in the upper-left corner of the screen. When you do so, the search window shown in Figure 2.2 appears. To search for a particular topic within the interview, follow these steps:

1. Enter your search request in the Find Topics field. Generally, your request should be limited to one or two words, such as "dependents" or "interest deduction."

2. Click the Search button to begin your search. The results of your search are displayed onscreen in the Step 2 box.

3. Within the Step 2 box, click the topic that you want to go to, and then click the Jump To button. You may also go directly to the topic by double-clicking the desired topic.

FIGURE 2.2.

You can access a specific interview topic using this window, if you are not sure where it is located on the Form 1040.

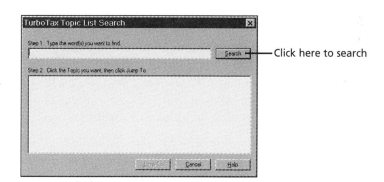

The EasyStep Interview format even allows you to take a look at the specific form that the information from your answers is being entered on as you are completing the interview. Simply click the Go to Forms tab at the bottom-right corner of the screen, as shown in Figure 2.3.

FIGURE 2.3.

The Interview screen shown here asks about interest income and the information provided is entered on the 1040 Form displayed in the window at the bottom of the screen.

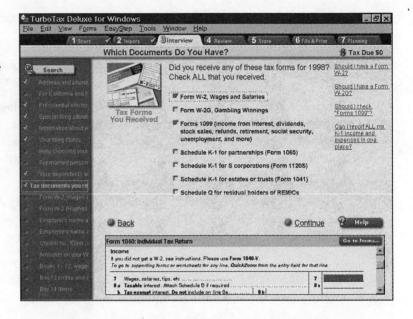

Although the questions presented in the EasyStep Interview are pretty straightforward, you might not be completely sure of the answers to all of them. If you are unsure or wavering about an answer, click the field that is giving you pause, and then click the Help option. You can also click a series of commonly asked questions that appear on the right side of the screen. For example, you may be asked on the Interview screen shown in Figure 2.4 whether you have any dependents. But you are not exactly sure whether you are entitled to claim your unemployed brother-in-law who lived with you for the entire year as a dependent. You can click the text link that reads "Who can I claim as a dependent on my tax return?" Alternatively, you can click the Help button, and the interview prompts you with additional information intended to provide insight as to whether your brother-in-law legally qualifies as your dependent. Good luck!

The EasyStep Interview even tells you whether you are going to owe money or are going to get a refund, as you enter the information. The amount you must pay or are getting back is posted in the upper-right corner of the EasyStep Interview screen, as shown in Figure 2.5. This amount changes as you progress through the interview, so don't rely on it until you have completed the entire interview.

Commonly asked questions

FIGURE 2.4.

Click the Help button or a specific question link for additional help as to how to answer interview questions, such as whether you have any dependents.

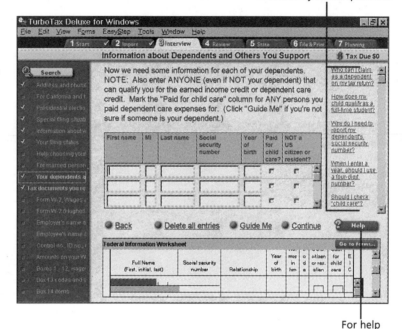

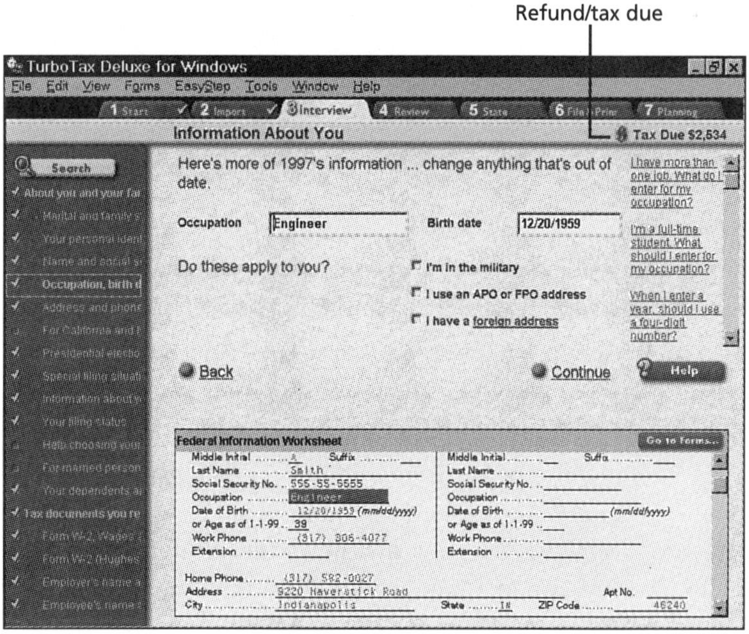

For help

Refund/tax due

FIGURE 2.5.

EasyStep keeps a running tally of what you owe and lets you access any form instantly.

2

The Forms Approach

The Forms method is a more challenging alternative for users who feel that they have a sufficient grasp of the process to enter information directly on the forms and schedules. You can switch from the EasyStep Interview to the Forms method at any time during the EasyStep Interview by clicking the Go to Forms button, shown in Figure 2.6, at any time during the interview.

FIGURE 2.6.

You can access the current federal income tax form at any time.

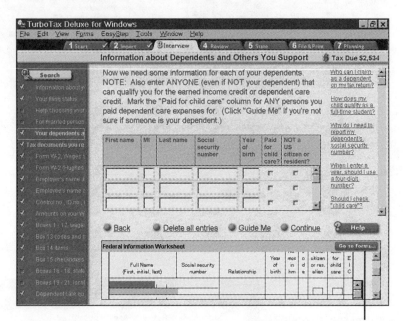

Click here to access Forms method

To prepare a return using the Forms method, you must first complete the Federal Information Worksheet.

To Do: Begin a Return with the Forms Method

1. Open the Forms menu and choose Open a Form.
2. Select Federal Information Worksheet from the dialog box that appears.
3. Click Open. The Federal Information Worksheet appears.
4. Complete the worksheet by clicking each field and filling in the necessary information. If you get stuck, look at the status bar at the bottom of the screen for additional information about what to type in a field.

5. When you have entered all the required information on the Federal Information Worksheet, open the Form 1040 by clicking the QuickZoom button at the bottom of the worksheet.

If you are unsure as to which forms to fill out, or are uncertain about the information that goes on them, use the EasyStep Interview.

TurboTax has a complete inventory of all IRS forms and schedules that accompany the Form 1040. You may access any form or schedule in much the same way that you opened the Federal Information Worksheet.

You can open only one form at a time, but you can have multiple forms open during your data entry sessions. All the opened forms can be accessed from the list found under the Window menu.

There are two option buttons for viewing the list of forms at the top of the Open Form window. If you select the Show My Return option, only the forms included in your tax return appear on the list. If you select Open a Form, the Open Form window lists all forms and worksheets available in TurboTax.

Do not enter zeros in any of the fields of the tax forms. Leave fields blank if there is not a number to be entered on them.

Getting Acquainted with TurboTax Help Features

TurboTax is more than a compilation of forms, schedules, and questions designed to ferret out the information that you need to enter on them. It is a complete system for preparing your personal income taxes, which means that it only provides information to assist you in keeping up with changes in the law and in IRS policy that may impact upon the information that appears on your return and your ultimate tax liability. You are provided with this expertise in the form of an extensive array of onscreen Help options, an easy-to-use database referencing new developments and planning alternatives, and even online support via the TurboTax Web site.

Getting Help with General Tax and Program Questions

For questions about using the program or on tax matters, click the Help menu option. The drop-down menu shown in Figure 2.7 appears.

FIGURE 2.7.

TurboTax provides an impressive array of Help options.

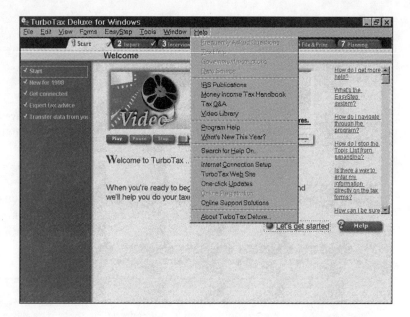

If you require help using the TurboTax program, you can select the Program Help option or simply click the Help icon, which always appears on the TurboTax screen. Program Help allows you to search for the answer using either a topical outline or click a search button to initiate a keyword query as shown in Figure 2.8.

Alternatively, if you need help interpreting tax laws and regulations as opposed to the mechanics of the program, from the Help menu select the Common Tax Questions or IRS Publications options to begin an appropriate search. These Help features also allow you to search by topical outline or using keywords and phrases.

FIGURE 2.8.

TurboTax allows you to search using a topical outline or by entering keywords as shown here.

Click the underlined text in the Help window to view more information about a particular topic.

Using the fewest possible words or letters results in a broad search that yields a greater number of search results. Adding more words narrows your search. For example, "deductions" brings up more topics than "interest deductions."

Getting Help Preparing a Specific Form

In addition to using Help for general questions, you can actually use TurboTax Help to guide you through the preparation of a specific form. You can use the Help menu options Tax Help, Government Instructions, and IRS Publications options for this purpose.

Assume, for example, that you are preparing a Schedule B for interest and dividend income, and you are unsure as to how to treat a certain type of interest payment that you received. If you click the Help button or select Tax Help from the Help menu, a screen appears that discusses the preparation of a Schedule B in lay terms, but not extensive detail.

If the Tax Help screen does not provide the answer that you are looking for, you can click the Government Instructions tab on the right side of the Help screen. You can then take a look at the official instructions the IRS or state tax authority has issued for preparation of the Schedule B.

Still in a state of confusion? Try clicking the IRS Publications tab to view a list of informational publications issued by the IRS that bear any mention of Schedule B. These little mini-treatises cover a variety of topics and can offer a great deal of insight when you have a not-so-common question.

The TurboTax Video Library

During the EasyStep Interview, you have an opportunity to view several informational videos specific to the questions that you are answering. You also may find it helpful to view a specific video if you are using the Forms method, or at other points in the course of preparing your return. To take a look at a video on a specific topic, use the following steps:

1. Choose Video Library from the Help menu.
2. Select a topic.
3. Click the title of the video that you want to view.
4. Click Pay.

Keeping Up with New Tax Developments

Tax laws are subject to constant change. Information that is only a few months old can easily be dated and obsolete. For this reason, TurboTax provides a number of different options to help you stay abreast of tax changes that may impact your return. Select the What's New This Year? option on the Help menu for a summary of all the 1998 tax changes.

For changes more recent than the last version of your software, you can rely upon the TurboTax Web site (http://www.turbotax.com). You can also utilize the TurboTax Fax Service to obtain answers to frequently asked questions, technical support, and information about late breaking tax developments. To use this service, follow these steps:

1. Call 1-800-766-5034.
2. Select an option from the menu provided. You can request a particular document or a catalog listing of all available documents and topics.
3. When prompted, enter your fax number and voice phone number.
4. Remain on the line while your request is being processed. The system automatically disconnects after your request has been processed, and you should receive your document within four hours. You can request up to three fax documents at a time.

To use the TurboTax videos and tax reference books and publications, you must have the TurboTax CD in the CD-ROM drive.

Summary

This hour introduced you to the two different approaches for preparing your income tax return using TurboTax. You can elect to use either the EasyStep Interview or the Forms Method.

The EasyStep Interview elicits the information needed to prepare your return through a series of straightforward questions. The program then determines which forms and schedules you need to file with your return and what amounts belong on them.

The Forms Approach is available for users having a greater level of comfort and familiarity with IRS Forms. This approach lets you pick and choose the forms to use.

In addition to becoming acquainted with the methods for preparing a return, this hour introduced you to an array of useful features and information sources. TurboTax provides several types of onscreen help to answer tax questions and address any issues that may arise in using the program. Additionally, both a Web site and fax update service ensure that you are privy to breaking tax developments subsequent to the latest release of the software.

Hour 3, "Personal Information and Filing Status," delves into those issues that taxpayers must resolve.

Q&A

Q How do I exit and restart the program if I do not finish my return in a single sitting?

A TurboTax allows you to stop working on your return and save your data for later at any time. Simply go the File menu and choose Exit. TurboTax asks you whether you want to save your file. Click Yes. The first time you do so, you are prompted for a filename. Enter it and click Save. When you restart the program, you are automatically taken to the point where you left off.

Q Can I use both the Forms Method and the EasyStep Interview or must I choose one or the other?

A You can safely switch back and forth between the EasyStep Interview and Forms Method at any time. Remember, all the information that you enter goes on the same return. You may find it convenient to initially prepare the return using the EasyStep Interview but use the forms method for later corrections and updates.

Q How can I view and edit the information that is being entered on my tax form as I complete the EasyStep Interview?

A During most parts of the EasyStep Interview, the form in use appears at the bottom of the screen. If you want to edit the information appearing on the form, click the field you want to change and type the new information.

HOUR 3

Personal Information and Filing Status

In this hour, we talk about you—your marital status, your income level, and your legal relationship with the people that live in your household. All these personal and familial characteristics determine how much tax you pay. It is a peculiarity of our tax system that rates are not constant for every individual but vary depending upon who you live with or whether they are your spouse. The IRS is similar to a nosy relative, but it does give you a break if you are elderly, blind, or a single parent.

This hour introduces you to the various tax rates to which you may be subject and the exemptions afforded to you. You also learn about the legal requirements for claiming another individual as a dependent.

Highlights of this hour include

- The definition and significance of filing status
- Personal exemptions—who gets to claim them and why
- Legal requirements for claiming a dependent

Electing Personal Filing Status

Your filing status is a function of your family situation, for example, whether you are married, single, or have children. It is used to determine what tax rates your income is subject to after it is computed. It is also used to determine issues such as the amount of Social Security benefits that are taxable or whether you are entitled to claim certain types of tax credits such as the child care credit or the credit for the elderly.

Taxpayers may elect one of the following five types of filing status:

- Single
- Married filing jointly
- Married filing separately
- Head of household
- Qualifying widow(er)

Single and Head of Household

You claim single taxpayer status if you are unmarried and do not have children that you are claiming as dependents. You are considered single if you were unmarried as of December 31, 1998, the last day of the tax year.

You can use the single filing status if you *do* have children, but the Head of Household status is generally a more favorable option. You may claim Head of Household status if you are not married and have at least one child or relative who qualifies as your dependent, as discussed later in this hour. You may also use Head of Household status if you *are* married, so long as you are filing a separate return from your spouse and meet the following additional conditions:

- You did not live with your spouse for the last six months of the tax year.
- Your residence was the primary home for one of your children who qualifies as a dependent for the tax year.
- You provided at least one-half the cost of maintaining your home during the tax year.

Head of Household rates tend to be significantly lower than single tax rates. The EasyStep Interview includes a series of questions directed at whether you meet the legal requirements for electing this more favorable status.

If you are divorced and you and your spouse alternate years claiming your child as a dependent, you may elect Head of Household filing status for the years that you are entitled to claim the dependency exemption under the divorce decree.

Filing Status Options for Married Taxpayers

If you are married as of the last day of the tax year, you have a choice of filing jointly with your spouse or filing using the Married Filing Separately tax status. The Married Filing Jointly status, in theory, combines the incomes and deductions of both spouses on a single return and applies a single tax rate. In contrast, couples using the Married Filing Separately status file separate returns and pay taxes at a special rate that is intended to approximate the tax that would occur if the couples were filing a single joint return. Couples who are separated or have special tax issues most often elect the Married Filing Separately status. Married couples generally pay less tax by electing to file jointly rather than Married Filing Separately.

Although married couples usually fare better by filing joint returns, there are rare exceptions to this rule. Most notably, it may be to your advantage to elect Married Filing Separate status if one spouse has most of the income and another spouse has a lot of deductions that are subject to limitations based on adjusted gross income. For example, medical expenses can be deducted only to the extent that they exceed 7.5% of adjusted gross income. By filing separate returns, a spouse with large medical expenses is able to deduct more of them if her adjusted gross income is a lot less than the combined income of the couple.

You may *not* file a joint return with your spouse if any of the following conditions exist:

- Your spouse files a separate return.
- Your spouse has been claimed as a dependent on someone else's return.
- Your spouse is a nonresident alien.
- You and your spouse have different tax reporting years.

Qualifying Widow or Widower with Dependent Child Status

If your spouse dies during the tax year, you are still entitled to file a joint return for your family, which includes your deceased spouse. You must meet the following requirements:

- You did not remarry during the tax year.
- You met the requirements for filing a joint return prior to the death of your spouse (even if you did not do so).
- You have a dependent child.
- You paid more than half the cost of maintaining your home.

Even if you do not meet all the above conditions for filing as a qualifying widow or widower, you may still meet the requirements for Head of Household status.

> If you are confused as to what your status might be and want to use the Forms method, check your prior year's return. Unless your marital, parental, or household situation has changed dramatically, it is probably the same as last year.

Personal Exemptions

Personal exemptions are often confused with dependency exemptions, but the difference between the two is not difficult to understand. Personal exemptions apply to the taxpayer and, if a joint return is being filed, to the taxpayer's spouse. On the other hand, dependency exemptions are claimed for persons dependent upon the taxpayer (and spouse) for support.

The amount that you and your spouse each receive as a personal exemption varies each year. For the 1998 tax year, this amount is $2,700 for each spouse. Exemptions are claimed on page 2 of the 1040, line 37, as shown in Figure 3.1. They appear on line 21 of the Form 1040A.

Exemption Phase-Out for High-Income Taxpayers

Unfortunately, not everyone is entitled to claim their personal exemptions. The exemptions are phased out for certain high-income taxpayers. The allowable exemption is reduced by 2% for every $2,500 (or fraction thereof) that your adjusted gross income (discussed in Hour 5, "Introduction to Personal Income Tax Forms") exceeds the amounts shown in Table 3.1.

FIGURE 3.1.

Personal exemptions are claimed on the Form 1040 as shown here.

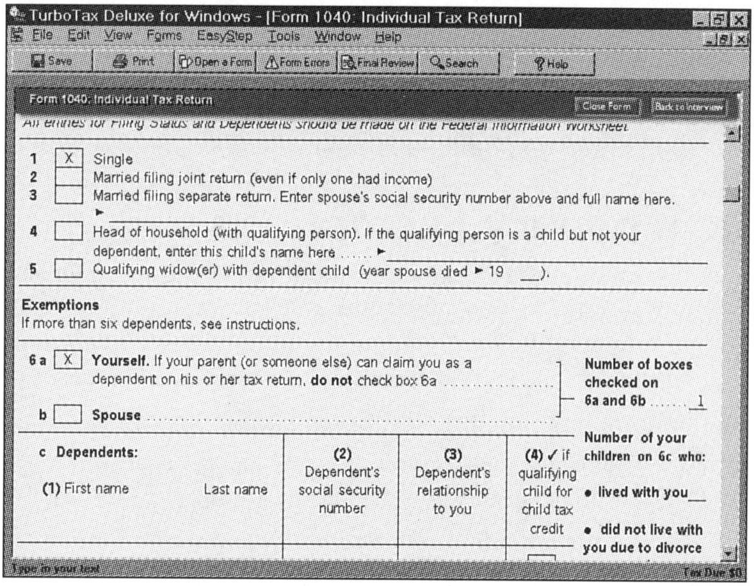

TABLE 3.1. PHASE-OUT FOR PERSONAL EXEMPTIONS.

Filing Status	AGI Threshold
Single	$124,500
Married Filing Jointly	186,800
Head of Household	155,650
Qualifying Widow(er)	186,800
Married Filing Separately	93,400

Other Limitations on Claiming Personal Exemptions

A husband and wife filing a joint return are each allowed a personal exemption. Generally, if spouses file separate returns, they must each take their own personal exemptions. If, however, you file a separate return with your spouse and have no income and are not a dependent of another taxpayer, your spouse may claim your combined personal exemptions.

Also, an individual who is taken as a dependent on another taxpayer's return may claim no personal exemption. This means, for example, that a student who works part time during the year may not claim a personal exemption if his parents take him as a dependent on their return.

A dependent who is not allowed his own personal exemption need not file an income tax return and is not taxed if he or she does not have more than $650 in adjusted gross income.

Dependency Exemptions

You are permitted to take an additional $2,700 exemption for any person for whom you provide care or support during the 1998 tax year and who meets the specific criteria set forth by the IRS. The IRS prescribes the following five basic tests for determining whether an individual in your household qualifies as a dependent:

- *The Gross Income Test.* The dependent must have less than $2,650 in gross income during the calendar year. This test does not apply if the dependent is under the age of 19 or is under 24 years old and is a full-time student.

- *The Support Test.* You must have provided over one-half of the dependent's support during the tax year.

- *The Relationship Test.* The dependent must be related to you as one of the following:
    - Son, daughter, grandchild, adopted child, or foster child
    - Sibling (by half or full blood) or stepsibling
    - Parent or stepparent
    - Niece or nephew
    - Aunt or uncle
    - In-law

Alternatively, if the dependent meets none of the preceding relationship criteria, they may still be claimed if they lived in your home for the full year, were a member of your household, and meet all the other tests for determining eligibility for the dependency exemption:

- *The Joint Return Test.* The dependent may not have filed a joint return with his or her spouse.

- *The Citizenship Test.* The dependent must be a citizen, national or resident of the United States, a resident of Canada or Mexico, or an adopted alien child who lived in your household for the entire year.

As with personal exemptions, dependency exemptions are phased out for high-income taxpayers. The threshold amounts for phasing them out were summarized earlier in Table 3.1.

Summary

This hour introduced you to the concepts of filing status and exemptions. Filing status is a function of your marital status, whether you have children, and other personal factors. Your filing status determines which tax rate is applied to your adjusted gross income (as discussed in Hour 5).

This hour also introduced you to the two types of exemptions: personal and dependency. A taxpayer may claim a $2,700 personal exemption in 1998, as may the taxpayer's spouse. Additional dependency exemptions may be claimed for persons who are members of the taxpayer's household and meet the other specific legal requirements discussed in this hour.

Q&A

Q **Do I need to have a Social Security number for each person that I am claiming as a dependent on my tax return?**

A Yes, you must include this information. The EasyStep Interview prompts you to provide this information. If you are using the Forms method, it is required to complete the Federal Information Worksheet. The IRS can impose a $50 fine for each omitted Social Security number.

Q **If I am determining whether I paid more than 50% of someone's support for purposes of including them as a dependent on my return, what types of expenses may I include?**

A You may count expenses such as medical, food, housing, clothing, transportation, and even entertainment. Compare the amount you paid to how much the dependent and others paid. If the amount that you paid is more than the total of what everyone else paid *and* you meet the other requirements discussed in this hour, you are entitled to claim the exemption.

Q **What if the status of someone I have claimed as a dependent in past years has changed during the most recent reporting year, for example as a result of death, divorce, or moving out of my household?**

A Generally, the IRS determines your tax status by looking at your situation as of the last day of the tax year. For example, if you are married on December 31, 1998, you file under a married status. Similarly, if you are single as of that date, you are considered single for the entire tax year for filing purposes. A child born one minute before midnight on December 31 may be claimed as a dependent, and so forth.

Hour 4

Gathering Tax Information

This hour lays the groundwork for completing a personal income tax return. The preparation phase can be daunting; most people find it more intimidating than the actual liability calculations. But in this hour, you confront the enemy by arming yourself with excellent checklists. More importantly, you gain an understanding as to why various information is required and, consequently, what to do if you are having difficulty locating some elusive bit of information needed to prepare your return.

You need the same documentation and information regardless of whether you are using the EasyStep Interview or the Forms method. This chapter tells you how and where to find it.

Highlights of this hour include

- Utilizing information from your prior year's returns
- Gathering information about your income
- Documenting expenses and deductions

- Checklists of required information
- What to do if you can't locate required information

Utilizing Information from the Previous Year

The most important source of information available to you in preparing this year's return is *last* year's return. You find much of the information that you need—such as filing status and dependents' Social Security numbers—conveniently summarized on the 1997 Form 1040. Of course, most of the numbers on the forms change from one year to the next, but it is useful to have a list of your income sources and deductions previously claimed.

It is *always* a good idea to save your prior year's return. Not only do these documents disclose information that would otherwise take precious time to track down, they sometimes memorialize economic events needed to accurately determine a current tax liability. For example, if you are selling an investment property, you want to know how much depreciation you have taken in prior years.

> If you prepared last year's return using TurboTax, you can easily import all relevant information using the procedures discussed in Hour 1, "Welcome to TurboTax."

Gathering Information About Your Income

Our tax system is based upon a concept of self-reporting. This means that the IRS relies upon *us* to tell *them* about all our income so that it can impose the correct amount of tax. But this system is not based entirely on trust. The IRS has certain verification systems in place. For example, federal tax law requires that the IRS receive a copy of your W-2, 1099, and K-1 Forms to verify that you have reported the income disclosed on these informational returns. The IRS matches the information submitted by those who prepare these forms with the liability you have reported on your return. This is sometimes referred to as the federal "matching system."

Of course, not all income sources are matched to IRS documentation, but you are still obligated to report them. This means that you must maintain your own records in addition to obtaining your W-2s, 1099s, K-1s, and other informational forms. The following is a list of sources to check to make sure you have reported all your income for the year:

- *W-2 Form.* Any employer who has paid you wages during the year is required to send you a W-2 Form. Copies of this form are sent to the Social Security Administration and retained by your employer. Several copies of it are also sent to you. You are required to attach a copy to your state and federal returns, and a copy is provided for you to retain for your personal records.

> It is a good idea to staple your reference copies of your W-2 and 1099 Forms to the copy of your tax returns that you keep for your records. This way you are less likely to lose those small pieces of paper used to print the 1099s and W-2s.

- *1099 Form.* Payers are required to mail this form to you to summarize the interest, dividend, rental, and miscellaneous income that you received from them during the tax year if it exceeded $600. You may also receive 1099 Forms disclosing events such as the sale of securities or real estate, or the amount of unemployment bene-fits received. You do not need to attach 1099 Forms to your income tax return; the payers mail a copy directly to the IRS. There are a number of variations of the Form 1099 and they are discussed in detail in Hour 6, "Introduction to W-2 and 1099 Forms."

- *K-1 Form.* This form summarizes income received from any ownership interest in partnerships, estates, and small business corporations. The K-1 also summarizes deductions and losses that you may be able to take as a result of your ownership interests in these entities.

- *Year-end bank statements.* Financial institutions are required to send you a 1099-INT or 1099-DIV if you received more that $600 of interest or dividends during the year. In the event that you received less than this amount or the required 1099 does not come in the mail, you can usually determine the correct amount of income attributable to these sources from your year-end bank or brokerage state-ment.

- *Year-end statements from brokerage accounts.* You are supposed to get a 1099 sum-marizing purchases and sales of securities, margin interest, brokerage fees, and interest and dividends. But it doesn't always happen, or the amounts appearing on the 1099s may be incomplete or inaccurate. So, at the risk of a little duplication, it is a good idea to locate your year-end brokerage account statements.

- *Year-end financial statements from businesses.* If you own your Schedule C busi-ness, farm, or a rental property, you need the year-end financial statements summa-rizing the business activity for the year. Taxable events for these types of entities show up on your personal income tax return.

4

- *Records of gambling winnings, prizes, and awards.* Again, in theory, someone should send you a 1099 conveniently summarizing these amounts. In case they don't, you need verification of these happy financial events in the form of bank deposit records or correspondence from the payer.

 Always save your gambling receipts in case you win big. Gambling expenses are deductible to the extent of gambling winnings.

Table 4.1 is a checklist of information required to accurately report your income from all sources. It includes all the preceding documentation, as well as the more obscure items, such as the information returns used to report interest from foreign bank accounts and contributions to IRA and SEP Plans.

TABLE 4.1. CHECKLIST OF INFORMATION—INCOME SOURCES.

Type of Document	Information Provided
W-2 Form	Wages, tips, and other compensation as well as withholding and deduction amounts
1099 Form	Interest, dividends, proceeds from sales of stock and real estate, unemployment benefits, and miscellaneous income
K-1 Form	Distributions from partnerships, estates, and small business corporations
Year-end bank statements	Interest paid to you in amounts of less than $600
Year-end brokerage statements	Interest, dividends, and capital gains
Records of gambling winnings, prizes, and awards	Taxable income derived from these sources
Form TD F 90-22	Interest from a foreign bank
Form 5498	Contributions to IRA and SEP Plans

Documenting Your Deductions

It is not surprising that the IRS generally does not audit people for the purpose of making sure that they have taken all their deductions. Of course taxpayers have every financial incentive to take all their deductions and tax credits. The IRS does, however, send you a notice (and appropriate refund) if it happens to come across a deduction it thinks you missed while it is processing your return.

It is important to realize that the burden of proof for deductions and expenses is on the taxpayer. You want to locate and retain the following information to substantiate your deductions:

- *Receipts for medical expenses and prescription drugs.* Save all the receipts for prescription drugs, dentists, doctors, and unreimbursed hospital expenses. Also, save canceled checks for any insurance premiums if you are self-employed or retired.

- *Canceled checks or receipts for property taxes.* Your property tax bill is not enough because it does not prove that the obligation was actually paid by you prior to year-end. You need your canceled check for this purpose.

- *Mortgage interest statement.* Your lender should send you a year-end statement summarizing the amount of mortgage interest you have paid during the year. If not, you can usually obtain it with a phone call. Your canceled mortgage check won't be sufficient because it doesn't separately break down the amounts attributable to interest and principal.

- *Documentation for charitable donations.* Save canceled checks and receipts for cash donations. For non-cash contributions, keep a log as to what you donated, to whom, and when. Be sure to get a receipt from the donee for the non-cash items. This may require having the donee sign off on a list of items that you have prepared.

You do not have to maintain records of charitable contributions or medical expenses if you do not itemize your deductions.

You can take mileage and other expenses associated with performing voluntary activities as a charitable deduction.

- *Records for business expenses.* The burden is on you to prove amounts you've paid for business travel meals and entertainment. A sample mileage log is provided in Appendix C for this purpose, and the complexities of this particular type of deduction are discussed further in Hour 14, "Business-Related Deductions." Receipts for meals must include information as to the date, who was entertained, and the nature of the business that you discussed. An appointment calendar can be used to keep track of this information.

Other business expenses usually show up on your Schedule C or as miscellaneous itemized deductions, as in the case of educational expenses. It is a good idea to retain both the bill for the expense, and a canceled check to show that it was actually paid during the year.

- *Vehicle registration receipts.* Some states charge an excise tax for the purchase of license plates. Save your receipt if your state is one of them, because this expense is deductible.

- *Records for miscellaneous deductions.* These deductions include tax preparation fees, union dues, business meals, uniforms, and safe deposit box expenses. They must exceed 2% of adjusted gross income to be deductible.

Table 4.2 summarizes the documentation needed to substantiate all your deductions. This table jogs your memory as to expenses you may have incurred and reminds you as to the information the IRS requires for meeting your burden of proof if they are challenged.

TABLE 4.2. CHECKLIST OF INFORMATION—EXPENSES AND DEDUCTIONS.

Type of Document	Information Provided
Canceled checks and receipts for medical expenses (medical, dental, insurance premiums, and so on)	Extent to which medical expenses paid during the taxable year exceeded 7.5% of adjusted gross income
Property tax receipts and/or canceled checks	Amount of property tax paid during tax year
Mortgage interest statements	Amount of interest paid for mortgage on personal residence
Charitable contribution receipts or logs	Charitable contributions of tangible goods, money, or expenses incurred in rendering services to qualified charities
Business mileage logs	Contemporaneous records of business mileage pursuant to IRS requirements
Entertainment receipts and appointment books	Records of expenses incurred for business entertainment and required documentation as to participants and matters discussed
Other business bills, receipts, and canceled checks	Documentation as to amounts paid for business purposes during tax year and nature of expense
Real estate closing statements	Expenses associated with the sale of investment or residential real estate
Receipts and canceled checks for legal and accounting services	Expenses attributable to tax preparation and planning and/or the production of income

Type of Document	Information Provided
Receipts for safe deposit boxes, uniforms, professional dues, and other miscellaneous deductions	Documentation as to miscellaneous expenses that must exceed 2% of adjusted gross income to be deductible

What to Do if You Can't Locate the Information That You Need

There are basically three options available to you if you can't locate a receipt or other documentation that you need to prove your expenses. First, you can reconstruct the expenditure from available records. Second, you can contact the payer or payee for a copy of his or her documentation. Third, you can make an estimate based upon *reasonable* calculations.

Reconstructing expenditures can be surprisingly easy. Your checkbook register and credit card statement are a good place to start. If these can't be located, you can request duplicate statements from your bank or credit card company.

Even if you paid cash, the receipts themselves can often be duplicated. Businesses and vendors routinely maintain customer receipts and records for a variety of purposes. It may take a few days to track down, but many businesses are willing to research their records of the transaction and provide a duplicate receipt. If the companies don't maintain records of specific customer purchases, you can at least research and document the *usual* cost of the item or service. This is persuasive to the IRS if you can also prove that you actually own the item or availed yourself of the service you are seeking to deduct.

In some cases the IRS accepts a cost estimate in support of a claimed deduction. For example, if you commute from one business location to another three times a week, you can estimate the number of deductible miles associated with this trip over the course of the tax year.

If you are waiting for information such as a W-2 or 1099 Form, try calling the accounting department or business office of the issuing company. Even if they have not yet mailed the form, they may be able to give you the information you need over the phone.

4

Summary

This hour was spent tracking down the documentation required to complete the TurboTax EasyStep Interview questions and tax forms. Your preparation time is minimized if you take the time to locate the items identified in Tables 4.1 and 4.2 before you dive into the substance of the return.

Tables 4.1 and 4.2 not only provide you with checklists to use as a starting point, they provide you with a bit of insight as to why the various items are needed. This hour also advised you as to viable alternatives for locating information that is missing or cannot be obtained via the usual sources.

In Hour 5, "Introduction to Personal Income Tax Forms," you learn more about how the information you have gathered is used to calculate your income tax liability. You also become familiar with the basic types of personal income tax reporting forms.

Q&A

Q **What if I can't locate a copy of the tax return that I filed last year?**

A You can contact the IRS to obtain a copy of last year's tax return by calling 1-800-829-1040. You can order either a transcript of your return, copies of the actual return, or something called a 1722 Letter. Either the copies of the return or the transcript provides you with all the information that you need. The 1722 Letter, which is a summary, is not sufficiently complete for your purposes because it does not break down the types of income and deductions that you reported on the prior year's return.

Q **How long should I save my receipts and documentation?**

A Generally, the receipts and documentation you have used to prepare you tax return should be saved for a minimum of three years from the April 15 deadline or the date on which you filed your return, whichever is later. You should save your documentation for a longer period of time if your return reflects deductions, carry forwards, or other tax events that impact subsequent years' returns. Examples include a gain on the sale of your house or a capital loss carry forward.

PART II

Overview of Forms, Schedules, and Worksheets

Hour

HOUR 5

Introduction to Personal Income Tax Forms

This hour provides an overview of the types of personal income tax reporting forms prepared by TurboTax: Form 1040 and Form 1040A. You learn to differentiate between the two types of returns and how TurboTax determines which one best meets your filing needs. You gain an understanding as to how the entries on each line of the return are used to calculate your liability or refund for the tax year. Even if you plan to use the EasyStep Interview exclusively and never confront a blank tax form or schedule screen, you still find it useful to know something about the anatomy of the Form 1040 and the essence of the calculations that determine your tax fate.

Highlights of this hour include

- The different types of 1040 Forms
- An overview of how the Form 1040 is structured
- The types of calculations that are used to determine tax liability based upon the information entered on the 1040 Form

- The concept of adjusted gross income
- How adjustments to income and tax credits effect liability

Types of 1040 Forms: Overview

Personal income tax liability is reported on Form 1040. It is available in three varieties: Form 1040, Form 1040A, and Form 1040EZ.

Form 1040A may be used by taxpayers who do not plan to itemize deductions and whose gross income does not exceed $50,000. It is essentially a shortened version of the Form 1040. This form is prepared by TurboTax.

The EZ Form is an option only for single taxpayers without any dependents or deductions and with limited sources of income. Because it is extremely easy to complete, it is not an option on TurboTax.

The Standard Form 1040

The standard Form 1040 is two pages long and is divided into nine informational sections: filing status, exemptions, income, adjusted gross income, tax computation, credits, other taxes, payments, and refunds. A Form 1040 is also generally accompanied by one or more supporting schedules.

Usually, supporting schedules are filed with the return to show how amounts entered onto the various lines were derived. For example, line 9 on the 1040, shown in Figure 5.1, shows an entry of $573 for dividends. Supporting Schedule B, shown in Figure 5.2, reveals that this amount is comprised of $301 from Standard Oil dividends and $272 from Pepsi Cola dividends. There are nearly two dozen types of supporting schedules that may be filed with a 1040 Form.

Form 1040A

Form 1040A is a shorter version of the Form 1040 and is shown in Figure 5.3. There are substantially fewer lines on the 1040A than on the standard 1040. Additionally, there are only three types of supporting schedules that can accompany it. These are designated as Schedules 1, 2, and 3. Only certain taxpayers, as described in the next section, are eligible to file a Form 1040A.

FIGURE 5.1.

An entry for $573 total dividends received by the taxpayer is shown here.

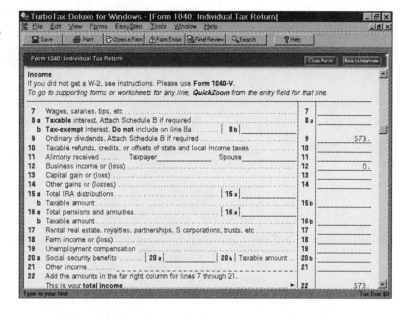

FIGURE 5.2.

This supporting Schedule B provides additional information as to how the amount shown on line 9 of the Form 1040 was derived.

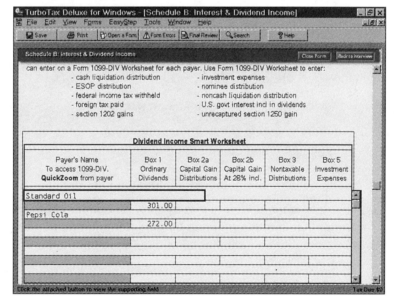

5

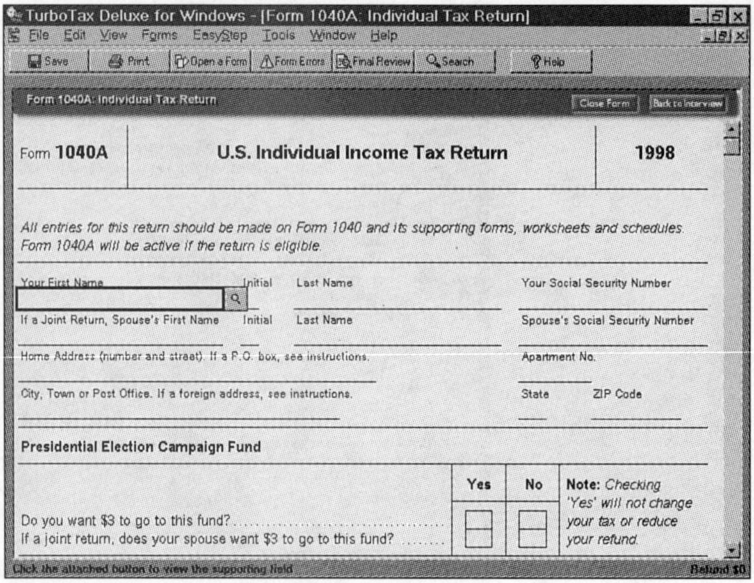

FIGURE 5.3.

Form 1040A is a simplified version of Form 1040.

Income Requirements for Filing Form 1040A

Taxpayers whose taxable income is less $50,000 may file a Form 1040A, provided that their income consists *only* of the following:

Wages, salaries, and tips

Scholarships and fellowships

Unemployment compensation

Dividends and interest

IRA and retirement plan distributions

This means, for example, that you cannot file a Form 1040A if any of your income comes from sources such as capital gains or revenue from rents and royalties. If you have more than $400 in interest and dividends, supporting Schedule 1, shown in Figure 5.4, must accompany the return.

Deductions

You cannot file a Form 1040A if you itemize deductions. You may, however, file the 1040A if you claim the child and dependent care credit, the elderly and disabled credit, or the earned income credit. These credits are calculated and reported on supporting Schedules 2 and 3.

FIGURE 5.4.

If you report more than $400 of interest or dividends on your Form 1040A, it must be accompanied by this schedule.

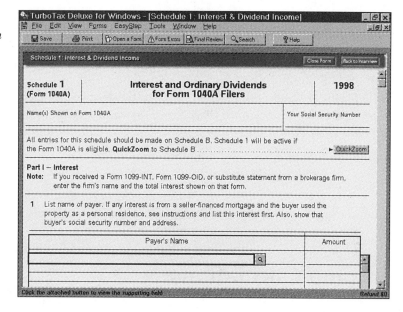

How Tax Liability Is Calculated

The Form 1040A is a simplified version of Form 1040, involving less reporting and fewer calculations. The basic tax computation for determining liability on both the Forms 1040 and 1040A is, however, essentially the same.

Determining tax liability involves a series of calculations, rather than just one. The format of both types of 1040 Forms is set up with these calculations in mind. This section helps you understand how the information entered on the form is used to perform the various calculations necessary to determine tax liability.

First, income from all sources is totaled, and certain amounts such as IRA contributions are subtracted to arrive at adjusted gross income. In fact, page 1 of the Form 1040 is devoted entirely to arriving at the adjusted gross income amount shown on line 32. This calculation can be summarized as follows:

```
Income - Adjustments to Income = Adjusted Gross Income
```

Deductions and credits are computed in the Taxes and Credits section on the second page of the return. Deductions and credits are subtracted from adjusted gross income to arrive at taxable income on line 38 of the form. This section of the return can be summarized by the following calculation:

```
Adjusted Gross Income - Deductions = Taxable Income
```

5

Your total tax liability, which is the amount of tax you must pay on the income that you earned for the year, is computed on line 39 of this section multiplying taxable income by the applicable tax rate as shown here:

```
Taxable Income x Tax Rate = Tax
```

Finally, the amount you owe or the refund to which you are entitled is determined by the information entered in the Other Taxes, Payments, and Refund sections also on page 2 of the return. The computations performed in these three sections of the return can be summarized as follows:

```
Tax Due - Credits and Prior Payments = Tax Owed or Refund Due
```

The calculation for the Form 1040A is simplified because it does not need to take into account the itemized deductions or most of the adjustments that appear on the face of the standard Form 1040.

Income Calculations

TurboTax performs three types of income calculations, the results of which are reported on the appropriate lines of the 1040 and 1040A Forms. TurboTax calculates total income, adjusted gross income, and taxable income. It is important to understand the differences among these reported income amounts.

Total income is the sum of all the income that you receive from any source during the year. The EasyStep Interview asks you questions about wages, interest and dividends, tax refunds, alimony income, business income, capital gains and losses, IRA and retirement plan distributions, unemployment compensation, and Social Security benefits.

Based on the answers you provide in the EasyStep Interview, TurboTax enters the appropriate amounts on lines 7–21 of the Form 1040 and on lines 7–14 of the 1040A. There is an "other income" line on the 1040 for amounts that don't quite fit into any of the foregoing categories. These amounts are added together to arrive at total income.

Certain amounts referred to as adjustments are subtracted from total income shown on line 22 of the 1040 to arrive at Adjusted gross income (AGI). Adjusted gross income is shown on line 32 of the Form 1040. It is derived by subtracting the amounts such as IRA, retirement plan, and medical Savings Plan contributions from total income.

Finally, taxable income is derived by subtracting deductions and exemptions from adjusted gross income. You then multiply taxable income by the applicable tax rate to arrive at tax due, before taking into account credits and prior payments.

Adjustments to Income

The concept of AGI is important because there are a number of deductions and credits that are computed based on a percentage of AGI. For example, medical expenses are generally not deductible unless they exceed 7.5% of AGI. Similarly, certain miscellaneous deductions cannot be taken unless the amounts spent exceed 2% of adjusted gross income.

It is important not to confuse adjustments with deductions. Adjustments are subtracted from gross income to reduce taxable income, regardless of whether a taxpayer itemizes deductions, as discussed in the following section. Additionally, certain deductions are subject to limitations based upon adjusted gross income.

Computing Itemized Deductions

TurboTax automatically totals your deductions based upon the EasyStep Interview questions or the amounts that you have entered on Schedule A. The program determines whether you are better off itemizing them or using the standard deduction amount. Similarly, if you decide to prepare your return by entering information directly on the schedules and forms, TurboTax totals the deductions you have entered and either opts for the standard deduction amount or uses the Schedule A itemization. TurboTax also determines whether you are entitled to take certain types of deductions that must exceed your adjusted gross income by a specified percentage, such as medical expenses.

Itemized Versus Standard Deductions

You are entitled to subtract from income the *greater* of total itemized deductions or the standard deduction amount to arrive at taxable income. You benefit by itemizing deductions on a separate Schedule A when the total of the deductions listed on the Schedule A exceeds the standard deduction amount that you are allowed.

Your standard deduction amount depends on your filing status. Table 5.1 lists the different standard deduction amounts for the 1998 tax year for taxpayers who are under age 65 and not legally blind.

TABLE 5.1. STANDARD DEDUCTION AMOUNTS FOR 1998.

Filing Status	Standard Deduction
Single	$4,250
Married filing jointly, surviving spouses	$7,100
Married filing separately	$3,550
Head of Household	$6,250

5

Consider an example of a taxpayer who is single and has $1,400 in real estate taxes and $2,100 in mortgage interest. The taxpayer's itemized deductions total $3,500, but the standard deduction amount is $4,250. TurboTax would use the standard deduction amount for this taxpayer because it is greater than the total of the itemized deductions.

Deductions Subject to Special Limitations

In addition to determining whether you should itemize or opt for the standard deduction amounts, TurboTax automatically computes the amounts that you are allowed to take for specific deductions that are limited to a percentage of your AGI. For example, medical expenses are deductible only to the extent that they exceed 7.5% of AGI. The EasyStep Interview asks you for information pertaining to the various medical costs that you have incurred and compares your total costs to your AGI to come up with the deduction you are allowed. Similarly, if you elect to enter amounts directly on the TurboTax forms, the program does not allow you to enter a deduction that exceeds the allowable amount according to your AGI.

Computing the Tax or Refund Due

Figuring out what you actually owe or if you have a refund coming is a three-step process that tracks the organization of page 2 of the 1040 and 1040A Forms. First, taxable income is multiplied by the applicable tax rate as determined by your filing status (for example, married, single, or head of household). Next, any credits to which you are entitled are subtracted from the liability amount. Finally, payments that you have already made during the year are applied to determine what you must pay or may elect to receive as refund or apply to the following year's taxes.

Step 1: Multiplying Taxable Income by the Tax Rate

First, you determine the total amount of tax that you must pay on the income that you earned during the year by multiplying taxable income by the appropriate tax rate. The tax rate is based on your filing status, your income level, and any special taxes (such as capital gains or alternative minimum tax) to which you may be subject. TurboTax uses the tax rate schedules if your taxable income is less than $100,000 and the tax tables if it is more than that amount. Different tables and schedules are in effect depending upon the filing status that you elect. TurboTax automatically references the correct one.

Additionally, TurboTax calculates special tax rates in effect for capital gains distributions, as discussed in Hour 11, "Income from Investments." Capital gains tax is calculated separately based on the information entered on Schedule D and is carried to line 13 on the first page of the Form 1040.

If you are self-employed and have net earnings of more than $400, you are subject to a special self-employment tax rate of 15.3%. The self-employment tax is discussed in Hour 10, "Taxation of a Business." The maximum amount of income subject to the self-employment tax is $68,400 for 1998. TurboTax automatically computes this tax based on the information entered on Schedule C or provided by you during the EasyStep Interview.

Step 2: Subtracting Tax Credits

Next, information on credits against tax liability is entered on lines 40-46 of the Form 1040. Common credits include the child care credit, credit for the elderly or disabled, and the foreign tax credit. Credits are discussed in depth in Hour 16, "Tax Credits."

A credit is different from a deduction. A credit reduces your tax liability dollar for dollar. In contrast, a deduction reduces *only* the taxable income on which the tax is computed. For example, assume you are in the 28% tax bracket and have the option of taking a $100 amount as a deduction or a credit. You want to take it as a credit and directly reduce your tax liability by $100. The same amount taken as a deduction would reduce your taxable income by $100, but would only decrease your ultimate tax liability by about $28. A credit has a more significant impact on tax liability than a deduction of the same amount.

The earned income credit is an odd type of credit. It is a "refundable credit," which means that even if you do not have tax withheld from your pay, you may receive a refund equal to the amount of the credit. The earned income credit is discussed in Hour 16.

Step 3: Taking into Account Payments Already Made

5

The final step in arriving at the amount that you owe is subtracting any payments that you have made during the year, such as through withholding, estimated payments, or refund amounts applied from a previous year.

Be sure to enter all information as to amounts witheld that appear on your W-2 and 1099 Forms. Also, be sure to include estimated tax payments during the year, and applied from the previous year's return, as well as any amounts that you may have paid when filing an extension.

Summary

This hour explained the basic structure of the Form 1040, Form 1040A, and Form 1040EZ. All these forms present and organize information in a format that reflects the calculations that are necessary to determine tax liability. Supporting schedules provide additional information and substantiate various amounts reported on the Form 1040.

This hour also discussed how total income, adjusted gross income (AGI), and taxable income are calculated. AGI is a particularly significant tax concept because it determines whether many types of expenses can be taken as deductions. For example, medical expenses can be deducted only to the extent that they exceed 7.5% of AGI, and certain miscellaneous deductions must exceed 2% of AGI.

Deductions are subtracted from adjusted gross income to arrive at your taxable income. TurboTax calculates the tax owed on your income for the year using the appropriate tax rate tables and schedules based on your filing status.

Ultimately, the program determines the amount that you send in with your return or receive as a refund subtracting credits and payments from the tax liability computed for the year.

Hour 6, "Introduction to W-2 and 1099 Forms," covers another type of tax reporting document: the Form 1099, which is used to track various payments made to you during the year.

Q&A

Q How do I decide whether to use the tax table or tax rate schedule for computing my income tax liability?

A You do not need to make this decision. TurboTax automatically computes the tax without giving you an option. In any event, there is no difference in the amounts arrived at using the tax table or tax rate schedule. But you cannot use the tax rate table if your taxable income exceeds $100,000.

Q TurboTax does a lot of automatic calculating and filling in of amounts on forms. How do I figure out where a number on a form came from?

A While in the Forms method, double-click any number in the tax form. The information upon which this number is based appears onscreen. If you click the number once, one of the following messages appears across the bottom of the screen: QuickZoom, Calculated Value, Date Field, CheckBox, Text Input Field, or Numeric Input Field. These options are discussed in Hour 2, "Preparation Options and Help Features."

Q Why do self-employed people have to pay a special tax?

A Employed people have half of their Social Security and Medicare payments from their paychecks and the other half paid by the employer. Self-employed people must pay both halves of the Social Security and Medicare taxes with their return.

Hour 6

Introduction to W-2 and 1099 Forms

This hour is spent reviewing two common types of information returns: the W-2 and 1099 Forms. These forms provide the information that you need to prepare your Form 1040, and copies are sent to the IRS so that it can verify the information that appears on your return.

This next hour acquaints you with how the W-2 is processed and distributed and the various types of 1099 Forms. You gain a sense of how this information is used by the IRS and other government agencies. Do not be surprised if this added insight enables you to catch an error or two in the information being reported.

Highlights of this hour include

- Who receives a copy of your W-2 Form
- What amounts are deducted from your wages
- What a wage base is
- The different types of 1099 Form

Understanding W-2 Forms

The W-2 Form (Wage and Tax Statement), shown in Figure 6.1, is used by employers to report wages, Social Security, and tips for workers who are legally classified as employees. Hour 9 provides the legal definition of an employee for tax purposes.

FIGURE 6.1.

A W-2 Form must be furnished by the employer to all employees who received any form of compensation during the year.

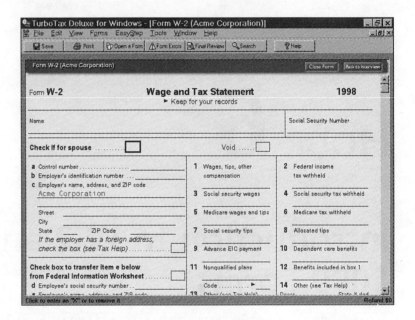

The term "wages," for purposes of the W-2 withholding requirements, is broadly defined and refers to any form of compensation paid to an employee. These amounts may include salaries, tips, bonuses, commissions, insurance premiums, or fringe or retirement benefits. The W-2 Form reflects sick pay, vacation allowances, moving expenses, and severance pay. It may also reflect travel and meal allowances, when applicable. Withholding of income and Social Security taxes is required on all these amounts.

Distributing Copies of Your W-2

Your employer furnishes copies of your W-2 directly to you and to the Social Security Administration. Generally, the 1998 forms must be provided to you by February 1, 1999. The Social Security Administration must receive its copy no later than February 28, 1999. The employer can request an extension of time to file with the Social Security Administration but may not extend its deadline for submitting a copy to you.

Contrary to popular belief, the IRS does not receive a copy of your W-2 directly from your employer. You are required to provide this document to the IRS by attaching a copy to your Form 1040. You are also required to submit a copy with your state income tax return.

If you notice an error or discrepancy on your W-2 on the amounts actually received by you or withheld from your pay, you should request that your employer provide both you and the Social Security Administration with an amended W-2.

Reading Your W-2 Form

Federal income taxes are not the only amounts withheld from your check during the year. Social Security, Medicare, and state and local taxes are subtracted as well. Your employee may also deduct state unemployment contributions and advance earned income credit payments, depending upon where you live and your personal situation.

It can be difficult to understand exactly what is being deducted given all the strange acronyms and terms that appear on the W-2 Form. Fortunately, TurboTax is designed so that you do not have to understand all the terminology on the W-2 Form or how the amounts were calculated to correctly enter them into the system. The screen shown in Figure 6.2 contains numbered fields that correspond to the numbered boxes on your W-2 Form. You find the following discussion of terms such as FICA, FUTA, and wage base useful, however, if you'd like to know the significance of the numbers that you are entering off of your W-2 Form.

Federal Insurance Contributions Act Tax

Under the Federal Insurance Contributions Act, your employer is required to withhold Social Security taxes from your wages. This tax, which includes a hospital insurance tax, is referred to on your W-2 Form by the acronym FICA. In addition to withholding this tax from your wages, the employer must match the amount of this tax withheld from your wages with its own contribution.

For 1997 the FICA tax rate is 7.65%. This rate is made up of two component taxes. Of the overall FICA assessment, 6.2% is attributable to the old age, survivors, and disability insurance tax, referred to as OASDI on your W-2. The hospital insurance component, referred to as the Medicare tax, consists of 1.45% or your wage base.

6

FIGURE 6.2.

The various types of taxes withheld and the wage base amounts used to compute them.

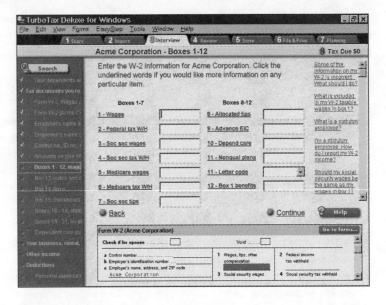

The term wage base refers to the amount of your wages used to compute the FICA taxes. The OASDI wage base for 1998 is $68,400. This means that the OASDI tax is only imposed on the first $68,400 of your wages. There is no limit on the wage base that can be used for computing Medicare taxes. Therefore, the Social Security and Medicare wage bases reflected on your W-2 Form may be different.

TurboTax automatically uses the correct wage base to calculate your Social Security tax liability. If your employer has erroneously withheld too much Social Security tax (or if you have multiple employers who withheld more than your wage base in the aggregate), don't worry. Any excess Social Security tax contributions are credited as an offset of your federal income tax liability.

State and Local Income Taxes

These amounts are also withheld from your paycheck during the year. The amount of withholding is summarized in box 18 for state income taxes and box 21 for local income taxes. You also notice that boxes 17 and 19 may reflect a wage base for state and local taxes that differs from the federal wage base. This is a function of the state and local revenue laws.

Federal State and Local Unemployment Tax Contributions

The Federal Unemployment Tax (FUTA) is paid by your employer and computed based upon the first $7,000 paid to you. The rate of the tax is 6.2%, but your employer may be allowed a partial credit against the tax for a contribution to state unemployment taxes.

This tax does not appear on your W-2 Form because it is paid entirely by your employer. It is mentioned here because it is commonly confused with FICA or state and local taxes.

Similarly, state unemployment taxes (SUTA) are also generally paid by the employer. But, there are a few exceptions. If you live in a state that permits employers to withhold SUTA, you see this reflected on your W-2.

Advance Earned Income Credit Payment

If you meet the qualifications for the earned income credit, discussed in Hour 16, "Tax Credits," you may have had part of it advanced to you by your employer during the year. If this is the case, these advanced amounts are reflected on your W-2.

Other Amounts Reflected on the W-2 Form

Other amounts may creep onto your W-2 Form. Box 13 can contain more than 20 different types of deductions, payments, or reimbursements designated by a letter code. Examples of box 13 amounts include 401(k) form deferrals, SIMPLE plan contributions, and moving expenses. Box 14 of the W-2 is sort of a "miscellaneous" reporting box and includes amounts such as educational reimbursement, insurance contributions, and union dues.

If you are unsure about the nature of an amount appearing in box 13 or 14 of your W-2, use the onscreen Help, illustrated in Figure 6.3, to pull up a list of codes and possibilities.

FIGURE 6.3.

If you can't figure out where a number on your W-2 came from, try the onscreen Help accessed from the W-2 interview or form screen.

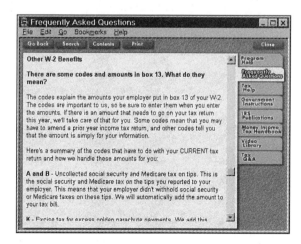

6

Understanding 1099 Forms

A 1099 Form is an information return filed to notify the IRS of specific transactions that occurred during the tax year. No tax is filed with an information return. The most common types of 1099 Forms are the 1099-MISC (reporting various types of non-employee compensation), the 1099-INT (reporting interest income), and the 1099-DIV (reporting dividend income). You can access the various types of 1099 Forms and the EasyStep Interview questions pertaining to them from the navigation bar on the left side of the screen, shown in Figure 6.4.

FIGURE 6.4.

Access the interview screens relevant to the various 1099 Forms by using the navigation bar.

Navigation bar

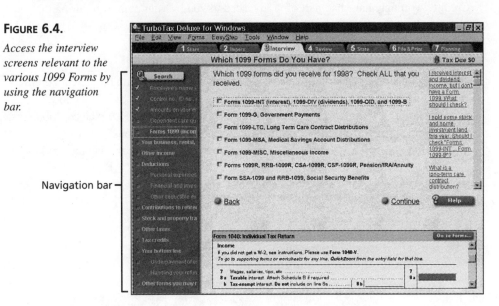

1099-MISC

You are supposed to receive a 1099-MISC Form from anyone who paid you more than $10 in royalties or other non-employee compensation or more than $600 for rents or services during 1998. If you do not receive a copy of this form from a payer, or if you receive one that is incorrect, you should take steps to obtain an accurate one. The reason for making the effort to do so is that a copy of the 1099 Form is sent to the IRS and the agency attempts to match the information on the 1099 with the information that you have reported on your return. Examples of amounts that appear on the 1099-MISC include the following:

- Payments for services to people other than employees, such as consulting fees
- Rental payments for real estate or equipment

- Commission prizes and awards
- Reimbursements of health insurance costs
- Proceeds from the sale consumer products valued at $5,000 or more
- Royalty payments to authors (my favorite)

A sample 1099-MISC Form appears in Figure 6.5. Income tax withheld on payments reflected on the Form 1099 appears in box 4 of the 1099 Form.

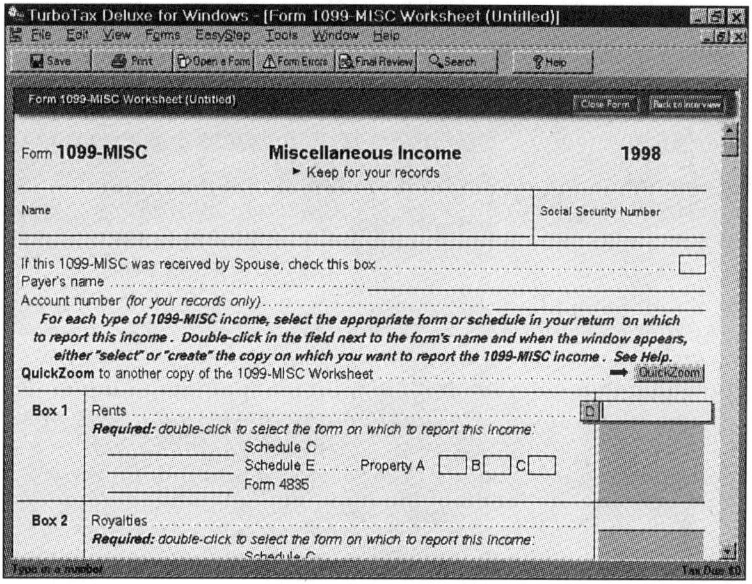

FIGURE 6.5.

Form 1099-MISC reflects payments for rents services and royalties.

The 1099-INT

A payer is required to provide a Form 1099-INT to each person who received more than $10 of interest. The 1099-INT is used to report interest paid on CDs, savings bonds, treasury bills, treasury notes, and treasury bonds. Additionally, interest paid by a trade or business totaling more than $600 during the year must be reported on the 1099-INT.

1099-DIV

Corporations issue the 1099-DIV to reflect a variety of distributions and payments. Most commonly, the Form 1099-DIV is used for reporting dividends, capital gains, and non-taxable distributions as a result of your ownership of stock in the company. These types of payments are reported in boxes 1a through 1d. Box 1e discloses investment expenses, which can be used to offset this income.

6

Boxes 3 and 4 of the 1099-DIV reflect foreign taxes that the company paid on dividends and other corporate distributions. These amounts are disclosed so that you can claim an appropriate credit.

Box 5 summarizes distributions that you may have received as a result of a corporate liquidation or dissolution. Box 6 tells you (and the IRS) the taxable value of any non-cash distributions you may have received.

It can be a complicated process to accurately report the many different types of corporate distributions reflected on the 1099-DIV. The EasyStep Interview streamlines the process with screens having numbered fields that correspond to the numbered lines on the 1099-DIV Form as shown in Figure 6.6.

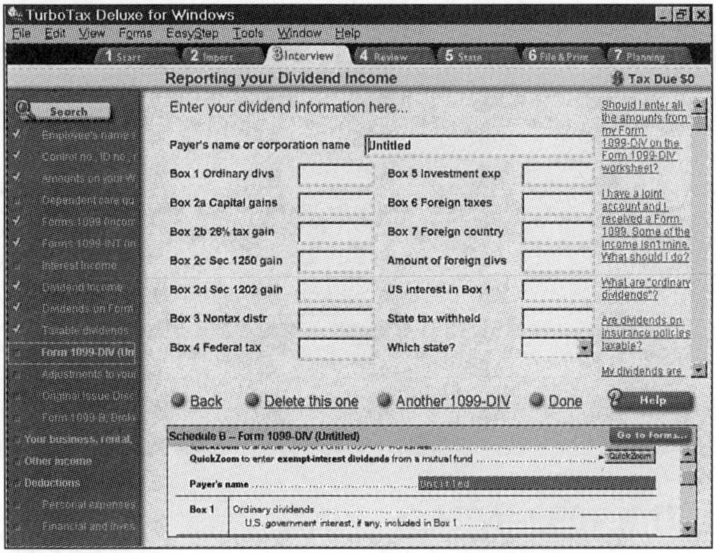

FIGURE 6.6.

EasyStep Interview simplifies the process of entering 1099-DIV information by providing screens with fields that correspond to the numbered boxes on the 1099-DIV Form.

You do not need to fully understand the basis for the computations or the nature of the amounts you are entering from the 1099-DIV to complete your return using either EasyStep Interview or the Forms method. You do, however, have a better handle on your financial situation and the performance of your investments if you understand the terminology used on the 1099-DIV Form. Accordingly, the various types of corporate distributions reflected on the 1099-DIV are summarized in Table 6.1.

TABLE 6.1. TYPES OF 1099 DISTRIBUTIONS.

Distribution Type	Explanation
Gross Dividends (Box 1A)	The aggregate of all distribution amounts reported on the 1099-DIV Form
Ordinary Dividends (Box 1B)	Earnings from dividends and short-term capital gains that are taxed at the taxpayers regular income tax rate
Capital Gains (Box 1C)	Distributions that are taxed at maximum 28% percent capital gains rate
Non-Taxable Distributions (Box 1D)	Distributions that are not taxable, usually because they represent a return of the taxpayer's initial investment
Non-Cash Distributions (Box 6)	The fair market value of goods or services received from the corporation
Liquidation Distribution (Box 5)	Distributions made upon dissolution of the business entity

Form 1099-B

Brokerage firms issue Form 1099-B to report sales of capital assets such as stocks and bonds. It is used to report proceeds from the sale of stocks, bonds, mutual funds, futures contracts, and other interests in securities. It is also used to report proceeds from foreign currency contracts and certain types of barter transactions. Generally, these transactions are taxed at capital gains rates and are reflected by TurboTax on Schedule D of the 1040.

Certain types of transactions reported on the 1099-B receive special tax treatment. The drop-down menu shown in Figure 6.7 lists these types of transactions and prompts you to select the classification that applies to you so that TurboTax can correctly determine your liability according to special rules that may apply.

Form 1099-G

Form 1099-G, shown in Figure 6.8, is used to report payments made to you by state and local government entities. It reflects amounts such as unemployment benefits, state and local income tax refunds, and taxable grant awards in excess of $600.

Form 1099-R

Form 1099-R, shown in Figure 6.9, is used to report distributions of $10 or more from retirement plans. Distributions from Individual Retirement Accounts (IRAs), Self-Employment Plans (SEPs), annuities, and certain types of insurance contracts are also reflected on this form.

6

FIGURE 6.7.

The types of sales transactions shown here are afforded special tax treatment.

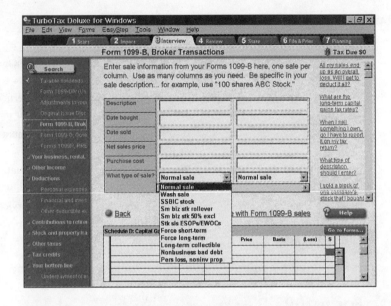

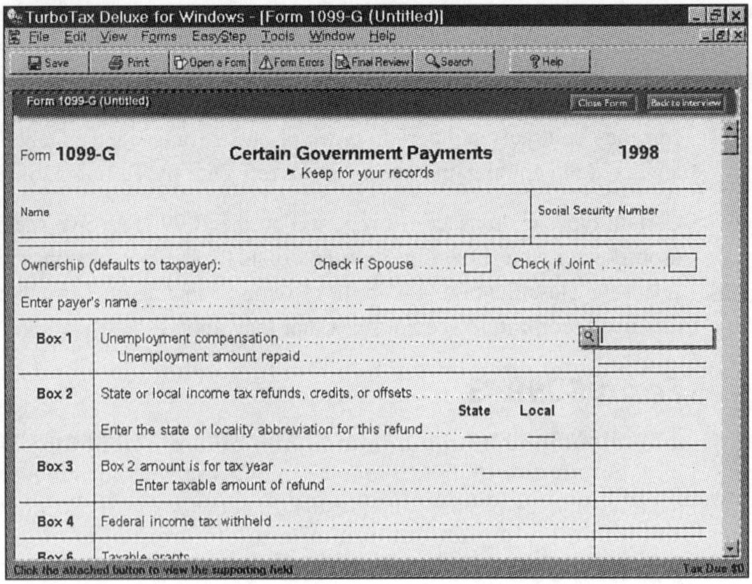

FIGURE 6.8.

Form 1099-G reflects payments made by government entities.

FIGURE 6.9.

Form 1099-R is used to report distributions from retirement accounts.

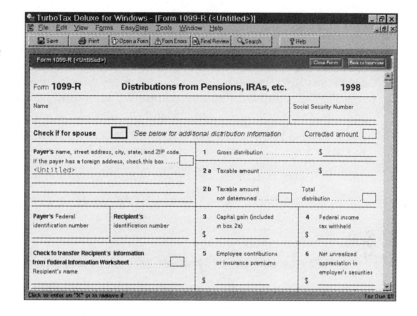

Forms 1099-LTC and 1099-MSA

These final two types of 1099 Forms are the new kids on the block, having been developed to reflect recent 1997 innovations to the Internal Revenue Code. Form 1099-LTC is used to report distributions under a contract for long-term care services for chronically ill individuals. Form 1099-MSA is used to report distributions from medical savings accounts.

> Medical savings accounts are discussed in Hour 13, "Non-Business Deductions."

Form 1099-S

Form 1099-S is used to report proceeds from the sale of real estate. If you sold your home during the year, you receive one of these forms. The person or entity responsible for closing the real estate transaction (such as the mortgage lender or title insurance company) is required to prepare and file it. The 1099-S reflects property tax obligations resulting from the transfer as well as the proceeds from the sale.

6

Summary

In this hour you learned to make some sense of the various information returns sent to you reflecting compensation that you received and transactions that you entered into during the year. The persons and financial institutions that paid these amounts to you prepare the W-2 and 1099 information returns. You are responsible for submitting copies of your W-2 to the IRS and to state and local tax agencies. Copies of 1099 Forms sent to you during the year are filed with the IRS by those who prepare the form. The IRS uses its copies of the 1099 Forms to verify the information you have provided on your return.

Hour 7, "TurboTax Schedules and Worksheets," provides additional insight on how amounts reflected on your 1099 Forms show up on your Form 1040.

Q&A

Q When am I subject to withholding for compensation that I receive for services?

A An employer is required to withhold taxes from the wages of any person legally classified as an employee rather than an independent contractor. Employee compensation and withholding are reported on Form W-2 and non-employee compensation, which is not subject to withholding, is generally reported on the 1099-MISC Form. The IRS has prescribed a 20-factor test for determining whether a worker is an employee or an independent contractor in Revenue Ruling 87-41. This test is discussed further in Hour 9, "Income from Employment."

Q Is it to my advantage to have my employer report my earnings on a 1099 Form without withholding taxes as opposed to issuing me a W-2 with all those payroll tax deductions?

A No! An employer is required to withhold Social Security taxes as well as federal income taxes from wages. More importantly, an employer must contribute *from its funds* an amount equal to the employee contribution. If you are not considered an employee, you lose the benefit of the employer contribution and generally must pay self-employment taxes on these amounts.

Q What is the "backup withholding" amount that appears on my 1099 Form?

A The backup withholding system requires the payer to withhold income tax from payments such as interest and dividends at a 31% rate if the taxpayer fails to provide the payer with his Social Security number, or the IRS notifies the payer that the Social Security number is incorrect. Backup withholding may also be required in cases where the IRS has notified the payer that the payee has underreported their income in the past. You can usually avoid backup withholding by filing a Form W-9 with the employer, which provides your Social Security number and requests that such amounts not be withheld.

HOUR 7

TurboTax Schedules and Worksheets

The sums and totals found on the final tax form you send to the IRS (your 1040, or perhaps 1040A), are the results of computations that occur on several worksheets and schedules. Ultimately, the taxman browses through and calculates numbers on very few forms you actually submit. However, if your taxes are complicated, the math that went into your computations could probably fill a small book. With TurboTax, you no longer have to shuffle through piles of schedules and worksheets, depleting bottles of white-out, trying to fix the math errors that pop up when you are trying to get these things in the mail before the post office closes.

One of TurboTax's nicest features is the seamless way that worksheet and schedule computations automatically appear on the tax forms you submit. Many lines and boxes you fill on your tax forms are the results of complex figuring that takes place elsewhere. With TurboTax, you not only can move between your tax forms and schedules with a click of a mouse, but you can zero in on an exact figure you decide doesn't look quite right to you, and instantly find the source of that figure, even if that source is an entirely different document. You can quickly determine whether there might be an error, all this before you lose your train of thought. In the time it *used* to take you to locate the correct worksheet and try to remember what you were doing, with TurboTax, you are already finished and have moved on to the next form.

Highlights of this hour include

- How TurboTax manages schedules and worksheets
- Understanding and including the correct schedules
- What is a schedule?
- Moving between worksheets, schedules, and tax forms

Why Schedules and Worksheets Are Important

In a nutshell, your tax forms are really nothing without the supportive documents that feed them. If you've ever looked at a 1040 from a couple years back, and wracked your brain trying to make sense of why a particular number is staring at you accusingly, you'd appreciate being able to go back and look at the documents that were responsible for that figure. Also, if you are audited, things may go your way if you can beat a clear path back to the computations that ultimately wound up on your tax form. The less guesswork, the better.

How TurboTax Manages Schedules and Worksheets

Perhaps you've noticed, while conducting the EasyStep Interview, that the top of the TurboTax screen asks you questions in plain English, while the bottom screen moves through the form you are actually filling out (see Figure 7.1). So you haven't quite escaped tax forms. They've been there all along, lurking underneath the friendly interview format.

And if your tax situation is complicated—for example, if you've a number of deductions that need a good deal of explanation—the EasyStep Interview winds you through a number of schedules and worksheets. Later, you'll see how TurboTax allows you to gracefully "jump into" these documents, without abandoning the comforting thread of the EasyStep Interview. But for now, let's take a look at what the schedules and worksheets are. We then explore how to move between them and how data from these documents ends up on your tax form. You see it's easy to edit that data if you need to.

FIGURE 7.1.

While asking you "plain English" questions, EasyStep is really filling out your tax form.

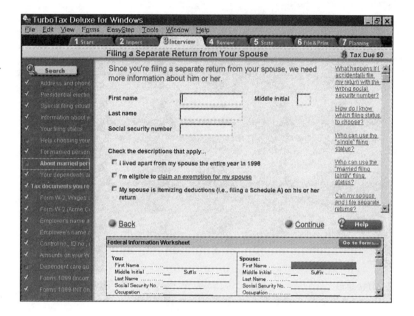

You'll also enjoy TurboTax's Supporting Details feature. With one mouse-click, you can create an accurate tax form entry from a long list of sums. Not only will you always be able to see where this grand total came from, you can just as easily add to it, if needed.

Understanding and Including the Correct Schedules

Figure 7.2 shows an example of moving through the EasyStep Interview, and suddenly, you are told that the Interview starts working with numbers from Schedule C. Based on how certain questions were previously answered, TurboTax decided that the tax form needed input from that particular schedule.

In moving through Schedule C, you are still using the Interview format. You are not abandoned in the netherworld of tiny boxes with inexplicable questions. However, as you can see from Figure 7.3, you *do* have to have some figures and documents at your fingertips.

7

FIGURE 7.2.

The TurboTax Interview takes a turn through Schedule C.

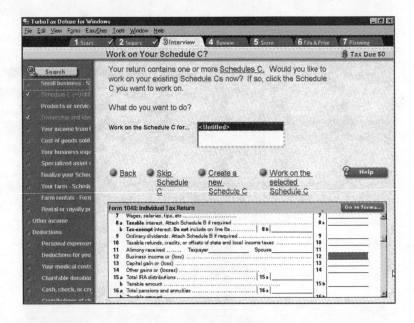

FIGURE 7.3.

While preserving the Interview format, you are asked questions from a particular schedule.

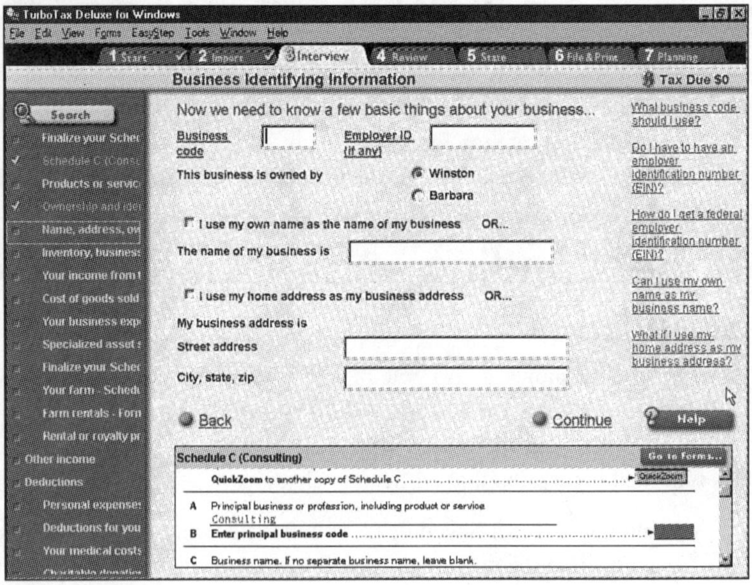

In the next sections, we explain the various schedules and the relationship they have to your tax return. We leverage only the detail needed so that, when TurboTax takes you on a side trip through one of those schedules, you have a bit of a map in hand.

For starters, not all schedules are created equal. Schedule A is important to every middle-class American taxpayer. It's divided into many segments. Others, such as Schedule B, are important to you only if you fall into a special category of earnings. Some of the schedules you may never need at all.

What Is a Schedule?

A schedule is a list of questions that most often require numeric answers. These answers snowball into a multi-faceted computation that finds its way onto the tax form you send to the IRS. Schedules are created to deal with common tax situations and are well-known in the accounting world by their alphabetical name: Schedule C, for example, deals with self-employment issues. Schedule D works out the kinks in your capital gains tax, if you are so lucky to have sold a house or business for a hefty profit. Each schedule creates computations that join the others on your tax form, and all of them become fodder for the answer to the big question: *How much do you owe this year, or how much are you getting back?*

In a benevolent stroke of kindness, TurboTax asks you questions on the schedule in plain English, adding up the multiple sums, rolling the equation forward, and quietly depositing the final answer on the correct line on your tax form. Still, you won't know the answers to typical schedule questions off the top of your head. So let's look at some of the major points of each schedule and later, when you see it coming, you'll know what sort of numbers to bring to the table beforehand.

Schedules are attached and sent along with your tax form to the IRS. Perhaps you've noticed the imperative at the top of any schedule: "Attach to Form 1040." Some read "Attach to Form 1040 or 1041."

Schedule A: Itemized Deductions

Soon after determining your filing status, you have to decide to take the standard deduction, or itemize. The amount you can deduct for yourself (which is the standard deduction) varies, depending on your filing status. After answering a few questions in the

7

EasyStep Interview, TurboTax helps you determine on which path lies the greater tax savings: taking the standard deduction, or itemizing. If you decide to itemize, a trip through Schedule A is in your future.

Some situations exist in which you might not qualify for the standard deduction, and thus, you'd have to itemize. For example, if you and your spouse are filing separately, and your spouse is itemizing, you also must itemize.

Schedule A quantifies and categorizes your itemized deductions. After working Schedule A, if the resulting sum is larger than your standard deduction, it is placed on line 36 of your 1040 Form (see Figure 7.4), although more calculations may intervene.

FIGURE 7.4.

If the sum from Schedule A is larger than your standard deduction, TurboTax automatically places the amount from Schedule A on the appropriate line on your 1040.

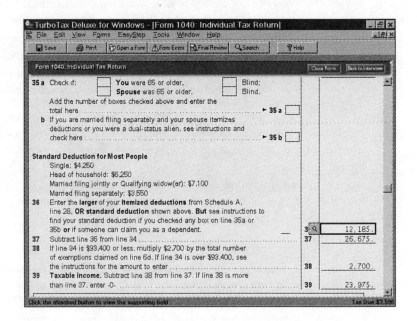

The following To Do section demonstrates how to open Schedule A in TurboTax, without the benefit of being asked to do so by the EasyStep Interview. The process discussed is the same for any other schedule.

To Do: Open Schedule A

1. Select the Forms, Open a Form menu command. The Open Form dialog appears (see Figure 7.5).

2. Scroll down and double-click Schedule A: Itemized Deductions. Schedule A appears and is larger than your screen can display.

3. Scroll down to see the rest of the form.

FIGURE 7.5.

Opening a form in TurboTax.

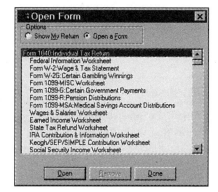

When a list has more entries in it than your screen can display, a scroll bar appears at the top right of that list. Check the down arrow at its bottom, and the screen displays the list entries that were previously not visible. Click the up arrow, and the first entries will reappear.

4. The headings in bold writing off to the left (such as Medical and Dental Expenses) represent *types of deductions* that Schedule A quantifies.

5. The numbers you fill in for each segment contribute to the entire deduction amount that is placed on your tax form. Press either the Tab or Enter key to move from line-to-line on the form.

6. To return to the EasyStep Interview, click either the Close Form or Back to Interview buttons at the upper right of the screen. Either option will save your information to your 1040 Form.

7

The following is an explanation of the main headings that appear on Schedule A, with answers to some of the most common considerations and decisions you have to make. Read through this section, and plan how you'd answer these questions when they arise on the EasyStep Interview. Retrieve the necessary paper documents beforehand, so you won't have to break the flow when you begin entering data into TurboTax.

 Working with Schedule A on the EasyStep Interview does not mean you have to directly enter data on this form. EasyStep walks you through it. It does help to be a little familiar with the form, if you care to make direct adjustments later.

Medical and Dental Expenses

You can deduct all medical and dental expenses that are above 7.5% percent of your *adjusted gross* income. This means that finding ways to reduce your adjusted gross income also makes it easier to reach that 7.5% threshold. Currently, if your annual income is more than $121,200 married or $60,600 single, there are limitations for medical deductions. You may deduct medical expenses for your spouse or dependent. Your spouse's medical expenses are deductible by you if you were married at the time you paid those expenses, or married at the time your spouse became ill, or both.

 Deductible medical expenses include the prevention, diagnosis, treatment, cure, and mitigation of disease.

Taxes You Paid

You may deduct state and local taxes, and property taxes, from your taxable income. (In Figure 7.6, notice TurboTax takes care of adding "lines 5 through 8," placing it on the correct line.) Part of your car or boat registration is also deductible. If you look closely at your car registration bill, you see that part of that registration payment is with regard to *the cost of the item.* That portion of your registration cost is deductible. State taxes you pay in this current year toward a tax liability of the previous year are also deductible (unless you paid them late). Special local assessments such as taxes for replacing sewage mains or streetlights may not deductible.

You can deduct all charitable contributions you make to qualified organizations, up to 50% of your income. Donations to certain organizations like Veterans groups are tax-free only up to 30%. If in the previous year, you exceed those limits, you may carry the remainder over to the current year, and take the rest of the deduction.

FIGURE 7.6.

TurboTax adds multiple-line equations for you, helping determine the deductibility of other taxes you paid.

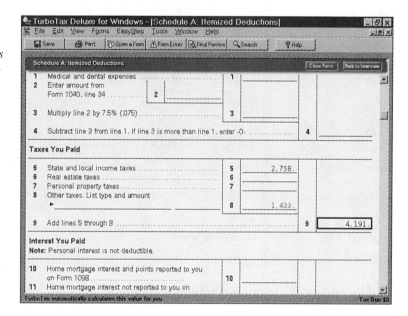

Interest You Paid

Interest you pay to purchase or improve your own home, as well as interest you pay to borrow money to invest, is deductible on Schedule A. Business expenses are deductible on Schedule C. Farm-related expenses are deducted on Schedule F. In most situations, you may also deduct points you are required to pay to secure a home loan. You may also deduct interest paid on a loan secured by your home equity, even if not all that money goes to remodel your house.

Charitable Contributions

The IRS regards your gifts to charitable and religious organizations as tax deductible. These would be financial donations, as well as material gifts, and even your driving on behalf of such organizations. The trick is that you receive nothing tangible in return for

7

("derived only spiritual benefit from") these gifts. If there's any possible question of the legitimacy of taking this deduction, have a letter from the receiving organization stating that no services were exchanged on behalf of your gift. This letter needs to be obtained and dated before the tax due date of the year the gift was made. There are yearly limits to how much you can deduct through charitable contributions, but you can carry the deduction over into the following year (see Figure 7.7).

FIGURE 7.7.

You can carry over charitable contribution deductions into the following year.

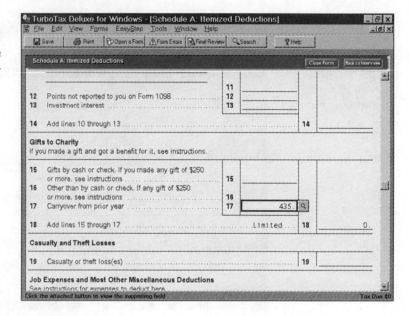

Casualty and Theft Loss

Your personal property losses as a result of theft, fire, accidents, or acts of nature are deductible. The hard part is determining the true cash value of a personal item that was lost. You may not deduct the first $100 of the value of that loss, and only losses that exceed 10% of your adjusted gross income may be deducted. Additionally, items covered by insurance may not be deducted, and if your adjusted gross income is too high, your ability to deduct is limited.

Unreimbursed Employee Expenses

This includes job-related travel, union dues, and job education costs (job travel does not include commuting to work). Only those deductions above 2% of your adjusted gross income are deductible. These expenses would include meals eaten while traveling on behalf of your job, and, in some cases, automobile upkeep. You're only eligible if your employer does not reimburse for these expenses, or if this reimbursement does not adequately cover what you spent.

Those are some of the main considerations that apply to Schedule A. TurboTax (and your accountant) has more details and specific information at its fingertips. The points listed above are far from comprehensive, and some of the thresholds referred to are apt to change with the new tax laws. There are a couple of themes common to all schedules, especially Schedule A, that are worth pointing out now:

- Do not take deductions that you cannot substantiate. Taking an overly large or unlikely deduction draws unwanted IRS attention to your tax form.

- Keep on hand hard-copy receipts, canceled checks, daily logs, detailed check vouchers, or any other documentation that helps substantiate deductions you are claiming.

- Watch the income ceilings for some deductions. If your adjusted gross income is too high, some deductions you might be planning on could become unavailable, or greatly reduced. Use IRAs, charitable donations, and extra mortgage payments to keep your adjusted gross income low enough to qualify for the deductions you have in mind.

- Take the time to learn the specific rules regarding deductions that you plan to take. Don't deal yourself out of the game just because you didn't read the fine print. While a particular schedule is onscreen in TurboTax, click the Help button to open articles pertaining to that schedule. For added details, click the links (blue text) that relate specifically to your deduction.

TurboTax automatically calculates all the sums on Schedule A. The correct amount for itemized deductions is placed on your tax form. Unless you are filing electronically, you have to print out this (and any other) schedule, attaching it to your tax form and mailing them in together.

Making Schedule Entries without EasyStep

As mentioned earlier, you are answering questions related to these schedules while still working with the EasyStep Interview. However, if you want to enter data right onto the schedule itself, you have two options:

- While the EasyStep Interview tabs are shown on the screen, work with the current form at the bottom of the screen. Only part of the form is visible, due to screen space limitations (see Figure 7.8). To view the rest, scroll down using the scroll bar. You can also enter data right onto the form, even while the EasyStep Interview is visible. Clicking the line Business Street Address (including suite or room number) causes the line to become a white box, as shown in Figure 7.8. The blinking cursor indicates you can type text in the area. Scroll anywhere on the schedule and enter data in this manner.

7

FIGURE 7.8.

You'll have to scroll to see an entire form.

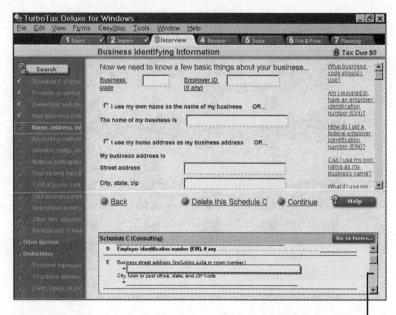

Worksheet scrollbar

- Abandon the EasyStep Interview for the moment, and work with the schedule full-page, as shown in Figure 7.9. Do this by clicking the Go To Forms button, found at the lower-right of the screen. When this button is clicked, the form in question fills the entire screen. None of the data you enter here disrupts the EasyStep Interview. After filling in some data this way, you can return to the interview by choosing Back to Interview from the EasyStep menu, at the top of the screen.

Schedule B: Interest and Dividend Income

Schedule B is for reporting annual income above $400 derived from interest or dividends. The schedule is divided into three portions: Income from interest, income from dividends, and foreign accounts and trusts.

Some distributions you may receive from investments are called dividends, but are actually interest. When walking you through this form, TurboTax asks questions about your earnings that help clarify this distinction.

FIGURE 7.9.

You can type data right onto a form, if you like.

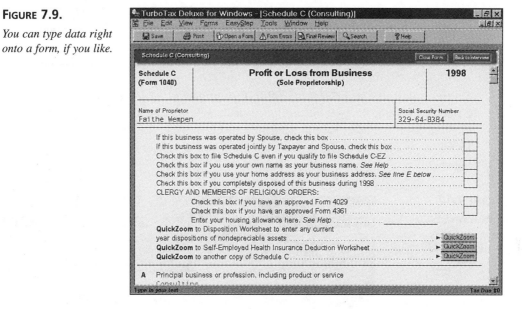

The following income sources should be reported as interest:

- Interest you receive from bank accounts
- Loans you make to others
- Interest from most other sources

The following income sources are called dividends, but should actually be reported as interest:

- Mutual savings banks
- Federal savings and loan associations
- Domestic building and loan associations

The following income sources should be reported as dividends:

- Money market funds
- Stock dividends and distributions

Interest you pay as a result of a penalty for early withdrawal from a deferred interest account may be deducted, although restrictions apply.

7

You must report the existence of foreign accounts to the IRS, even if such accounts earned you nothing during that year.

Several worksheets, such as form 1099-INT, contribute to Schedule B. As you complete a worksheet, TurboTax uses the resulting calculations, placing the new figures in the required form. You don't have to open the schedule or enter the numbers yourself (see Figure 7.10). Later in this hour, you learn about how schedules and worksheets work together.

FIGURE 7.10.

TurboTax makes it easy to move between worksheets and schedules.

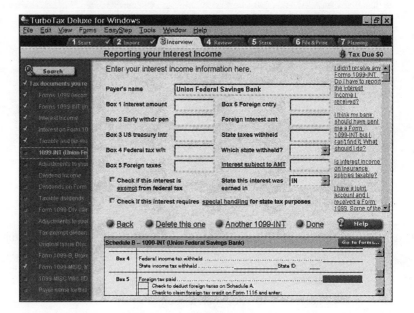

Schedule C: Profit or Loss from a Business

There are several types of Schedule C Forms. The one that TurboTax picks for you depends on whether you own the business alone, or with partners, as well as the type of business. Some Schedule C Forms are brief and require fewer details. The complexity of your tax situation determines whether you are eligible to use the simpler schedule.

For Schedule C, the following are a few important things to keep in mind:

- TurboTax asks for your business code and employer ID (if your company has employees).

- The extent of your participation in this business of yours is greatly related to the type of deduction you can take, if your business has shown a loss.
- You have to show you've been paying your own Social Security and Medicare taxes.
- If you've paid someone more than $600 that year to work for you, you must send them and the IRS a 1099 Form. (TurboTax walks you though this process.)

It must be reiterated that Schedule C and related forms take pains to differentiate between you as a *passive participant* in a business (you put up an initial amount of money and are not otherwise involved), and an *active, day-to-day* participant. If you plan to show a loss for this business on your taxes, you may need to produce evidence of your active involvement.

Attention must also be paid to how equipment purchased for your business is to be depreciated. Most business equipment must be depreciated over a five to seven year period and not deducted all in the same year. When deducting vehicular expenses related to your business, maintain careful accounting between personal use of a vehicle and driving costs related to your business. If you do not have a vehicle solely for business use, keep good odometer and mileage records to justify your business driving deductions.

Schedule C asks you to specify which accounting method you use for your business: Cash (the money you have right now is what you're counting on) or Accrual (the money you owe or are owed is what you're counting on). The advantages of one particular accounting method vary depending on your business type. Trouble is, after you inform the IRS of your choice, you cannot change it without the IRS's permission. You may, therefore, want to consult an accountant before making this choice.

Schedule D: Capital Gains and Losses

This schedule is where you declare profits or losses from the sale of property. Not every sale of property necessarily shows a taxable profit, and provisions abound, sheltering you from having to be heavily taxed every time you sell a residence, business, or some other type of property. The following are some points to consider regarding Schedule D:

- The actual capital gains you must report is offset by the amount of improvements you made to the property (called the "adjusted basis"), so you'd rarely have to show your entire sales profit as a gain.

7

- Distinctions are made between making a repair to a property (fixing a leaky roof) and improving a property (installing expensive skylights and fixtures). Repairs are written off and depreciated the same year you make the repair. Improvements add to the "adjusted basis" of the property and help to shelter you from a high capital gains figure on your tax form, when you *do* sell.

- Sale of primary residence is not subject to capital gains tax, although the exact profit threshold above which you can be taxed changes frequently.

> Starting this year, if you are married filing jointly, you can acquire up to $500,000 dollars when you sell your home and not pay capital gains tax on that amount. If you're single, up to $250,000 dollars from a home sale is not subject to capital gains tax.

- Conversely, you can never claim a capital loss if you have to sell your home at a loss. (You are expected to tough it out until the market improves.)

- Special rules apply to property held for less than one year (see Figure 7.11).

FIGURE 7.11.

Schedule D makes a distinction between property held less than or more than one year.

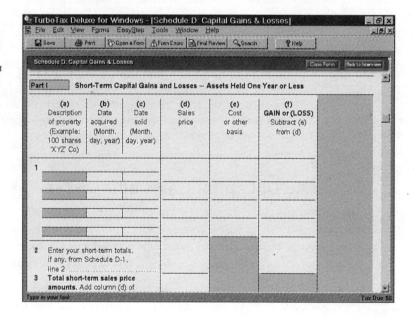

Schedule E: Supplemental Income and Loss

Income and losses resulting from rental property, royalty payments, and patents are declared on Schedule E. This schedule pertains to supplemental sources of income, profits resulting from royalties earned, patents, and other intellectual property that you acquired. Rental income and loss is also declared here.

Please note that this schedule does not pertain to patenting *your own* inventions or royalties from a book *you* authored. Schedule E is for intellectual property *you acquired*, not as a result of your own labor. For example, if you went out and bought the publishing rights to the song catalogue of an artist, you would report that income on Schedule E.

Schedule E also applies to renting out your vacation home or letting a film crew come and use your house for a movie. Short-term, as well as long-term, rental of your property is covered in Schedule E.

Schedule EIC: Earned Income Credit

If you are a single parent and earn below a certain income threshold, you may not only be exempt from taxes, but can receive money back from the federal government. This schedule takes pains to determine whether a child qualifies as a dependent, because grandchildren and other children under your care may also qualify you for EIC (see Figure 7.12).

FIGURE 7.12.

Some situations can earn you an Earned Income Credit.

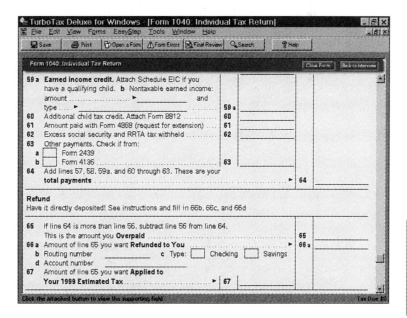

7

If you can show you qualify early enough in the year, you may also be eligible for Advanced Earned Income Credit, in which your employer pre-pays your Earned Income Credit on a per-paycheck basis. Your employer would then report these payments to you and reduce his own tax liability.

Schedule SE: Self-Employment Tax

This is a very important schedule to the self-employed. It verifies you paid all your taxes as a self-employed person, and helps substantiate a loss of income, if you spent more than you earned toward your business during that year. Worksheets associated with this schedule include the Health Insurance Deduction Worksheet, which reduces the amount of income you must declare as a result of having to purchase your own health insurance.

> The Health Insurance Deduction Worksheet can be important to you as well, if you work at a job that does not offer insurance. You may be able to deduct the amount of money you spent on insurance, if you can substantiate that none was available through your spouse's job, or your own employer. If you have two income sources (one from self-employment, and the other from your "job"), this form may clarify whether you can stop paying Social Security at some point during the year, because Social Security does have an upper-income threshold.

Schedule H: Household Employment Tax

Currently, you are taxed if you pay more than $1,000 per year to any one person; however this threshold varies depending on age, and current tax law. This schedule wants to know if you've been paying Social Security tax and Medicare for this employee, among other things.

Schedule K: Business Partnerships

Schedule K is for business partnerships. The IRS is looking for the same type of input as with Schedule C, the extent of your involvement with this business, proper depreciation of business equipment, proper relationship to employees, and such. You are also asked whether any of your business partners are foreign nationals.

Schedule R: Credit for the Elderly Disabled

This schedule is to assess your own personal eligibility for credit due to advanced age or disability, not for establishing that such a person is under your dependent care.

This concludes the section reviewing what to expect from certain schedules. Again, nothing in this section is meant to be comprehensive. TurboTax provides a lot of in-depth, detailed information for individual schedule lines and calculations. Let's look at how to access schedules and their data in TurboTax.

Choosing a Schedule Not Offered By the Interview

If the EasyStep Interview does not offer you a schedule or worksheet that you think would hold some advantage to you, simply fill it out yourself, and TurboTax includes the results on your tax form, even though it "didn't come up" in the Interview.

To Do: Open a Schedule

1. Select Open a Form from the Forms menu, and scroll down to the form you want to open.

2. Double-click it and enter a Description of this form in the dialog box provided (see Figure 7.13). This description is for your identification purposes only. The schedule or worksheet fills the screen.

FIGURE 7.13.

Type in a description of a worksheet, for your own recognition.

3. Just click any box to type in the data. Move from box to box by clicking them or by pressing the Tab key.

4. Amounts that appear in the Totals area also appear in the appropriate lines of your tax form.

5. To move back to the interview, choose Back to Interview from the EasyStep menu, or press the Back to Interview button on the upper-right corner of the form.

7

Adding Schedule Data On Your Own

As mentioned earlier, you'll probably never need to locate a schedule on your own because the EasyStep Interview draws out the necessary documents that pertain to your tax situation as it unfolds during the interview. But to find a form yourself, choose Open a Form from the Forms menu, and scroll down the list, double-clicking the form you want to open.

Even though EasyStep Interview did not invite data from this schedule, computations that result from you completing this schedule appear on your tax form where appropriate, nonetheless.

To Do: Type Onto a Schedule Line

1. Within an opened form, click any line. If that line can receive direct data from you, the data field for that line turns white and a blinking cursor appears.

2. Type the appropriate numbers or data. (Later, we discuss how TurboTax deals with errors.)

3. You may notice a white "form" icon to the left of where you type (see Figure 7.14). That's for Adding Supporting Details, which we explore shortly.

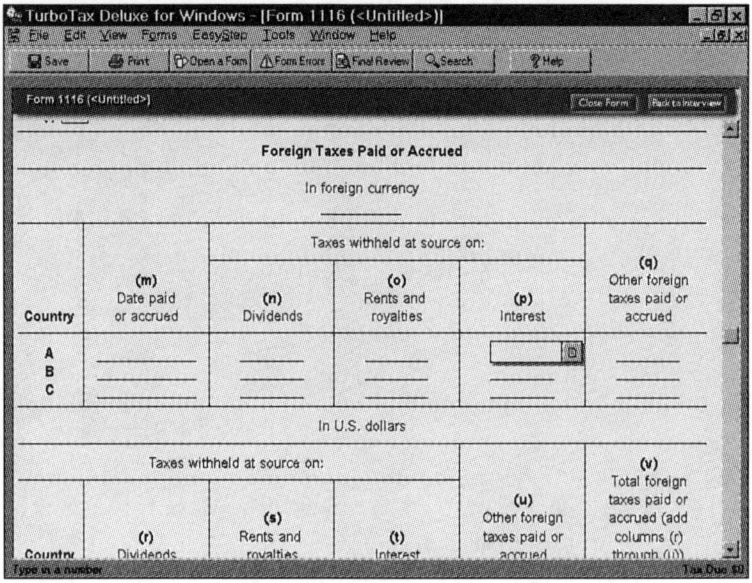

FIGURE 7.14.

The tiny white "form" icon is for adding supporting details.

4. Press Enter or the Tab key to finalize the data. The white data entry box will automatically jump to the next relevant field.

5. Some fields require only that you type an X (see Figure 7.15) in one of the choice boxes. Using your mouse, click once in the box, and an X appears. Click again, and the X is removed.

FIGURE 7.15.

Some fields require that you "X" a form by clicking the appropriate field.

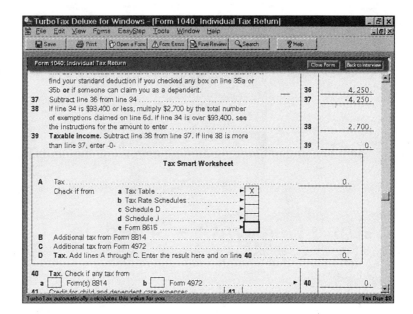

When a Schedule Line Won't Allow Direct Typing

Many schedules, worksheets, and tax forms have fields that are not for you to type in. The data that appears there is computed from other lines in the schedule, or even another form or worksheet altogether. If a field is surrounded by a solid black rectangle and does not show a blinking cursor when you click inside it (see Figure 7.16), data from that field is called from other lines. Numbers appear when those supportive lines are filled out.

7

FIGURE 7.16.

A field surrounded by a solid black rectangle receives data from another TurboTax form or schedule, not by you typing it in.

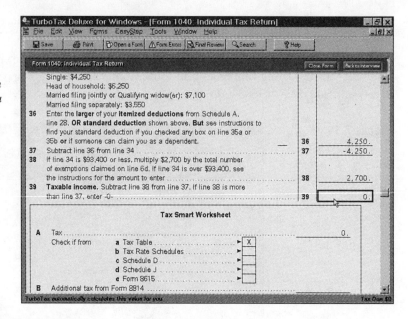

Getting Help with a Schedule

When you are faced with a cryptic schedule line, the type that manages to look intimidating and totally inscrutable at the same time, you are not alone. TurboTax provides many ways to get help understanding what is being asked. This help ranges from descriptions of the entire form, to line-by-line "What do I do now?" hand-holding.

If you are looking at a schedule from the full-page view, or if you've simply clicked View Current Form during the Interview, you still follow the same steps to get help with your schedule:

- To read a general explanatory description of any schedule, click once on the schedule, but outside any field. Then click the Help question mark at the upper-right of the screen (see Figure 7.17), and a Tax Help article pertaining to that schedule appears.

- To get help with a specific line, click that line and click the Help question mark at the upper-right of the screen. You either see a detailed description of that particular line, or a link to a description of that line. (A clickable link is blue. Click it and the article describing the line or field opens.)

- For more help with a particular line, right-click the schedule or field you are having trouble with, and click Guide Me (see Figure 7.18). You are walked through this form in an EasyStep Interview format.

FIGURE 7.17.

For many types of help, click the Help question mark at the upper-right of the screen.

Help button

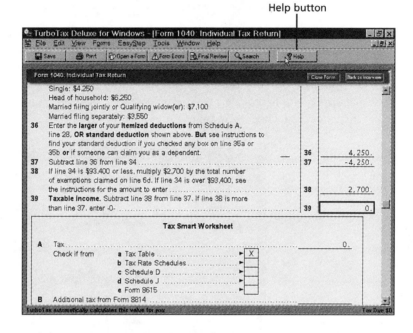

FIGURE 7.18.

To move through a worksheet or schedule in an EasyStep format, right-click and select Guide Me.

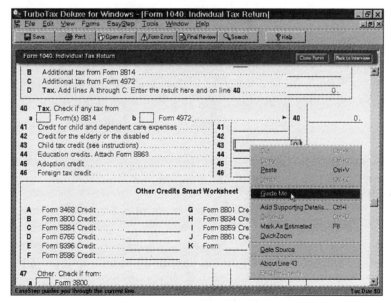

7

Reading the Government Instructions

Addition help on most schedule or worksheet items is available by placing your cursor in the schedule or line you need help with and choosing Government Instructions from the Help menu (see Figure 7.19). This Help menu simply displays the instructions that the IRS includes in a booklet with the schedules. (By the way, if you can get over the fact that they refuse to provide a table of contents, the *IRS Forms and Instructions* booklets are not too bad. Order them from www.irs.ustreas.gov.)

FIGURE 7.19.

Click the Government Instructions tab to read the IRS's standard instructions on any form.

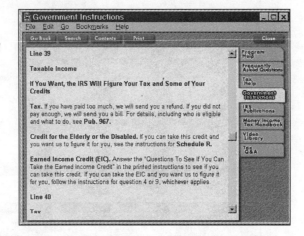

Later in this hour, we explore QuickZoom and the Add Supporting Details feature, which help connect your schedules to its related worksheets and other data sources.

As mentioned earlier, the resulting computations from your schedule appear appropriately on your tax form. Now let's explore worksheets, what they are, and how they can help you.

TurboTax Worksheets

Like schedules, worksheets provide computations that end up on your final tax form. But they are more for your convenience. They help with the math and are not sent in with your tax form, as schedules are. Schedules provide computations that are mandated by tax laws. Worksheets are just helpful. Worksheets are good to keep on file, if you ever want to know how you arrived at certain numbers. With TurboTax, you need not litter file cabinets with these documents. TurboTax keeps track of them for you and can be retrieved with a single mouse-click.

How Worksheets Help

Figure 7.20 gives a good example of how a worksheet contributes to your tax form's accuracy. Shown here is the Itemized Deductions Limitations Worksheet. It determines whether your income is high enough to limit your total allowable itemized deductions.

FIGURE 7.20.

The Itemized Deductions Limitation Worksheet determines whether your income places you out of bounds for certain deductions.

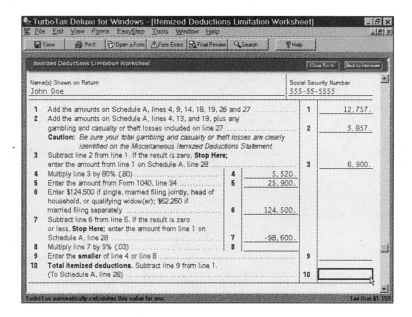

Notice the mouse cursor is highlighting line #10 (to Schedule A, line 28). This indicates that the results of this worksheet are funneled over to Schedule A.

From Schedule A, the calculations contribute to your tax form. If you've ever scanned a tax form, marveling at how anyone could possibly keep track of all these mitigating, and/or calculations, you are quite pleased at how TurboTax allows you to focus on setting a good tax strategy, and takes care of where all the figures are placed.

Examples of Worksheets

Most often, the EasyStep interview makes it clear when you need to stop and answer questions on a worksheet before proceeding with your form (we learn how that's done momentarily). However, if you think working through one of the worksheets would be helpful, just click Open a Form from the Forms menu, and scroll down, selecting the Worksheet you want to work with. It's not possible right now to name all the worksheets TurboTax provides. The following are a few examples:

7

The Federal Information Worksheet. This worksheet parallels the questions TurboTax asks you at the beginning of the interview. If you realized you've entered your Social Security number in error, or made some other mistake, just click Open a Form from the Forms menu, and scroll to the very top. Double-click the Federal Information Worksheet and add data where appropriate.

Which Forms to Complete Worksheet. This worksheet is second from the top of the list and asks simple language questions about tax-related issues. After filling out the questionnaire, TurboTax lists the forms you need to complete to accurately get a picture of your taxes.

In the Forms list, space does not always permit the entire listing of a worksheet's name. In such cases, "Wks" is substituted for worksheet. For example, in that list, clicking Health Insurance Deductions Wks opens the Health Insurance Deductions Worksheet.

The Vacation Home Worksheet. This form helps to determine your income liability for money you received from renting out your vacation home or similar property.

The MSA Worksheet. This document is used to compute the maximum contribution limit for a Pre-tax Medical Spending Account.

Learning About a Worksheet

Like getting help with schedules, TurboTax provides both general descriptions of worksheets, as well as line-by-line walk-through help.

- To read a general description of a worksheet's purpose, click any blank area of the worksheet, not inside a field or on a line. Then, click the Help question mark at the upper right of the screen.

- For help with a specific field or line, click directly on the area you want help with, and again, click the Help question mark at the upper-right of the screen.

Now that you're acquainted with worksheets and schedules, let's explore how to get around between them.

Moving Between Worksheets, Schedules, and Tax Forms

In TurboTax, you don't simply flip back and forth between forms in an arbitrary way. You follow the numbers and trace where a certain sum came from (or is going to be recorded). If, when filling out a tax form, TurboTax determines data is needed from a particular schedule or worksheet, you are able to click and move there immediately. You are not left to search through a list, hoping to open the right one. Additionally, if a number appears on a worksheet and you have no recollection of typing it there, that's because TurboTax already calculated that number elsewhere and made it available to you on this form. The following is how to get around schedules, worksheets, and forms:

- You move between TurboTax documents by using a feature called *QuickZoom*, which is a tiny magnifying glass that appears next to a set of numbers on a line.

- Click that magnifying glass, and the source of that computation (the numbers next to the magnifying glass) opens. An example is given in the following To Do list.

To Do: Find Data Sources

1. In Figure 7.21, line 1 of an Itemized Deductions Limitation Worksheet is highlighted. It reports a figure of $4,191.

2. Notice the magnifying glass to the left of the sum. That's the QuickZoom icon. Click it, and the *data source* for that number opens.

FIGURE 7.21.

This form reports an amount that originated on Schedule A.

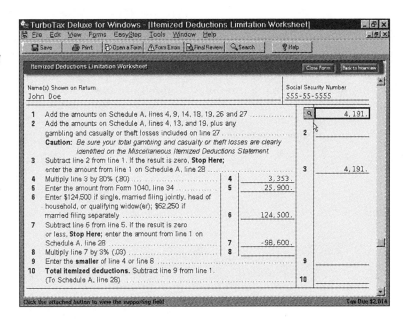

3. Note that the amount on Schedule A is the same as the one found on the worksheet we were just looking at.

> When you've opened a new worksheet or schedule using QuickZoom, it's easy to return to the form you were previously working on. Just click the Close Form button at the upper-right of the screen.

Understanding the Numbers

Now let's say that, after noticing these two like figures, one on your 1040 and the other on a Schedule B worksheet, you're really not sure of their meaning. Perhaps you answered some questions in the EasyStep Interview that related to these forms, but now you'd like to understand more about what you've been answering, or perhaps make adjustments. How can you find out what these numbers mean?

- Click the Help question mark in the upper-right corner of the screen. Make sure the QuickZoom magnifying glass is visible. That way, Help knows for which set of figures to provide an explanation.

- QuickZoom also provides a link to another related form or worksheet. In Figure 7.22, you see the Estimated Taxes and Form W-4 Worksheet. This form helps calculate how many allowances you should claim, which influences the taxes deducted from your paycheck. It's important not to get overwitheld or underwitheld. To get more information, click the QuickZoom link to the information form.

> Just as with schedules, if you click a tax line in a worksheet and it appears surrounded by a thick black rectangular line, you are not able to edit that line. It means that number is calculated elsewhere. To find out more about why you are not able to edit a particular line, and how the numbers can be adjusted, click the line once, and then click the Help question mark at the upper-right.

FIGURE 7.22.

QuickZoom to a related form.

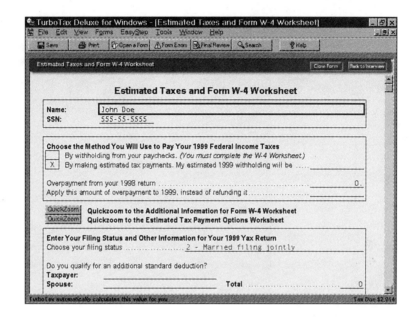

Dividing Entries into Supporting Details Lists

TurboTax aims to make it easy for you (or the IRS) to determine where a particular number on your tax form came from, and how a certain figure was arrived at. Wouldn't it be nice if you could click a number in a tax form and see a breakdown of that sum, and a list of the figures that added up to *that* number? How about a description next to each number, so you could know what you *meant* by it at the time? That's exactly what TurboTax has done.

In Figure 7.23, you see the Medical Expenses Worksheet. On the first line you indicate how much you spent on prescription medication.

7

FIGURE 7.23.

The Medical Expenses Worksheet includes a figure derived from Supporting Details.

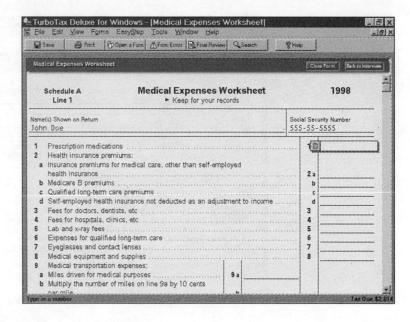

To Do: Add Supporting Details

1. Instead of typing in a number, click the tiny Form icon that appears to the left of the number field. What appears is an empty list (see Figure 7.24).

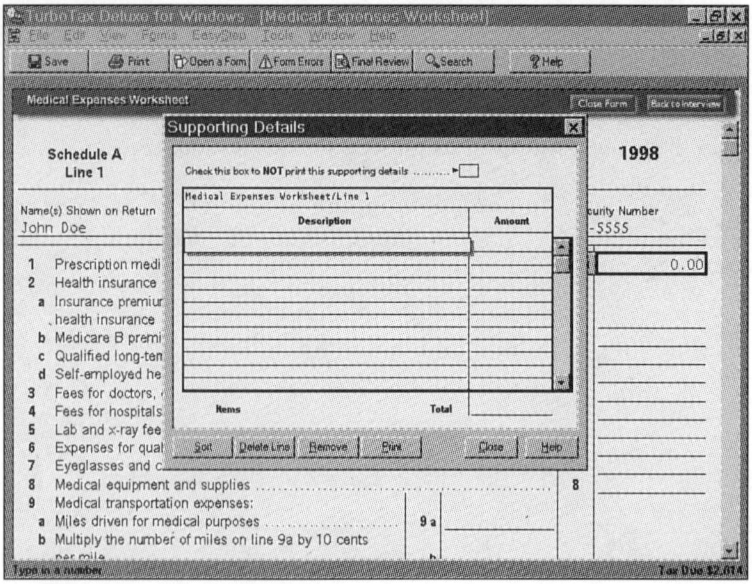

FIGURE 7.24.

Click the Form icon to open the Add Supporting Details list.

2. On each line of this list, type a description (in this example, a single medical prescription name). Press Tab to get to the Amount field for that item.

3. Also, type in an amount associated with that item (in this case, the amount for the prescription drug that was paid for at some point during the year).

4. Each amount contributes to a sum, which continually updates itself at the bottom of the list when you add a new number.

5. This sum also automatically appears on the tax form itself, on the line you clicked.

Later, when you want to look up the sum developed with the Add Supporting Details list, right-click the line and select Add Supporting Details (see Figure 7.25). The Supporting Details mini-worksheet appears, filled with the numbers and descriptions you originally typed in. Also, when you print out this tax form, the Add Supporting Details worksheet also prints out.

FIGURE 7.25.

Right-click Add Supportive Details to verify the sum on your form.

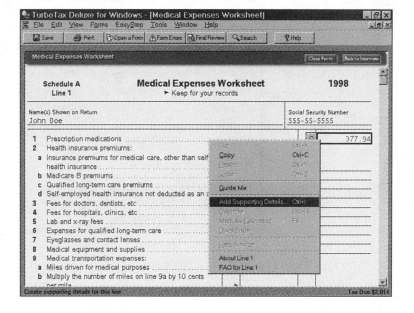

If you don't want to print these mini-worksheets when you print your tax forms, check the checkbox at the top of the Add Supporting Details dialog box. It specifies that you should check it if you do NOT want these supportive details printed. In other words, if you do not click that checkbox, these details will be printed when you print your tax forms.

7

Changing Entries on Schedules and Worksheets

Changing a number or entry on a tax form is often not just a matter of clicking the line and typing a new value. When you click on the line you want to change, a QuickZoom magnifying glass may appear, indicating that this number originates on a different schedule or worksheet (see Figure 7.26). You may be able to type in a number, even if the QuickZoom icon appears, as long as no previous data is found on the *source* schedule or worksheet.

FIGURE 7.26.

Click the QuickZoom icon to view source figures on another form.

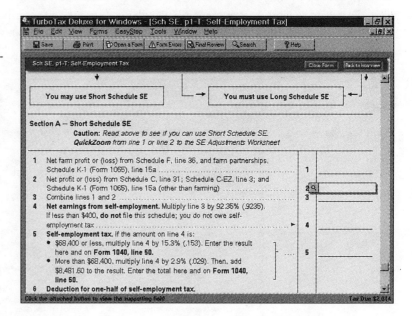

To Do: Use QuickZoom To Locate and Change an Entry

1. Within an opened worksheet or form, double-click on a line. Click the QuickZoom magnifying glass, which opens the source worksheet or schedule.

2. Type the new entry. The entry you wanted to fix on your tax form is also changed.

3. To see your tax form again, click Close Form or Back to Interview button at the upper-right of the screen.

Limits to Directly Typed Entries

At times, TurboTax does not let you type data directly into a line if you have opted to do electronic filing (see the Error Alert dialog in Figure 7.27). TurboTax does tell you, however, where the entry should originate from (in this example, the source would be Form 4972).

FIGURE 7.27.

Selecting Electronic Filing causes TurboTax to be more cautious about what you can type directly into a form.

At other times, when you type an amount that is supposed to originate from a schedule, TurboTax issues a warning (see Figure 7.28) indicating that the appropriate schedule has not been prepared yet. You are allowed to leave the suspect value in that field (it appears in red), if you insist. Later, when you are about ready to finish your file, TurboTax reviews errors, and, once again, prompts you to remove the inappropriate value.

FIGURE 7.28.

You can sometimes type data into a form reserved for a computation from elsewhere, but TurboTax warns you.

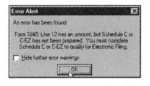

Also, if you get around to working through the schedule mentioned in the warning, your value is just replaced by the resulting calculation from the schedule.

Most often, you are not able to change personal data such as name, address, and Social Security number unless you open the Federal Information Worksheet form. Do this by selecting Open a Form from the Forms menu, scrolling to the top, and clicking Federal Information Worksheet, which will be second from the top.

7

Summary

Schedules and worksheets are a big part of the tax return process. As you have seen in this hour, TurboTax makes it simple to keep track of the myriad of schedules you might have to fill out. In the next hour, you find out TurboTax can help you fill out your state tax return. By using the information from your federal return, it makes the state return process a breeze!

Q&A

Q What are schedules for?

A Schedules provide guidance for calculated values that are then placed on your tax form.

Q What are worksheets?

A Worksheets help you calculate important figures such as assessing your eligibility for certain deductions. Unlike schedules, worksheets are not turned in to the IRS with your tax form.

Q I see a number on my TurboTax form, but I don't know how it got there. I'd like to put in a different number.

A In TurboTax, just like with paper tax forms, schedules and worksheets feed into your tax form. Additionally, worksheets provide numbers used in schedules, which are then fed downstream into the tax form itself. Often TurboTax won't allow you to type a number in a space reserved for a computation from another source.

Q Can I override data that TurboTax places on my form from another source?

A Yes you can. Right-click the space you want to type your own number, and select Override. You are then able to type something in, but it appears in red. Later, right before TurboTax finalizes your form, the program reviews all your overrides and warns you about letting this data remain in place.

HOUR 8

Completing Your State Tax Return

This hour covers the information that you need to complete your state income tax return. Regardless of which one you are filing in, the state return is based on the same information you have compiled to prepare your federal return. In fact, many states ask you to include a copy of your federal income tax return when filing.

It may come as a surprise to you that if you spent considerable time or worked in more than one state, you may need to file multiple state tax returns. Your obligation to do so depends on whether your activities during the year constitute the legal "nexus" that is necessary for a state revenue agency to have jurisdiction over you.

Highlights of this hour include

- How to obtain a TurboTax state program
- How to complete a state tax return
- Filing multiple state tax returns
- Making changes to your state tax return

Obtaining Your State Tax Package

To complete your state income tax return, you must purchase a separate state income tax product from TurboTax. This is easily accomplished in either of two ways. You may call Intuit and order the product directly at 1-800-Intuit. Alternatively, you can access the TurboTax Web site.

To Do: Order State Tax Software Online

1. Make sure that you have activated your modem connection.
2. Click the State tab on the EasyStep interview screen (see Figure 8.1).

FIGURE 8.1.

You can access the TurboTax Web site and order the product directly from this screen.

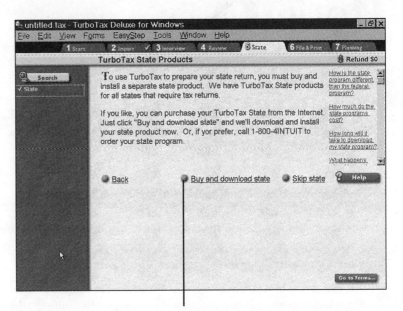

Click here to access Web site

4. Click the Buy and Download State button, and proceed to enter the required information to purchase your product.

Have your credit card information handy regardless of whether you are ordering the state tax package by telephone or from the Web site.

8

You can also access the TurboTax Web site by entering the following URL into your Web browser: http://www.turbotax.com. After you have entered the required information, you are provided with instructions as to how to directly download the TurboTax state tax product. TurboTax state tax products are available for all states that impose state income taxes except the following:

Alaska

Nevada

South Dakota

Texas

Washington

Wyoming

If you decide to prepare your state tax return without the benefit of the TurboTax product and need to locate a form, refer to Appendix B. This appendix contains contact information for all state taxing authorities.

Completing a State Tax Return

Before you begin your state tax return, you need to complete your federal return. Because you need to import a lot of data directly from the federal return, it is a good idea to complete the Final Review of your federal return (discussed in Hour 17, "TurboTax Review Features") prior to beginning your state return. This hour discusses how to make changes to your federal return after modifying your state, but because it takes time to make the changes, you want to avoid having to do so.

You'll find that it is most time-efficient to finalize your federal return before beginning work on your state return.

To Do: Prepare a State Tax Return

1. Go to the EasyStep menu and select State from the drop-down menu that appears. A series of onscreen interview instructions appear. Follow these instructions to access the State Assistant.

2. The State Assistant guides you through most of the adjustments and additions that you need to make to your federal information to complete your state return.

▲ 3. To review your state form, click the state Review topic and click Review.

> You can access the State Review function at any time from anywhere in the program.

To Do: Print a State Return

1. Go to the EasyStep menu and select File & Print from the drop-down menu that appears.
2. Click Print My Return to mail it.
▲ 3. Choose your state tax return from the list that appears.
4. Click Print.

Filing Multiple State Tax Returns

You are required to file multiple state returns if you were a resident of more than one state during the year. For example, if you were employed in Wisconsin and accepted a new job in Illinois mid-year, you are required to file income tax returns for both states. The Wisconsin 1040 provides, as an example, a form requiring apportionment of income among states.

You may have an obligation to pay taxes to a state even if you were *never* a resident of the state. If you engage in income producing activities or have property that generates income (such as real estate or bank accounts), you may be obligated to file an income tax return in that state. Each state has different requirements for finding that a taxpayer has "nexus," which is a sufficient legal connection with the state to warrant taxing them. If you are unsure as to your tax obligations to a particular state, check the filing instructions for the state form.

Generally, states require withholding of personal income taxes from payments of wages earned by resident and non-resident employees within their borders. However, many states enter into reciprocal agreements to forgo withholding taxes on a resident of another state who works within their borders.

It is a good idea to check the filing instructions for a state if you are unsure as to whether you have a filing obligation before ordering the TurboTax state package. You can usually obtain a copy of the state form by calling the taxing authority for the state. Mailing information, telephone numbers and Web site information are available in Appendix B.

Filing Multiple State Tax Returns with TurboTax

To prepare tax returns for multiple states using TurboTax, you must purchase and install the state TurboTax packages for all the states that you need.

If your obligations in one or more states are minimal and require few calculations other than those that have already been performed on the federal form, you may want to try to simply fill in the state tax form without ordering the TurboTax state package. Refer to Appendix B to obtain tax forms and instructions directly from the states you need.

> If the task of completing state tax forms manually proves too daunting after you get the forms from the state taxing authority and attempt to complete them on your own, you can download the state tax package from the TurboTax Web site literally on a moment's notice.

After you complete your first state tax return, to progress to the next one, take the following steps:

1. Go to the EasyStep menu. Choose State from the drop-down menu that appears.

2. Select the return that you want to complete from the list that appears.

TurboTax automatically saves all state tax forms that you complete to the same file, along with your federal Form 1040.

Making Changes to Your State Tax Return

It is important to remember that most of the information on your state tax return is based upon the information entered on your federal income tax return. If you make changes to your federal return and want them to be correctly reflected on the state tax return, follow this procedure:

1. Open your federal tax return in the Forms Method. If you are in the EasyStep Interview, click the Go to Forms button.

2. Select the state return that you want to open from the list that appears (if you have more than one).

The current information from your updated federal form is automatically inserted in the state form *unless* you have "override" amounts on your state form. Override amounts are entries that you changed on the state form using the Override option. You may handle the updating of Override amounts in one of three ways:

- You can use the Cancel Override option. This option is accessed from the Forms menu. After you cancel the Override, TurboTax automatically imports the updated federal information to the state form.

- You can delete the Override entries and leave the fields blank. TurboTax automatically imports the updated federal data into the blank state fields.

- You can update the Override fields manually.

> If you make changes to your federal return, remember to update *all* affected state tax returns.

Summary

Generally, state tax returns are prepared from data and calculations appearing on the federal Form 1040. TurboTax state programs can be ordered by telephone or downloaded from the Internet. You can also obtain state tax forms and instructions directly from the various state tax authorities. Contact information for these agencies is provided in Appendix B. You may be subject to tax in more than one state, and it is a good idea to confer with the state tax authorities or an accountant familiar with multi-state income issues when in doubt.

Chapter 5, "Introduction to Personal Income Tax Forms," acquaints you with the component parts of the 1040 Form that is the basis for most state tax filings.

Q&A

Q My wife and I file separately for state purposes. Can I create a second tax return for the same state?

A Yes. Use the Save As option from the File menu to save two copies of your federal return under different names. You can then proceed to prepare a separate state tax return from each federal tax return file.

Q Can I move back and forth between my state and federal tax return?

A Yes. If you are in the Interview, click the topic you want. In the Forms Method, go to the File menu and select the tax form that you want to access.

Q How can I get state specific information when using TurboTax?

A Review the state Read Me file that accompanies your TurboTax state program.

PART III
Income from All Sources

Hour

HOUR 9

Income from Employment

This hour addresses the factors that determine how much money you take home when you work for someone else. Obviously, this is a function not only of what is paid to you by your employer, but what is withheld for payment to various government agencies.

In this hour, you learn which types of workers and amounts are subject to withholding requirements, and which are exempt. This hour also guides you through the process of entering W-2 wage information into the TurboTax system. You even learn about some amounts that are not included on the W-2 Form, but which are taxable as wages nonetheless.

Highlights of this hour include

- The distinction between employees and independent contractors
- How to enter wage information from your W-2 into the TurboTax application
- The importance of the elections made on your W-4 Form

- Taxable compensation that does not appear on your W-2
- Types of compensation exempt from withholding requirements

Employees Versus Independent Contractors

The company that you work for has determined whether you are classified as an employee or independent contractor long before you sit down to do your 1998 tax return. But this issue directly affects the amount of your after-tax income, and it is to your advantage to make sure that you are classified properly.

Whether your company deems you an employee or an independent contractor determines how much of your Social Security tax is paid by your employer as opposed to being paid by you. Additionally, this classification determines your rights, under the laws of your state, to unemployment benefits and worker's compensation insurance.

Employers are required to withhold income and various other taxes from the wages of workers classified as employees. Wages and withholding for employees are reflected on the W-2 Form. Conversely, if a worker is categorized as an independent contractor, the employer is not required to withhold and report taxes; a 1099 Form rather than the W-2 is used to summarize and report compensation.

An employer is required to pay a portion of the Social Security tax withheld from the wages of an employee subject to W-2 reporting. This means that the employer shares the burden of this tax. In contrast, an independent contractor must pay the full amount of his or her social security tax.

Rather than having income and Social Security taxes withheld from wages, an independent contractor must pay them in the form of self-employment tax. This tax is discussed in Hour 10, "Taxation of a Business," and includes the full portion of the worker's Social Security and Medicare tax. It is reported Schedule SE. The short form Schedule SE is shown in Figure 9.1.

How do you know whether you are an employee or an independent contractor for tax purposes? The legal distinction between employees and independent contractors focuses on the level of control an employer has over the worker. Generally, an employer is able to control the times, location, conditions, and circumstances under which an employee works. In contrast, an employer does not exert control over an independent contractor over the manner in which the work is done. The employer has only an interest in the work product. Examples of independent contractors include writers and consultants. The IRS prescribes a 20-factor method for classifying workers as either employees or independent contractors in its Revenue Ruling 87–41.

FIGURE 9.1.

Schedule SE is used to calculate Social Security and Medicare taxes for independent contractors whose wages are not subject to withholding.

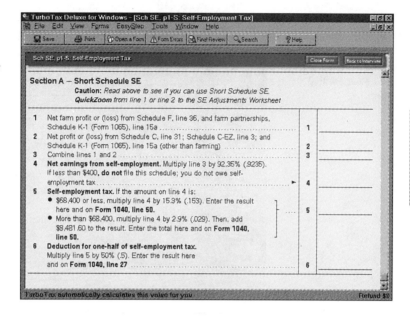

9

If you have been classified as an independent contractor and believe that you meet the criteria of an employee, you should inquire about being reclassified because it is to your advantage to have your employer contribute Social Security and Medicare taxes on your behalf. You may be an employee even if you have several jobs.

Entering Your W-2 Information

TurboTax asks you, at the beginning of the EasyStep Interview, if you have received any tax forms during the year. It lists several types of tax forms, including W-2 Forms. If you have checked the W-2 box, you will be asked on the next screen to confirm that you have received one or more W-2 Forms during the year. Then you can proceed to the following To Do section.

To Do: Enter W-2 Information

1. If you indicated that you received a W-2 Form, you see the form shown in Figure 9.2.

2. If you have imported data from a prior year's return, the name of your employer automatically appears on the interview screen. If your employer has changed during the year, you need to enter information from additional W-2 Forms.

FIGURE 9.2.
FIGURE 9.2.

Entering your employer's name and address is a key beginning to filling out the W-2 Form.

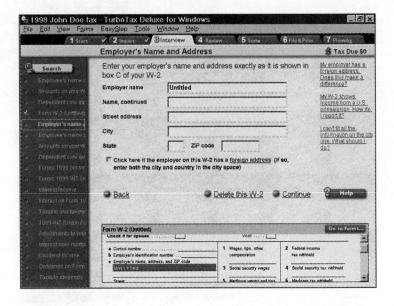

If you have more than one employer, you are prompted to enter information from additional W-2s after you have completed the process of entering the information from the first W-2.

3. Enter the name and address of your employer on the screen, and click Continue.

4. If your own name and address appears, confirm them and click Continue.

5. When prompted for the control number and other information, enter it and click Continue.

6. Enter the information from your W-2 Form in the fields shown in Figure 9.3.

7. Click Continue. The screen shown in Figure 9.4 appears, prompting you to enter the amount and code that appear in box 13 of the W-2 Form. An employer can enter information about approximately 20 different items in Box 13, and a letter code is used to indicate what the amount shown represents. For example, a letter R code indicates a contribution to a Medical Savings Account.

To view a list of all coded items that may appear in box 13, access the drop-down list provided on the TurboTax W-2 Form screen, as shown in Figure 9.4.

FIGURE 9.3.

The numbered fields on this screen correspond to the fields on the W-2 Form.

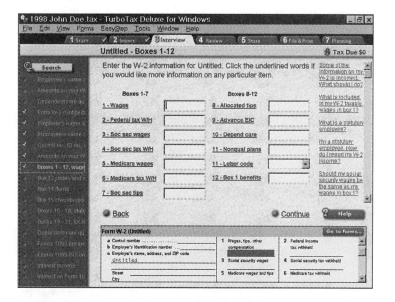

FIGURE 9.4.

This drop-down list describes the amounts associated with the codes in Box 13.

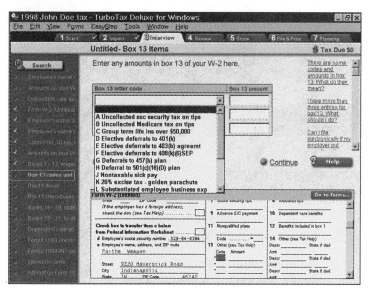

8. When you have entered all the amounts shown in box 13, click Continue.

9. Enter any amounts and codes that appear on box 14 of your W-2 Form. These include amounts and information the employer thought you might want to know about and include dues, health insurance premiums, educational payments, and state disability insurance paid.

10. When you have entered all the amounts shown in box 14, click Done With Box 14 to advance to the screen shown in Figure 9.5.

FIGURE 9.5.

These check boxes contain additional information about your legal status as a tax-payer. Onscreen Help defines these terms.

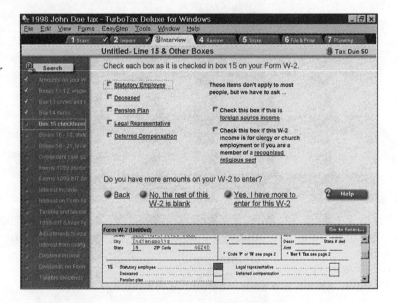

To find out more about the box 15 information, such as is meant by a "legal representative" or "statutory employee," click the onscreen Help option.

11. Check each box onscreen that is checked in box 15 of your W-2 Form.

12. After you have checked the appropriate fields as shown in Figure 9.5, click No, the Rest of This W-2 Is Blank.

13. If you have more W-2s to enter, click Yes, Enter a New W-2. Otherwise click No, I'm Done with W-2s.

Form W-4 Withholding Exemption Certificate

Form W-4, shown in Figure 9.6, is filed by employees to advise their employer as to how many exemptions they are claiming for federal income tax purposes. Your level of compensation, filing status, and number of exemptions claimed are used to determine how much federal income tax should be withheld from your paycheck. (Filing status and personal exemptions were discussed in Hour 3, "Personal Information and Filing Status.")

If two different taxpayers have identical salaries and exemptions but one is single and one is married, the single taxpayer is subject to a higher rate of withholding.

FIGURE 9.6.

This form is filed by an employee at the time of hire to determine withholding.

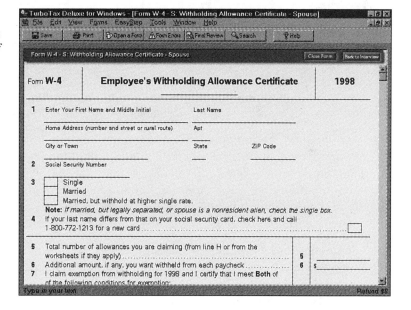

Usually, employers use the same W-4 Form to compute both federal and state income tax withholding. If you are claiming a different number of exemptions for federal and state income tax purposes, you need to fill out two different forms.

If you claim an excessive number of exemptions, or in other words, more than the number of exemptions to which the IRS feels you are legally entitled, the agency can intervene. It can impose a $500 fine and issue its own determination as to how many exemptions you are entitled to claim. Your employer is legally bound by the IRS determination.

If you did not owe any federal income tax last year and do not expect to owe any this year, you can file a Form W-4 claiming an exempt status. If you do so, your employer does not withhold tax from your wages. A form with an exempt status expires every year and must be renewed with your employer annually.

Compensation That Is Not Subject to Withholding

Income that you receive as an independent contractor is not subject to withholding, but is taxable and subject to the self-employment tax that is discussed in Hour 10. If you are an employee, you may also receive payments during the year that constitute taxable compensation but are not subject to withholding for one reason or another.

Certain taxable benefits provided by your employer are not subject to withholding. If your employer provides you with a group term life insurance benefit in excess of $50,000, the cost of the benefit over this amount is taxable to you as compensation. This taxable benefit is not, however, subject to withholding. Similarly, if your employer reimburses you for deductible moving expenses, these amounts are not subject to withholding even though they must initially be reported as income on your tax return.

Scholarships and grants may also be taxable as self-employment income if you perform services to receive them, such as teaching or research. Unemployment benefits are also included in income. Similarly, sick pay and disability payments are generally taxable if you did not purchase the plan that is making the payments. However, these amounts may not show up on your W-2 if someone other than your employer is making them.

Tip income is another common source of compensation that does not show up on a W-2 Form. If you have less than $20 per month in tip income, you are not required to report it to your employer; withholding is not required. This income is, however, taxable as compensation. TurboTax prompts you to enter information as to any tip income that you did not report to your employer.

It is important to be aware of the categories of taxable compensation that may not appear on your W-2 Form. Not only are these amounts subject to federal income tax, they increase your wage base for purposes of the Social Security and Medicare taxes. TurboTax prompts you to enter most of these amounts as miscellaneous income during the interview. It also provides a screen for any types of taxable compensation that may not have specifically been addressed during the interview, shown in Figure 9.7.

FIGURE 9.7.

This screen is available to enter any types of taxable compensation that were not specifically addressed during the EasyStep Interview.

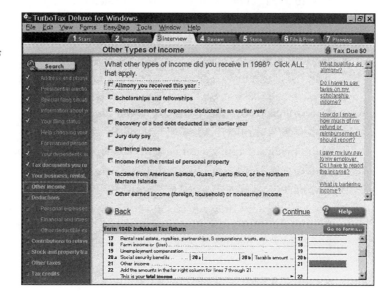

Summary

This hour introduced you to the legal distinction between employees and independent contractors. Employers must withhold payroll taxes from the wages of workers legally classified as employees but are not required to do so for independent contractors. More importantly, employers are required to contribute to the Social Security and Medicare taxes paid on behalf of employees, whereas independent contractors must bear the full burden of these taxes.

It is also important to be aware of taxable compensation that does not show up on a W-2 Form even though you are an employee. Examples include certain scholarships and grants, unemployment compensation, and group term life insurance. Even though these amounts do not appear on your W-2, you must report and pay tax on them. TurboTax prompts you to enter the necessary information into the system for this purpose.

Hour 10 goes into greater depth on how the self-employment tax that independent contractors pay is computed.

Q&A

Q What happens if, for some reason, my employer does not withhold enough from my paycheck to cover my federal income tax liability at the end of the year?

A Under-withholding can subject you to interest and penalties. To avoid it, you must be sure to pay either withholding or estimated taxes equal to the lesser or current year's liability or 90% of the prior year's federal income tax liability.

Q What withholding issues arise if you work for more than one employer?

A Because each employer is withholding Social Security taxes and does not know what the other employers are withholding, it is possible that they may withhold amounts in excess of the Social Security wage base. Any excess Social Security taxes withheld are simply treated on your return as advance federal income tax payments, and you are given an appropriate credit by TurboTax.

Q What penalties apply to an employer who fails to withhold tax from an employee's wages?

A An employer is liable for Social Security and Medicare taxes regardless of whether they are collected from wages. An employer who fails to withhold is liable for payment of the employee's portion of these taxes, as well as applicable interest and penalties. This liability is relieved, however, if the employer can show that the employee paid the tax.

Hour **10**

Taxation of a Business

This hour is spent on tax preparation issues faced by entrepreneurs—people who work for themselves rather than for others. Your business venture may be a sprawling enterprise employing dozens of workers, or it may the sort of activity that occupies your free time and some space in your garage.

Regardless of which category your revenue-producing efforts fall into, you need to report your income. Schedule C is the logical choice for a solely owned business that is not incorporated (unless you are a farmer who uses Schedule F for this purpose).

Highlights of this hour include

- The basic format of the Schedule C
- The material participation and at-risk rules
- The self-employment tax
- Reporting income from farm activities

Introduction to Schedule C

Schedule C is used to report income and expenses from a business or profession. To use Schedule C or Schedule C-Z, your business must be considered a sole proprietorship. A sole proprietorship is a business that is owned by one person, and the income and expenses of the business are reported on the owner's Form 1040. A sole proprietorship is not considered a separate legal entity; its earnings are reported using your Social Security number. Corporations and partnerships are considered separate legal entities, and you must file a separate tax return for them rather than using Schedule C.

The Schedule C is one of the most confusing forms included with a 1040. It is filled with complicated elections that have significant consequences as to your liability. It is a good idea to use the EasyStep Interview when preparing this form, even if you opt to use the Forms method for completing the rest of your 1040.

The Schedule C, shown in Figure 10.1 is a summary of all the revenue and expenses for your business. As such, it is a sort of income statement for your business, and copies of it are often requested by banks and financial institutions in making decisions as to whether to extend credit to the business.

FIGURE 10.1.

Schedule C, used to report income from a business, is divided into three sections.

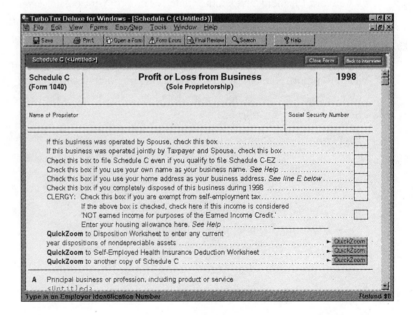

Schedule C is divided into three sections. The top portion includes pertinent background information about your business and its accounting methods. Part I is used to report income for the business. Part II summarizes the expenses of the business. You notice that the order of the questions in the EasyStep Interview tracks the organization of the Schedule C.

Entering Information About Your Business

The first section of the Schedule C provides information about the name and location of your business, its method of accounting, and other essential information used by the IRS for classification and processing.

To Do: Enter Information into the Schedule C

1. Scroll through the interview outline at left of the screen, and double-click the topic "Your business, rental, and farm activities." The screen shown in Figure 10.2 appears.

2. Select those types of schedules that apply to you.

3. Click Continue to progress through the next screen; and then Continue again to bypass the video.

4. When prompted, enter a description of your business, such as computer consulting. Then click Continue.

FIGURE 10.2.

Begin processing your Schedule C by selecting the check box in the top row of this screen.

▼

5. Read the information about business codes and click Continue.

6. The next screen, shown in Figure 10.3, prompts you to enter an official IRS code for you business. You can either enter the code used on last year's return, or click the words Business Code to bring up a list of codes.

FIGURE 10.3.

Tell TurboTax a little bit about your business.

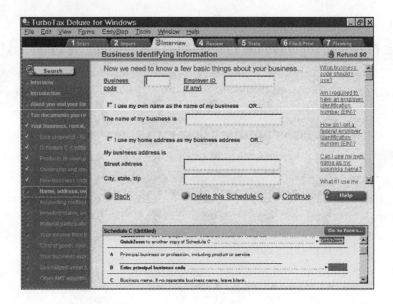

7. Enter your employer identification number, if you have one. Generally, you do not have a separate taxpayer identification number for your business and instead use your Social Security number for this purpose. An exception to the general rule occurs if you have a Keogh or plan (discussed in Hour 22, "IRAs, Pension Plans, and Annuities"). Additionally, this form may be required if your business files excise, fiduciary, alcohol, firearms, or tobacco tax returns.

8. Next, you specify whether you use your own name for the business. Either mark the check box or enter the business name.

If you need to obtain a taxpayer identification number for your business, you need to file Form SS-4. These forms are available at IRS and Social Security Offices.

▼

▼ 9. Enter the mailing address for your business, or simply indicate that it is the same address that appears on the Form 1040. Click Continue. The screen shown in Figure 10.4 appears.

10. Enter your method of accounting, either by referring to last year's return or by selecting one of the following options:

- *Cash.* You do not recognize income until you receive payment, or expenses until you pay them.

- *Accrual.* You record your receipts when they are *earned* as opposed to when they are received.

- *Other.* Any other logical and consistent method that you apply consistently from year to year.

FIGURE 10.4.

Select the method of accounting used by your business by selecting an option from this screen.

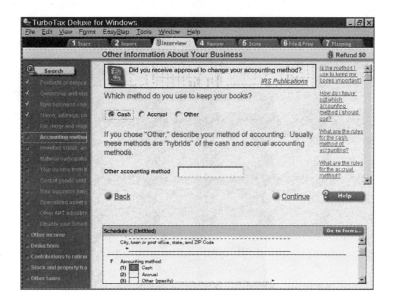

10

 After you select an accounting method for your business, you cannot change it without first requesting permission from the IRS. IRS Form 3115 is used for this purpose. Click the IRS Publications link at the top of Figure 10.4 for more information.

▼

▼ 11. TurboTax also prompts you to indicate whether your business carries an inventory, whether you started the business during the tax year, and whether you sold or disposed of the business in this tax year. Mark and of these check boxes that apply, and then click Continue.

12. If you indicate that your business carries ending inventory, the screen shown in Figure 10.5 appears. Enter your method of valuing ending inventory, which is the inventory that you have on hand at year-end, and the beginning and year-end values in the appropriate fields. You are prompted to select one of the following valuation methods:

- *Cost.* You specifically track the actual cost of each item, including acquisition costs such as shipping.

- *Lower of Cost or Market.* You value your inventory at the *lower* of its actual cost to you or at its present fair market value.

- *Other.* Any method other than cost, or lower of cost, or market.

FIGURE 10.5.

TurboTax gives you three options for valuing your year-end inventory.

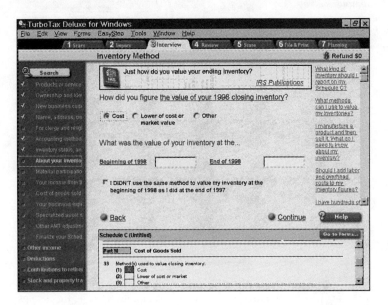

> The methods used valuing your *ending* inventory on hand at the close of the tax year are different from the methods used for determining the cost of goods *sold during the year.* Valuation of cost of goods sold during the year is discussed in the next section.

▼

▼ 13. When asked if you materially participated in the business, click Yes or No, or click Guide Me to get more help determining this.

 What the IRS really wants to know by asking you about material participation is whether you actually worked in the business or hired someone to conduct the business. If you did the latter, the major disadvantage is that Schedule C losses may be reclassified as "passive losses" and may be deducted only to the extent of passive activity income, instead of in their entirety to reduce *all* your taxable income.

▲

Reporting Income from Your Schedule C Business

10

TurboTax asks you whether anyone who pays the business reports the payments on a Form 1099-MISC. If your response to this question is yes, TurboTax prompts you to enter information from each 1099-MISC Form using the screen shown in Figure 10.6. TurboTax offers you a choice of entering the total amount of your gross receipts, to be reflected on line 1 of Schedule C, or of entering income reported on 1099 Forms separately. Income entered either way is ultimately treated the same. Whether you decide to break these amounts out separately or report them on one line, as shown in Figure 10.7, and explained in the next section, is purely a matter of personal preference.

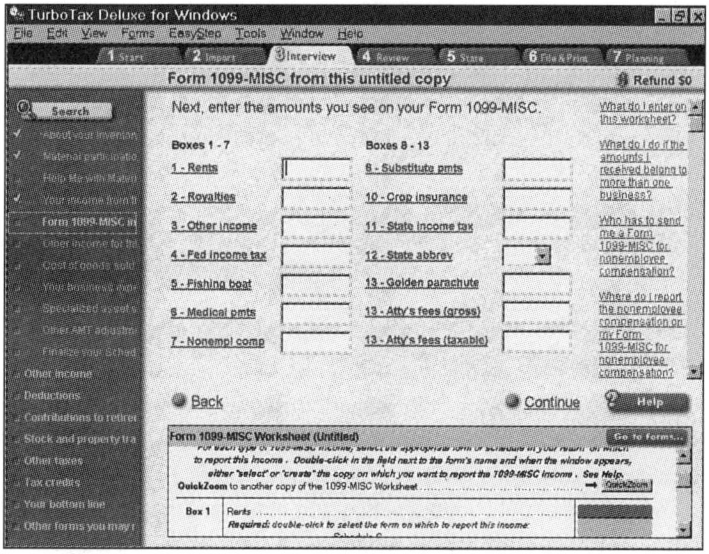

FIGURE 10.6.

You must report 1099-MISC separately so that it can be matched to the information supplied to the IRS by the payer.

Gross Receipts Less Returns and Allowances

If you have income that is *not* reported on the 1099-MISC Form, you are prompted to enter it using the screen shown in Figure 10.7. You are also provided with a field in which you enter the amount of returns and allowances. Returns and allowances include discounts and refunds. These amounts are subtracted from Gross Receipts because they are not properly included in determining the gross income for the business.

FIGURE 10.7.

Returns and allowances are entered on this Interview screen as a positive number.

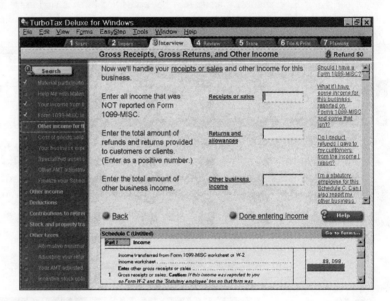

Determining Cost of Goods Sold

The cost of the inventory or goods that you sold during the year is subtracted from gross receipts on the Schedule C to arrive at gross profit.

 You can generally ascertain the correct figure for beginning inventory by looking at the value for ending inventory shown on the prior year's return.

If you purchased or produced inventory during the year, you also need to include all the costs of production in your valuation figures. For example, if you sell hand-painted eggs, be sure to include the costs of paint, labor, and the eggs themselves in determining the cost of goods sold. The screen shown in Figure 10.8 prompts you to enter all applicable costs. Based on the amounts that you enter on this screen, TurboTax computes your cost of goods sold and carries the number to line 4 of the Schedule C.

FIGURE 10.8.

This screen prompts you to enter all of the component costs of inventory produced or purchased during the year.

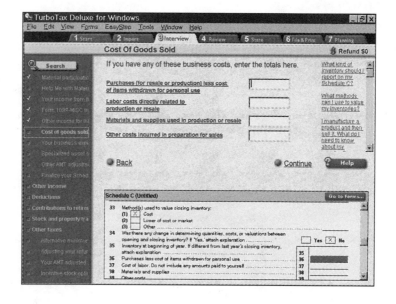

Other Gross Income Amounts

TurboTax asks you any other gross income you may have received during the year such as bad debts, interest income, and fuel tax credits. "Other gross income" can also include amounts received from activities that are not a part of your normal business. For example, if you are a physician asked to testify in a medical malpractice case, you might report your fee for this service as "other gross income." These amounts appear on line 6 of the Schedule C Form.

Entering Other Business Expenses

Expenses other than the costs attributable to maintaining your inventory are reported on Part II of the 1040. These expenses are entered as positive numbers on several successive screens.

Some business expenses are subject to limitations, and TurboTax automatically takes these limitations into account and calculates them. For example, meal and entertainment expenses are subject to a 50% limitation.

The various specific business expenses are discussed in Hour 14, "Business-Related Deductions," because employees may also deduct many of these types of expenses.

At-Risk Rules

After you have entered the income and expenses for your business, TurboTax asks you if the investment that you have in the business is "at risk." Your answer to this question, entered on the screen shown in Figure 10.9, is reflected on line 32A of the Schedule C.

FIGURE 10.9.

If you are unsure of the answers to the questions on this screen, take advantage of the Help links located on the right side of the screen.

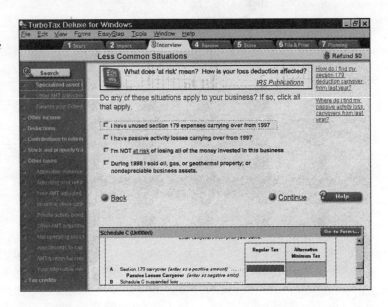

The at-risk rules require that you may take deductions and losses only to the extent that you contributed your own funds to the business or are personally liable for the amount your borrowed. Section 465 of the Internal Revenue Code prevents you from taking losses in excess of the amounts you actually have at risk.

Schedule C-EZ

If you have income that you derived from self-employment, but don't really have a full-fledged business, or your business doesn't have a lot of activity, you may be eligible to file Schedule C-EZ. The Schedule C-EZ is a simplified version of Schedule C. TurboTax gives you the option of filing either the complete Schedule C or the Schedule C-EZ if you meet the following requirements:

- Your business expenses are less than $2,500.

- You use the cash method of accounting.

- You do not take a home office deduction, depreciation, passive losses, or a net loss relating to the business.

- You don't have any employees or inventory.

Your tax liability is unaffected by the election to file Schedule C or Schedule C-EZ. It is strictly a matter of personal preference as to how you want to see the information presented.

The Self-Employment Tax

The self-employment tax is automatically computed by TurboTax and reflected on Schedule SE of your 1040 Form, as shown in Figure 10.10. This tax is imposed *in addition* to the federal income taxes. The self-employment tax rate is 15.3%, which consists of 12.4% OASDI (Social Security) tax and Medicare tax of 2.9%. For 1998 the OASDI wage base is $68,400, which means that the 12.4% rate is not imposed on wages in excess of this amount.

Income from Farm Activities

The IRS views farmers as a special type of entrepreneur. Farm activities are reported on Schedule F rather than Schedule C. The process for completing Schedule F is not significantly different than the process for Schedule C. Rather, it is the *type* of income and expenses that differs. Farms have expenses—such as the costs of seeds and fertilizer—that don't apply to the majority of Schedule C filers. Farmers also get a special gasoline credit that is computed by TurboTax.

Similarly, a farmer's income can include federal subsidies, commodity credits, and insurance proceeds from damaged crops. A copy of Schedule F appears in Figure 10.10. As you can see, its basic structure is similar to the Schedule C.

10

FIGURE 10.10.

Schedule F is used to report income from farm activities.

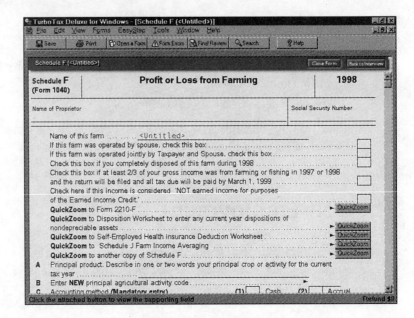

Summary

In this hour you examined Schedule C, used for reporting income and losses in business activities. Schedule C is used only for reporting the income of a sole proprietorship. Partnerships and corporations are separate legal entities that file their own tax returns.

In addition to disclosing income and expenses, Schedule C must disclose other information about their practices. Specifically, the Schedule C contains information about inventory valuation methods, your participation in the business, and the amount of investment you have "at risk."

Other forms used to report business activity include Schedule C-EZ and Schedule F. The C-EZ form is a simplified version of Schedule C for businesses with limited activity. Schedule F is used to report income from activities.

Hour 11, "Income from Investments," discusses investments that do not involve your active participation.

Q&A

Q **If you barter some of your business services for a payment made in services from another business in lieu of cash, does this constitute income?**

A Yes, you must report the fair market value of the services received on your Schedule C.

Q **If I change my inventory valuation method during the year, how do I inform the IRS?**

A You must request permission from the IRS and can do so by attaching a statement to your tax return. You can use a special blank form from the Open Forms window for this purpose. Additional information about filing this statement is included in IRS Publication 538.

10

HOUR 11

Income from Investments

This hour focuses on the types of income that you don't work for in the traditional sense: income from your investments. In this hour, we use the term investment to refer to any type of property, other than an interest in a business you actively manage, that you hold for the purpose of making money.

In the next hour you become familiar with issues associated with the taxation of the interest, dividends, and capital gains distributions you receive from your investments. You'll consider the special rules associated with rental real estate and are introduced to the relatively unpopular passive activity loss limitations and at-risk rules that limit the amount of losses you may deduct from these types of investments. You also gain an understanding of the amounts appearing on the K-1 Form distributed by partnerships, estates, and small business corporations in which you have an interest.

Highlights of this hour include

- Treatment of income and dividend income
- Rental income

- Rules pertaining to vacation properties
- Passive income and losses
- Material participation requirements
- At-risk rules
- Entering information from K-1 Forms

Reporting Investment Interest

Interest includes any compensation that you receive for the use of your money. Any time someone pays you or gives you something of value in exchange for the use of your money, it is considered taxable interest. For example, if you loan money to a relative and are repaid with interest, the interest is taxable to you. If you receive a plastic cooler for opening a new bank account, the fair market value of the plastic cooler is also taxable interest paid for the use of your money!

Investment income from bonds, savings accounts, and other types of interest producing investments is reported on Schedule B, shown in Figure 11.1.

FIGURE 11.1.

Income from interest is reported on Part I of Schedule B.

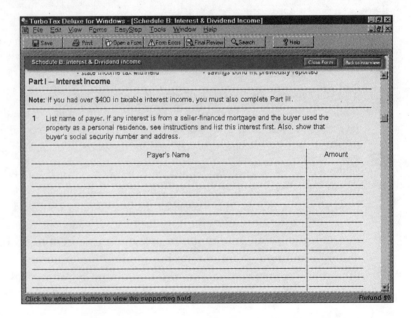

In theory, you should receive a 1099-INT from any institution that paid you more than $10 in interest or dividends during the year. But it is easy to lose track of these forms, and the obligation is on you, as the taxpayer, to report *all* your income, even if you don't receive the required 1099 Form.

If you don't receive a 1099 Form, but should have, enter the information into TurboTax that should have been disclosed on the Form 1099.

As shown in Figure 11.2, TurboTax prompts you to identify all the types of 1099-INT Forms you have received during the year.

FIGURE 11.2.

Check off all types of 1099-INT Forms you received during the year.

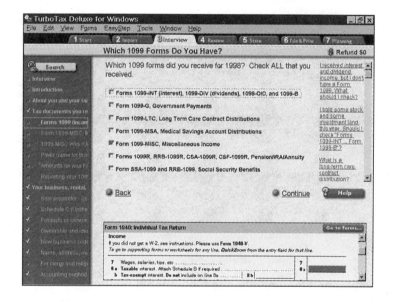

If you did not receive a 1099 Form, contact the paying entity. Often they are able to provide the information that you need over the phone, rather than requiring you to wait for a duplicate.

Different types of interest may receive different types of tax treatment. Examples of interest afforded special tax status include the following:

Original Discount Interest (OID). This type of interest is generally reported on a 1099-OID Form. The taxable amount shown on the 1099-OID is attributable to the difference between the price you paid for the bond and its "face" amount. For example, assume that you purchased a 10-year $10,000 bond for $9,000. The $1,000 discount is taxable to you as interest over the life of the bond—in this case $1,000 a year.

OID calculations can get a little tricky. It is best to try to wait for your 1099 from the issuer telling you how much OID interest to report each year, rather than trying to compute it yourself.

State and Local. Interest on these types of bonds is generally tax exempt. The 1099 should indicate whether it is or not.

Municipal Bond Interest. Interest earned on municipal bonds is generally exempt from state and local taxes, as well as federal income tax, provided the bond was issued in your state. If in doubt, check with the issuing authority or your financial advisor.

Interest paid on U.S. Treasury Bonds, notes, bills, and zero coupon bonds is taxable on your Form 1040, but it is *exempt* from tax on your state return.

Interest on Series EE Savings Bonds. If you cashed EE bonds issued on or after December 31, 1989, you may be able to exclude all or part of the interest if you used the proceeds to pay college expenses.

Some amounts referred to as "dividends" on a statement from a financial institution are actually interest. If you are paid for the use of money sitting in an *account*, such as a credit union account, the amount that you receive is appropriately reported as interest. If you receive some money from investments held in a *fund* that pools the resources of its investors to invest in securities, the amount that you receive is most likely a dividend. This is the case even if the fund erroneously refers to it as interest.

A copy of each 1099 Form issued to you is sent to the IRS so that the agency can match this information to what is reflected on your return. Be sure to report each interest or dividend source separately, using the name of the payer appearing on the 1099 Form to avoid generating a notice from the IRS.

Reporting Dividends

Dividends are a return on your investment in stock; they represent your share of corporate earnings and distributions. Dividends are taxable and are reported on Form

1099-DIV. TurboTax prompts you to enter the information shown on the 1099-DIV directly into the system using the interview screen shown in Figure 11.3.

FIGURE 11.3.

Enter information from the 1099-DIV Form using this screen.

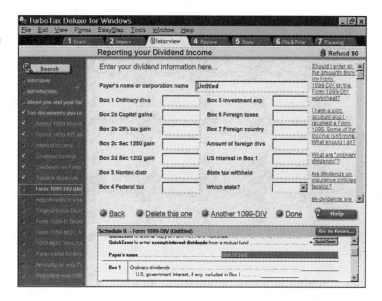

There are three basic types of dividend income. It is very likely that you receive more than one kind each year from the same entity. Each type of dividend income receives a different type of tax treatment as follows:

Ordinary Dividends. These distributions represent your share of taxable corporate earnings. They are subject to the same tax rate to which your other income is subject.

Capital Gain Dividends. This type of distributions represents income from a sale of business assets, rather than business earnings. They are taxed at a maximum rate of 28% in 1998. (Capital gains and losses are discussed in Hour 12, "Income from the Sale of Property.")

Non-taxable Dividends. Generally these dividends represent a distribution of business assets or a return of capital.

You also see the term gross dividends on your 1099-DIV Form and the TurboTax screen used to enter this information. This term refers to the aggregate of ordinary dividends, capital gain distributions, and any non-taxable dividends.

11

Investment expenses, also reported on the 1099-DIV, can be used to off-set the amount of taxable dividend income.

If you have used TurboTax in previous years, the names of the companies that have paid you dividends in the past appear on the system this year. This is a very useful tracking device, forcing you to account for all the stocks you had last year. If a stock listed from last year's return has not been sold, you should have a 1099-DIV reporting its activity for the year.

Rental Properties

If you own land or buildings and rent them out to other people, the income that you receive is reported on Schedule E.

TurboTax allows you to create up to 10 copies of Schedule E with your return and report up to three properties on each schedule. The program asks you to identify the property for which you are entering information, using a separate interview screen for each one.

Passive Activity Rules

TurboTax asks you a series of questions in connection with each rental property for the purpose of determining whether you actively and materially participated in the management of the real estate. Income or losses that you generate from real estate rentals are presumed by the IRS to be passive income, meaning that you did perform work to generate them. Generally, passive losses can only be deducted to the extent that there is income from other passive activities to offset them. Passive income may be subject to the alternative minimum tax rules discussed in Hour 21, "Additional Types of Taxes Imposed."

You can overcome the IRS presumption that income and losses from rental activities are passive. To do so you must either demonstrate that you materially participated in the activity for at least 750 hours during the year *or* that at least 50% of your income came from rental activity.

Deducting Rental Expenses

You are entitled to deduct expenses associated with your rental property—cleaning, repairs, maintenance, advertising, and so on. If you own less than 100% of the rental property, you cannot deduct all the expenses associated with it against your income. TurboTax automatically determines the amount of the deduction you are entitled to take.

> Try the Tax Help or Money Income Tax Handbook options in the onscreen Help if you are unsure of the legal requirements for taking a specific type of expense associated with your rental properties.

TurboTax also asks you about amounts that you have at risk with regard to each rental property and provides a series of questions to help you make this determination if you are not sure. The at-risk rules are designed to keep taxpayers from claiming losses that exceed the amounts they actually have invested in the business.

Vacation Properties

Vacation properties are subject to a series of complicated rules that are anything but leisurely in their application. Basically, the deductions you are permitted are determined by the amount of time that you occupied the property during the year.

If you *used* the property for more than 14 days in a year or 10 percent of the total number of days that it was rented, you cannot deduct expenses for the property that exceed the amount of income recognized from it. On the other hand, if you *rented* the property for less than 15 days, you don't have to report any of the income you earned on the property; you also may not deduct any of the expenses associated with it.

Royalties

Royalties are passive income associated with ownership in oil, gas, and mineral properties, as well as certain copyrights and patents. They are also reported on Schedule E. They are payments for the right to extract natural resources or to use your "intellectual property."

> Royalties that you earn as a self-employed writer are *not* considered passive income. They should be reported on Schedule C rather than on Schedule E.

Entering Income from K-1 Forms

If you own an interest in a partnership or small business (Subchapter S) corporation, you receive a K-1 Form each year. The K-1 summarizes the income and losses from the entity that are "passed through" to you and reported on your individual return. Income and expenses for each entity in which you own an interest are entered separately. Figure 11.4

11

depicts the interview screen used to begin a series of questions about partnership activity that has been reported on a K-1.

FIGURE 11.4.

TurboTax prompts you to enter relevant information about the K-1s that you receive.

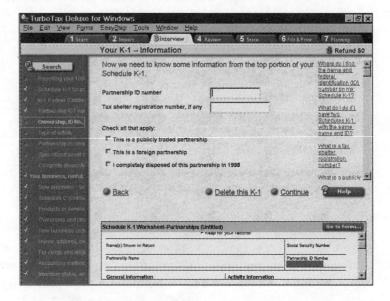

The income reflected on the K-1 Form is generally passive and reported with other passive losses on Form 8582 shown in Figure 11.5.

FIGURE 11.5.

Passive losses are reflected on Schedule 8582.

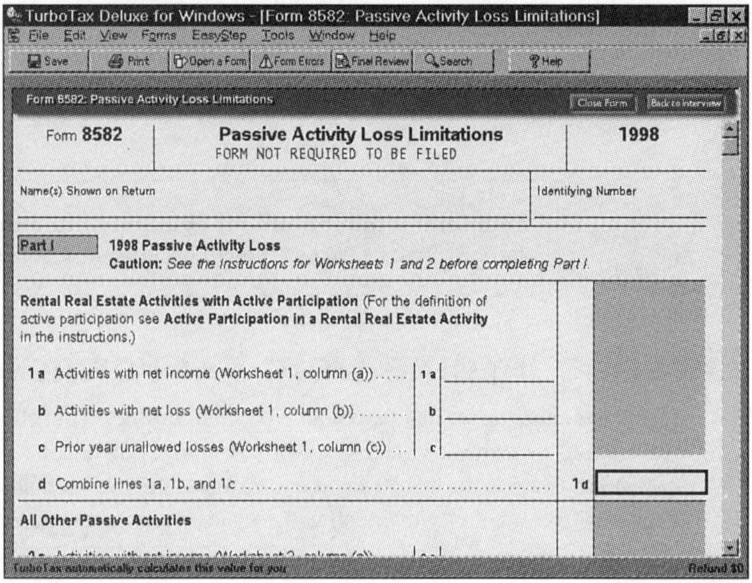

If you are a beneficiary of a trust or an estate, you also receive a K-1 Form reflecting income earned on the assets of the trust or estate and deductions for its expenses. Whether you must pay tax on trust income that is not actually distributed to you is a question for the attorney or accountant preparing the K-1 Form. The K-1 Form is a summary of information to be entered on your tax return based on complex legal and accounting determinations someone *else* had to make.

Summary

This hour analyzed the various types of income reported on your Schedule E: rents, royalties, partnership, Subchapter S corporation, and trust and estate income. Income and losses from these sources is generally considered passive and may be subject to alternative minimum taxes and limitations on deductibility. Passive gains and losses are reported on Form 8582.

This hour also introduced you to the concept of material participation and the at-risk rules. If you materially participate in an activity by spending more than 750 hours per year engaging in it, you can rebut the presumption that the income is passive.

The at-risk rules limit the deductibility of losses from the business. The purpose of these rules is to ensure that you do not attempt to deduct losses in excess of your actual investment.

Hour 12, "Income from the Sale of Property," continues to analyze the tax treatment of income from various sources and contains a discussion of the capital gains tax rates.

11

Q&A

Q What if I have passive losses in excess of passive income?

A After you have determined the amount of passive losses that you can deduct in the current year using Form 8582, any balance gets carried forward to the next year. You can deduct the passive losses carried forward to the extent of passive income for that year.

Q Do security deposits constitute rental income?

A No, security deposits are not rental income, nor are they included as an expense when you return them. They are funds belonging to the tenants and do not have any bearing on your income tax liability. However, if a security deposit is applied to rent, it is counted as rental income.

Q Can I deduct travel and meals on Schedule E?

A You may deduct expenses for travel and meals on your Schedule E if you travel away from home to conduct your rent or royalty activities. Report these expenses on line 18 as "other" expenses.

HOUR 12

Income from the Sale of Property

This hour provides you with a working knowledge of special tax laws that apply when you sell assets, such as your home or investment property. When you sell an asset, there is generally a gain or loss associated with the transaction. Gains are taxed at different rates depending on the purpose for which you have used the asset and how long you have owned it. Losses are subject to a variety of recognition rules: Some losses are deductible in full, some in part, and others are not recognized at all.

This hour helps you understand the distinction between capital and ordinary income and some of the rationale behind that distinction. It also introduces you to the complex capital gains tax rate structure, the installment sale rules, and the TurboTax approach to correctly identifying and calculating the tax liability for a variety of property transactions.

Highlights of this hour include

- Computing gain or loss on sales of assets
- Capital versus ordinary income

- The capital gains tax rates
- Treatment of installment sales
- Tax on the sale of your personal residence
- Casualty and theft losses

Calculating Gain or Loss on the Sale of an Asset

When you sell an asset, there is usually a gain or loss associated with the transaction. Those gains and losses are subject to recognition rules and special tax rate, which are discussed in the remainder of this hour. But before you can begin to apply recognition rules and rates, you need to know *how much* gain or loss is associated with the transaction.

Gain or loss is determined by subtracting the basis of an asset from the amount of money that you receive for the asset. This computation is summarized as follows:

```
Gain/Loss = Sales Proceeds - Basis
```

Basis is the amount that you paid for the asset, plus other costs of acquiring it, such as shipping, commissions, and assembly. You can also add the costs of certain improvements to basis, such as an addition on your home.

Assume, for example, you have purchased a $5,000 custom-shelving unit for your office conference room. You pay a delivery and assembly charge of $500, but decide the shelving is not big enough when it is delivered. You resell it to another business for $6,000. Your taxable gain is $500, computed as follows:

```
$6,000 (proceeds) - Basis ($5,000  + 500)
```

It is advantageous for tax purposes, to have as high a basis as possible. A high basis minimizes taxable gain and maximizes deductible losses.

To correctly report your gain on the sale of stocks and bonds, you need to enter the date that you purchased the stock and how much you paid for it. You can also add certain costs of acquiring your stock to its basis, such as commissions and recording fees. Basis also includes reinvested dividends. You should be sure to track and include all these amounts on the TurboTax screen shown in Figure 12.1.

FIGURE 12.1.

Be sure to enter all purchase costs associated with an asset to maximize basis.

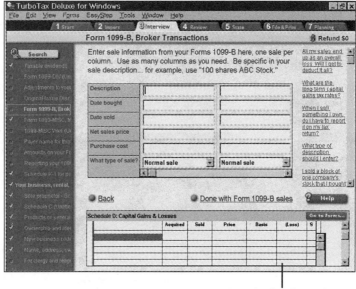

Enter basis information

Basis is reduced by the amount of any depreciation deductions taken. These amounts are *recaptured* at the time of sale. The reduction in your basis increases your taxable income.

Capital Gains and Losses

Assets held for long-term investment purposes are, generally, taxed at lower, more favorable rates. The rationale for this policy is to encourage investment and stimulate our national economy. The resulting complexity of the tax rate structure and accompanying forms also serves to keep a lot of lawyers and accountants employed.

Definition of a Capital Asset

Capital assets are defined in Section 1221 of the Internal Revenue Code as property held for investment, such as stocks, bonds, or real estate, with some very notable exceptions. Inventory is not a capital asset, because it is considered for sale to customers in the normal course of business, rather than for investment. Similarly, depreciable business property is generally not considered to be a capital asset. However, if the business property qualifies as "1231 property" (aptly named for Section 1231 of the Internal Revenue Code), it may receive special capital gains treatment.

12

Personal property (such as your auto or home furnishings) is afforded capital gains rates if you sell them at a profit. But you are not permitted to deduct losses from the sale of personal capital assets. Sale of a personal residence is discussed in greater detail later in this hour.

Sales of capital assets are reported on Schedule D, shown in Figure 12.2. The gain or loss shown on Schedule D gets carried to line 13 of your 1040.

FIGURE 12.2.

Schedule D is used to report capital gains and losses.

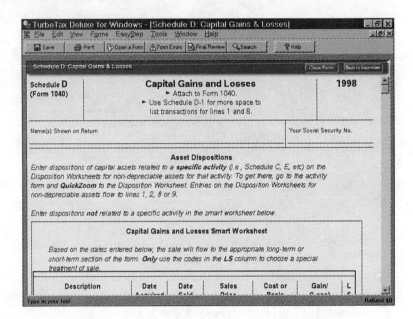

Depreciable business property (1231 property) is not considered a capital asset, even if it is fully depreciated. Sales of this type of asset are reported on Form 4797, shown in Figure 12.3. These types of assets are often sold on an installment basis and are also discussed further in this hour under the topic of installment sales.

Capital Gains Tax Rates

Different tax rates and rules apply to sales of capital assets depending upon how long you have owned them. The amount of time that you have owned a capital asset is referred to as its holding period. Capital assets sold after July 29, 1997 are categorized and taxed according to three different types of holding periods, as follows:

- *Short Term.* The holding period for short-term capital losses is 1 year (12 months or less).

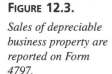

FIGURE 12.3.

Sales of depreciable business property are reported on Form 4797.

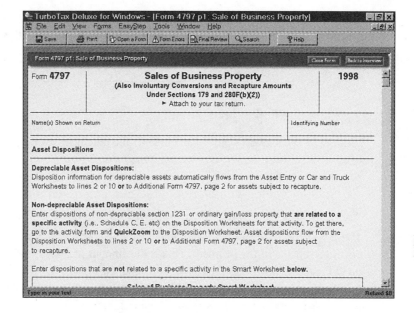

- *Mid Term.* This holding period applies to property sold after July 28, 1997 and includes property that is held for more than one year but not more than 18 months. These assets are taxed at a maximum rate of 28%.
- *Long Term.* Assets held more than 18 months (sold after July 28, 1997). Assets included in this category receive the most favorable tax treatment.

Long-term capital gains rates, for gains incurred after July 28, 1997, are substantially lower than ordinary income tax rates. The maximum long-term capital gains tax rate for assets held more than 18 months is 20%, with only a 10% tax being imposed on taxpayers in the 15% bracket.

To compute your holding period, begin counting the day after you purchased the property, and include the date that you sold it in your computation. If you inherit property, your holding period is long-term regardless of when the decedent acquired it.

Tax Treatment of Capital Losses

Capital losses are reported on Schedule D, along with capital gains. They are subject to special limitations. Deductions for capital losses are first offset against capital gains. Losses in excess of capital gains may be used to offset up to $3,000 of other 1040 income. Losses in excess of this $3,000 amount get carried forward to future years and are called capital loss carry forwards.

12

> Capital gains and losses are added up together without regard to whether they are short- or long-term for purposes of determining the $3,000 offset to ordinary income and any capital loss forward.

Installment Sales

Installment sales involve payments made by the purchaser over a period of time, instead of all at once. Because you are receiving the income over a time frame that may extend beyond the current tax year, you don't have to include it all on your 1998 tax return. You can defer some of the tax liability to subsequent years when you actually receive the payments.

The proportion of installment payments that are taxable each year depend upon the gross profit percentage of the payment. This is the amount of the payment that represents gain on the sale, as opposed to return of your initial cost basis. TurboTax calculates your gross profit percentage and advises you of proportion of installment proceeds using the information that you enter on the screen shown in Figure 12.4.

FIGURE 12.4.

The installment sale percentage is applied to principal payments to determine your taxable gain for the year.

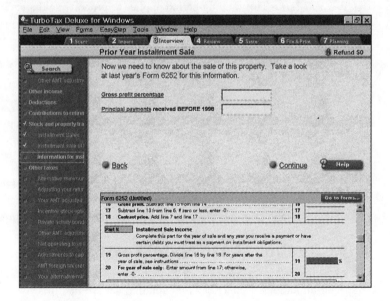

Special rules apply to installment sales of depreciable *business* assets. These rules are extremely complicated. Unfortunately, TurboTax does not calculate the potential recapture of depreciation expenses, but instead refers you to the instructions for Form 4797.

Sale of Your Home and Personal Property

Generally, when you sell non-business gain, such as your car or your stereo, the IRS wants to know about it. Gain from the sale of a non-business asset is taxable. Because you do not get to deduct *losses* from sales of personal property, you do not even need to disclose loss transactions on your tax return!

> To avoid confusion, do not list personal items, such as the exercise equipment that was gathering dust or the home computer you don't use for business purposes, on your Schedule D if you sold them at a loss.

A personal residence is subject to special rules. Gain on the sale of a personal residence is not taxable if the following requirements are met:

- The gain is less than $250,000 for single filers ($500,000 for married, filing jointly).
- You have lived in the home for two of the preceding five years.
- You claim this exemption from income only once every two years.

This exclusion has proved to be a tremendous benefit for people who upgrade and renovate their homes, because the increase in value is not taxed upon sale. The proceeds from the sale of a personal residence are reported to the IRS on Form 1099-S, discussed in Hour 6, "Introduction to W-2 and 1099 Forms," and matched to the amounts reported by you on Form 2119 of your tax return, shown in Figure 12.5.

The exclusion of gain on sale of a home discussed in this section replaces the old rules permitting exclusion of gain by taxpayers over the age of 55. Gain in excess of the $250,000/$500,000 limitation is taxable and can no longer be rolled over into the sale of a new (more expensive) home. If you owned your home less than a year, the gain is short-term and reported on line 4 of Schedule D. If you owned it for more than a year, it is long-term and goes on line 11 of Schedule D.

12

FIGURE 12.5.

Report a gain from the sale of your personal residence using this form.

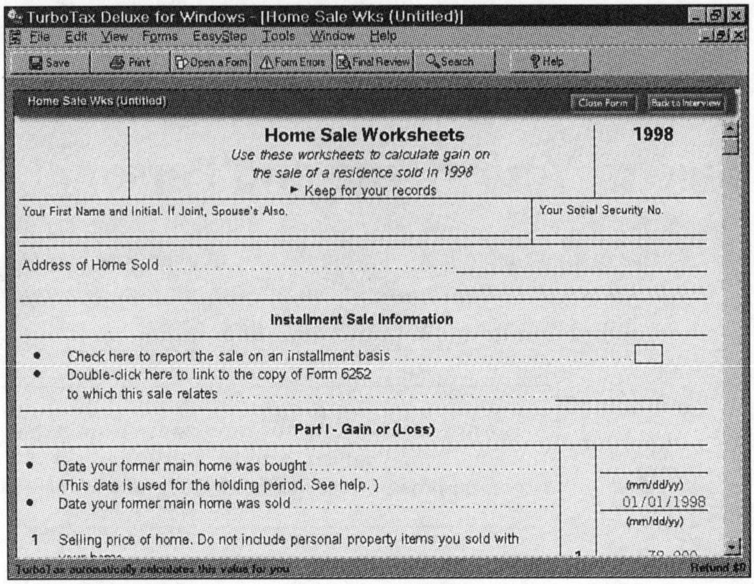

Casualty and Theft Losses

Casualty and theft are events that destroy assets. You may recognize a gain in the event of a casualty or theft if, for example, insurance proceeds exceed the amount of your cost basis in the asset. Casualty and theft losses are subject to special limitations.

Casualty and theft losses are reported on Form 4684, shown in Figure 12.6. Schedule A of the form is used to report losses on personal property. Schedule B is used for business or other income-producing property. If you had more than one theft or casualty loss during the year, you must submit a separate copy of this form for each one. The gains and losses reported on Form 4684 may flow through to Schedule A as itemized deductions or to Schedule D used for reporting capital gains and losses. They may also show up on Form 4797 related to business/income property.

A casualty is the damage, destruction, or loss of property as the result of a sudden, unexpected, but identifiable event, such as a flood or an earthquake. A theft is the unlawful taking and removing of money, for example, robbery, larceny, or embezzlement.

FIGURE 12.6.

Casualty and theft losses are reported using this form and may flow through to Schedule D, Form 4797, or Schedule A.

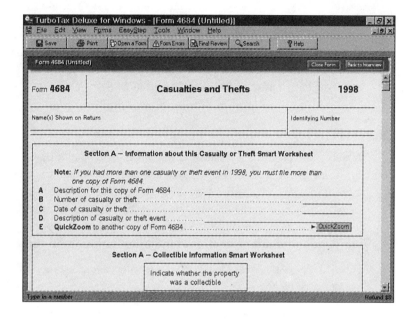

 You may *not* take a casualty loss deduction for damage caused by termites, disease (for example, plants), rust, corrosion, or drought.

Casualty and theft losses are subject to special limitations. The total amount of loss is reduced by the following:

- $100 for each casualty and theft loss event
- 10% of the taxpayers adjusted gross income

Only one $100 reduction applies to each casualty and theft loss event. Therefore, if someone sets your house *and* your car on fire, only $100 is subtracted for that event.

Worthless Securities and Bad Debts

If a company that you have invested in goes belly up, you are entitled to deduct a capital loss equal to the amount of your basis of the investment. As with other capital losses, your deduction is determined by your holding period, as previously discussed.

12

A non-business bad debt can also be deducted, subject to certain limitations. For example, you might be able to deduct money you loaned to a friend to start a new business that has failed. Bear in mind, the IRS generally requires some good evidence that the debt will not be repaid, such as bankruptcy or the debtor's death. Non-business bad debts are treated as short-term losses and reported on Schedule D.

Summary

It is to your economic advantage to minimize the amount of gain that is recognized as the result of a sale of an asset, as well as to ensure that the transaction qualifies for the more favorable capital gains tax rate when possible. Capital gains are a special *type* of income, subject to particular recognition rules and tax rates. Similarly, payments made to you in installments are subject to their own idiosyncratic reporting recognition rules, as are losses attributable to theft, casualty, and worthless investments.

Hour 13, "Non-Business Deductions," identifies additional opportunities for reducing your taxable income.

Q&A

Q How does TurboTax report capital gains that appear on my 1099-DIV Forms?

A The entire amount of gross dividend appears on Schedule B with the rest of your dividend income. On Part II of Schedule B, the capital gains portion of the dividends entered, reducing the total dividend by that amount. This capital gain portion then gets carried over to line 13 of Schedule D.

Q How are gains and losses on mutual fund shares that have been purchased on many different dates calculated?

A TurboTax averages the cost of all shares in a mutual fund to arrive at an average cost basis used for determining gain or loss.

Q What is the difference between the *trade date* and *settlement date* reported on my 1099-B Form? Which one is used for determining my holding period for capital gains tax purposes?

A The trade date is the date that the sale actually occurs. The settlement date is the date the proceeds are placed in your account. The trade date is the date that is entered on your Schedule D.

PART IV
Deductions and Credits

Hour

HOUR 13

Non-Business Deductions

This hour introduces you to Schedule A, which is used to list itemized deductions. Not all taxpayers have to go to the trouble of completing this schedule. You are also offered the alternative of taking a standard deduction rather than specifically calculating and disclosing each and every deduction to which you are entitled.

This hour helps you decide which approach works to your best tax advantage. You also gain insight as to the various types of deductions permitted by the Internal Revenue Code and how aggressive you should be in claiming them.

Highlights of this hour include

- Whether to itemize or take the standard deduction
- Medical expense deductions
- Tax payments you are allowed to deduct
- Deducting interest expenses

- Tax on the sale of your personal residence
- Charitable contributions
- Miscellaneous deductions

Choosing the Standard Deduction Versus Itemizing

Every taxpayer is entitled to a standard deduction. The theory behind the standard deduction is that every taxpayer has *some* deductions. It is time-consuming for the IRS to have to review a lot of individual returns containing relatively small-itemized deduction amounts. Allowing a large proportion of taxpayers to take a presumed amount as a standard deduction streamlines IRS processing and verification considerably. It also seems equitable to allow *everyone* to deduct something.

How the Standard Deduction Is Reported

The standard deduction is taken on page 2 of your 1040 Form, as shown in Figure 13.1. It is subtracted from your adjusted gross income from line 33 to arrive at your taxable income, which appears on line 39 of the 1040.

FIGURE 13.1.

Report the standard deduction on page 2, line 35, of your tax return.

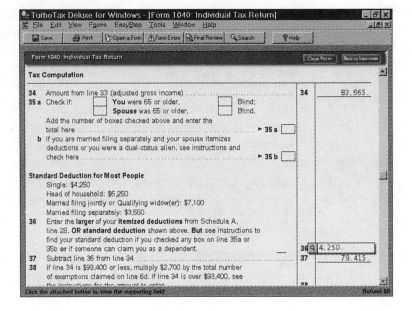

You are not permitted to take both the standardized and itemized deductions; you must choose between the two. You are not allowed to itemize deductions if you are filing a Form 1040A or Form 1040EZ. You must file the 1040 long form to itemize.

> If you think that your itemized deductions come pretty close to the standard deduction amount, calculate them and make sure. Double-check to make sure you haven't overlooked any allowable itemized deductions before deciding which one to take.

Determining the Amount of the Standard Deduction

The amount of the standard deduction that you are allowed to take depends upon your filing status (discussed in Hour 2, "Preparation Options and Help Features"). TurboTax automatically determines the standard deduction to which you are entitled based upon your filing status; the interview does not need to ask you any specific questions. The standard deduction amounts are increased annually. The allowable standard deduction amounts for 1998 are reflected in Table 13.1.

TABLE 13.1. STANDARD DEDUCTIONS ARE BASED ON FILING STATUS.

Filing Status	Standard Deduction
Single	$4,250
Married Filing Jointly	$7,100
Married Filing Separately	$3,550
Surviving Spouse	$7,100
Head of Household	$6,250

Standard Deduction Amounts for Dependent Children, Elderly, and Blind Taxpayers

13

If you are preparing a tax return for a child whom you are claiming as a deduction on your own return, the child is entitled to a standard deduction. The child is entitled to a minimum deduction of $650 and a maximum deduction equal to the lessor of the child's earned income or the amount reflected in Table 13.1. Earned income is income earned from employment, as opposed to investments. A child can claim itemized deductions in lieu of the standard deduction amount if they exceed it.

Taxpayers who are blind or elderly are entitled to increase their standard deductions. Taxpayers who are age 65 or older are entitled to add an additional $1,050 to their standard deduction amounts. Taxpayers who are blind are also allowed to tack on an additional $1,050. Taxpayers who are *both* blind and elderly may boost their standard deduction amounts by $1,600. There is no corresponding tax bonus available for blind and elderly taxpayers who itemize their deductions.

You are considered legally blind for tax purposes if your vision is not better than 20/200 in your *best* eye.

Deciding to Itemize Deductions

Itemizing your deductions is a lot more work than simply opting for the standard deduction. TurboTax tries to streamline the process, but no software program (or accountant, for that matter) can pull together your receipts and documentation for you. The EasyStep Interview prompts you to enter the information needed to complete Schedule A using question screens such as the one shown in Figure 13.2. The questions on these screens, straightforward as they may be, are going to require some research.

FIGURE 13.2.

The interview screens pertaining to itemized deductions require you to track down your receipts and reconstruct your expenses for deductible items.

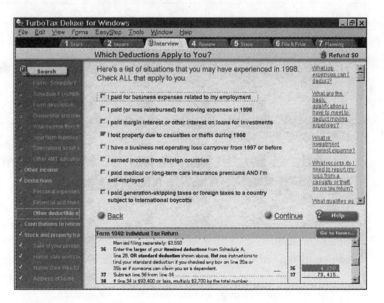

Medical Expense Deductions

Topping the list of deductions appearing on Schedule A are medical expenses. To take a deduction for medical expenses, not only must your itemized deductions exceed the standard deduction, you must demonstrate that your total medical expenses add up to more than 7.5% of your adjusted gross income. (Adjusted gross income is defined in Hour 5, "Introduction to Personal Income Tax Forms.") This means, for example, if your adjusted gross income is $80,000, you must have at least $6,000 of medical expenses before you are allowed to deduct any of them. This is, obviously, a very restrictive policy that excludes a large portion of medical expenses incurred by taxpayers each year.

The policy with regard to the types of medical expenses allowable is more liberal. In fact, taxpayers often overlook many deductible expenses, such as the cost of transportation incurred in obtaining medical care. Prescription medicines and drugs and the cost of insulin are deductible. Special schooling for a child needing psychiatric treatment is deductible, as is inpatient treatment for alcohol or drug addiction.

A standard mileage rate of 10 cents a mile (plus parking fees and tolls) is used in computing the transporting expenses deductible as medical expenses.

Nursing home care is deductible if the need for medical care is the primary reason for the individual's placement in the home. Capital expenditures and additions that are added primarily for medical care are also deductible, but only to the extent the cost of such modifications exceeds the amount of any increase in value of the property.

The following list shows some of the types of frequently overlooked medical expenses that you can deduct on Schedule A.

Deductible Medical Expenses Often Overlooked

Prescription birth control pills

Ambulance

Cosmetic surgery for purposes of reconstruction, disfigurement, or to correct a congenital abnormality

Alcohol and drug abuse treatment

Eyeglasses, contact lenses, and eye exams

Artificial limbs

Hearing aids

13

continues

Deductible Medical Expenses Often Overlooked—Continued

Laboratory fees

Legal abortion

Lodging related to medical care (limited to $50 a night)

Weight-reduction programs prescribed by a doctor

Special schooling for the mentally or physically disabled

Psychiatric treatment

Mileage for travel to receive medical care

Vasectomy and tubal ligation expense

Nursing home, assisted living, and retirement community costs
when medical care is provided

Seeing-eye or hearing-ear dogs, including all expenses of maintaining the animal

Telephone equipment or visual enhancing equipment for
hearing or visually impaired persons

Physical therapy

Sexual dysfunction

Orthodontics treatment

Examples of medical expenses that are *not* deductible include nonprescription medicines and drugs, unnecessary cosmetic surgery, and weight reduction programs that are not prescribed by your doctor. Generally, you cannot deduct the cost of programs calculated to improve health or prevent disease, such as a workshop to stop smoking, unless a physician prescribes them. Similarly, other types of preventative treatment, such as vitamins and dandruff shampoo, cannot be deducted unless a doctor prescribes them.

There is an issue as to what type of credentials an individual must possess to be considered a doctor by the IRS. The following is a partial list of health care providers that can prescribe deductible medical services.

Partial List of Types of Doctors Recognized by the IRS

Opticians, Optometrists, and Opthalmologists

Gynecologists and Obstetricians

Dentists and Orthodontists

Pediatricians

Dermatologists

Partial List of Types of Doctors Recognized by the IRS

Chiropractors and Osteopaths (if licensed)

Physical Therapists

Plastic Surgeons

Podiatrists

Psychiatrists and Psychologists

Anesthesiologists

Orthopedists, Internists, Urologists, and Endocrinologists

Health and accident premiums can also be deducted, subject to the overall 7.5% limitation to which all medical expense deductions are subject. Self-employed persons can deduct 40% of amounts paid for health insurance from gross income.

 The basic cost of Medicare Insurance (Part A) is not deductible. However, the cost of extra Medicare (Part B) coverage is deductible.

Taking Deductions for Tax Payments

Taxpayers who itemize are entitled to deduct state and local taxes, real and personal property taxes, and foreign income taxes paid during the tax year. Other types of taxes are not deductible. Table 13.2 distinguishes between deductible and non-deductible tax payments.

TABLE 13.2. DEDUCTIBILITY OF TAXES IMPOSED.

Deductible	Non-Deductible
State income taxes	Sales taxes
County, municipal, and school district taxes	Cigarette, firearms, and alcohol
Real estate taxes	Estate and gift taxes
Personal property taxes	Utility company taxes
Property tax portion of vehicle license fee	Special assessments (such as street and sewer repairs)
Foreign income taxes	Social Security taxes
Unemployment taxes	Medicare taxes
Permit and license fees	

13

You are allowed to take a deduction for all real estate taxes paid during the year. The taxes do not have to be paid on your principal residence; you may deduct real estate taxes paid on one vacation home. To claim these amounts as deductions, add up all the amounts paid for real estate taxes on line 6 of the Schedule A, or enter them using the EasyStep Interview as shown in Figure 13.3.

FIGURE 13.3.

All real property taxes paid during the year are deductible in full.

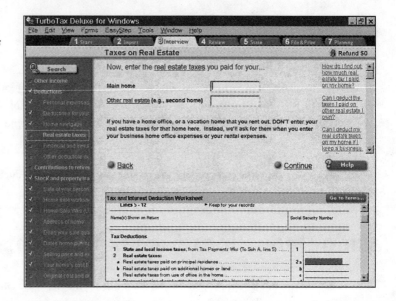

 If you bought a new home during the year, check your closing statement for additional real estate taxes paid.

Personal property taxes, if you paid any, are also deductible. Personal property taxes are sometimes difficult to distinguish from other types of taxes. The earmarks of a personal property tax include the following:

- Based solely on the value of the property
- Imposed directly on the property
- Charged on an annual basis

Personal property taxes are most commonly associated with vehicles and boats. Report them using the Interview screen shown in Figure 13.4.

FIGURE 13.4.

Report personal property taxes using this screen.

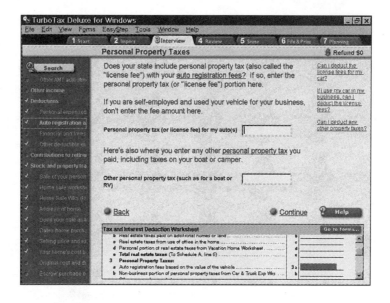

If you pay a vehicle registration fee or tax in your state, you may only deduct the portion of the fee that is attributable to personal property tax. You may not, for example, deduct any portion charged for license plate renewal.

Deductions for Interest Expenses

Certain types of interest expenses are deductible in full. Whether interest is deductible is determined by the purpose for which the debt was incurred. Interest deductions may be subject to limits and phase-outs as to the amount that may be taken as a deduction.

Home Mortgage Interest

13

A deduction for home mortgage interest may be taken on line 10 of Schedule A. Points paid to secure a loan are deductible as interest, if the loan is for your principal residence. Late payment penalties charged by a bank may be deducted as home mortgage interest—these, too, are a cost of borrowing money.

You should receive a Form 1098 from the bank or financial institution to whom you paid interest during the year. A copy of the 1098 is also sent to the IRS so that it can verify the amount that you report on your return.

Mortgage interest is deductible only if it is paid on your principal residence or on a second vacation home. Mortgage interest paid on additional homes is not deductible. Enter deductible mortgage interest using the EasyStep Interview screen shown in Figure 13.5.

FIGURE 13.5.

Home mortgage interest is generally deductible in full.

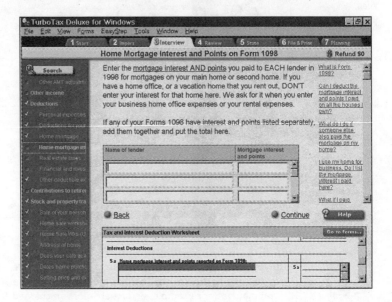

 Your deduction for mortgage interest may be limited if your mortgage exceeds $1,000,000.

Student Loan Interest

A limited amount of interest on student loans is deductible, beginning in 1998. A deduction is allowed for up to $1,000 of interest paid on qualified student loans, during the first 60 months that interest payments are required on the loan. Loans must be for educational expenses for tuition, fees, and books. The deduction is phased-out for taxpayers with adjusted gross incomes between $40,000 and $55,000 single taxpayers and between $60,000 and $75,000 for married taxpayers. Report student loan interest on the screen shown in Figure 13.6.

Investment Interest

Interest borrowed to finance investments is deductible in full. Investment interest includes interest paid on loans to finance purchases of stocks, bonds, and investment real estate. It is reported on line 13 of Schedule A and entered using the EasyStep Interview screen shown in Figure 13.6.

FIGURE 13.6.

Investment interest may be deducted to the extent of investment income.

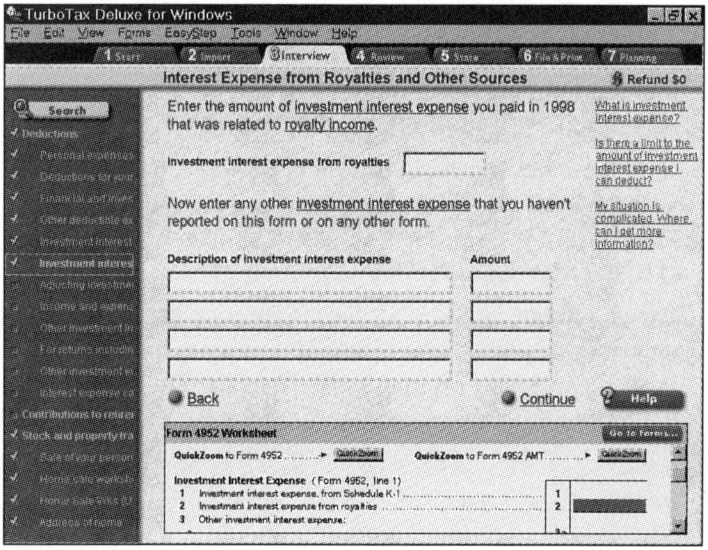

The amount of your investment interest deduction is limited to your interest income. It is taken as a miscellaneous deduction and subject to a 2% floor as discussed later this hour, under the topic of miscellaneous deductions. The deduction limitation is reported using Form 4952, shown in Figure 13.7. If you are not able to deduct all your investment interest in 1998 due to this limitation, you can carry forward the unused interest deduction to future years.

FIGURE 13.7.

Unused interest deductions can be carried forward for this purpose.

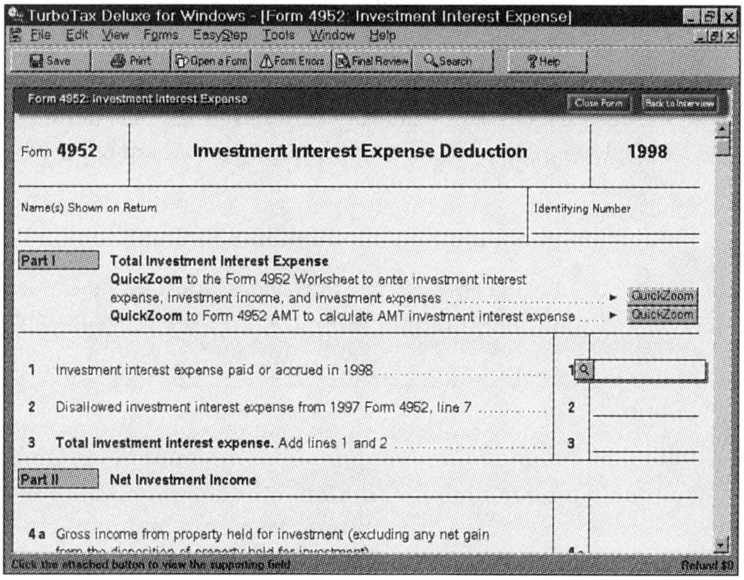

13

Taking a Deduction for Charitable Contributions

The Internal Revenue Code encourages charitable giving. Not only does Congress presume that altruistic behavior should be rewarded, but the existence of strong not-for-profit lobby groups all but ensures that charitable giving retains a protected tax status.

Qualified Charities

You are permitted to take a deduction for contributions made to a qualified charity during the tax year. A qualified charity is an organization, which has fulfilled the IRS requirements for tax exempt status. Examples of tax exempt organizations include the Girl Scouts, the American Cancer Society, churches, and synagogues. Direct payments to individuals do not qualify as charitable deductions.

To determine whether an organization is a qualified charity, you can do one of the following:

- Call the organization
- Call the IRS
- Go to the IRS Web site (www.irs.ustreas.gov/prod/search/eosearch.html) that lists qualified organizations

Limitations and Required Documentation

You are required to document any single contribution in excess of $250; do not aggregate contributions made to different organizations for this purpose.

If you purchase goods or event tickets from a charitable organization, you may take a deduction only to the extent that you received less than fair market value for your purchase. For example, if you purchase candy for $2 that normally sells for $1, your deduction is limited to $1.

You are permitted to deduct mileage and other expenses incurred in connection with any volunteer services that you perform for qualified charities. The mileage rate for this purpose is 14 cents.

Donations of Non-Cash Items

If you donate used items to a charitable organization, you may take a deduction for non-cash contributions. Form 8283, shown in Figure 13.8, is used to report these types of contributions. You are required to keep detailed records of what you contributed and must obtain a receipt for any contribution in excess of $250 to a single recipient. Non-cash contributions are valued on the Form 8283 at the amount that you would expect to pay for similar used merchandise.

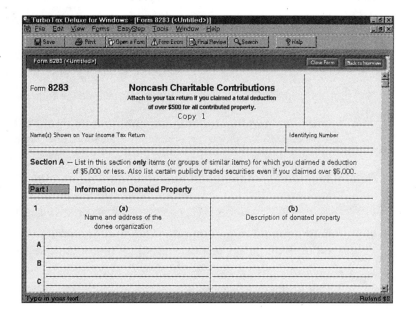

Gifts of Appreciated Property

Gifts of appreciated property give rise to special tax issues. Appreciated property is property such as artwork, stock certificates, antiques, and other types of property that generally (hopefully) increases in value. It is property that would generate a capital gain or loss if you sold it. Donations of appreciated property are also reported on Form 8283.

The amount of charitable deduction that you are allowed to take is equal to the fair market value of the property. This is a tremendous tax benefit. Assume you bought a painting of $100 and it is now worth $5,000. If you sold it, you would have to pay capital gains tax. But if you donate it, not only do you escape the tax liability, but generally you are entitled to a $4,900 deduction. If the organization sells the painting, however, instead of displaying it, your deduction is limited to your basis in the painting ($100).

13

If you are making a gift of appreciated property to a charitable organization, try to donate it to an organization that uses rather than sells the property for cash. This enables you to deduct the full fair-market value of the property.

Miscellaneous Deductions

Miscellaneous deductions are essentially those deductions that do not fit into any of the categories discussed previously during this hour. They are reported on line 27 of Schedule A. The most important thing to know about miscellaneous deductions is that you cannot take them at all unless they exceed 2% of your adjusted gross income.

Commonly reported miscellaneous deductions include the following:

- *Employee Business Expenses.* These expenses include travel, entertainment, automobile, dues, subscriptions, continuing education, job search expenses, and a host of others that are covered in depth in Hour 14, "Business-Related Deductions."

- *Investment Expenses.* You can deduct the cost of maintaining your investments. Brokerages fees, safe deposit box rental, business publications, and professional advice are all deductible expenses that fall under this category.

- *Tax Preparation Fees.* You can deduct all costs related to the preparation of your tax return, including professional advice, postage, and accounting services.

- *Gambling Losses.* You may take a deduction for gambling losses to the extent of your gambling winnings.

Retain evidence of gambling expenses such as used lottery tickets and bingo cards.

Miscellaneous deductions should be documented in the same manner as other deductions.

Do not categorize deductions as miscellaneous if you can take them somewhere else on the Schedule A and avoid the required floor amount of 2% of AGI.

Summary

Taxpayers are given the option of specifically itemizing their deductions or taking the standard deduction. The standard deduction is based on the assumption that everyone has some deductions and should be entitled to deduct a presumed amount without researching actual deductions. The amount of the standard deduction to which you are entitled varies depending upon your filing status. Itemized deductions are permitted when your deductions exceed the standard deduction. Miscellaneous deductions are subject to a floor of 2% of your AGI. Hour 14 continues the discussion of deductions that you can use to offset your income.

Q&A

Q Can I deduct the cost of the TurboTax software and this book?

A Yes, you can. These expenses are deductible as tax preparation fees. They are reported as miscellaneous deductions on line 27 of Schedule A and subject to the 2% floor.

Q If I do not have enough deductions to itemize this year, can I save them up and take them on next year's return?

A No, you cannot. Expenses must be deducted in the year that they are incurred. You can, however, alternate the years that you itemize and push deductible expenses into the same year. For example, you may want to pay two years of property taxes in one year to push you over the standard deduction amount.

13

HOUR 14

Business-Related Deductions

This hour is dedicated to the topic of business expenses. The IRS takes a partner-like attitude toward expenses that are incurred in producing revenue, allowing you to deduct such amounts with the understanding that it gets its share of the income you ultimately produce. But like any partner with an interest in the business, it wants to see the documentation of your expenditures.

The toughest issues with regard to business expenses arise in situations where it is difficult to tell whether an expense is *really* for business. This is particularly true for expenditures that may have been made for more than one purpose and have to be allocated accordingly.

Highlights of this hour include

- Employee business expenses versus Schedule C expenses
- Home office deductions
- Automobile expenses

- Entertainment
- Education and training
- Moving expenses

Employee Business Expenses Versus Schedule C Expenses

The IRS takes a different view of your business expenses, depending on whether you work for someone else or are self-employed and file a Schedule C. Schedule C filers are generally entitled to deduct all business expenses (other than travel and entertainment) in full. Employees, on the other hand, must report these types of expenses as miscellaneous deductions on Schedule A, as shown in Figure 14.1.

FIGURE 14.1.

Employee business expenses are reported on Schedule A as miscellaneous deductions.

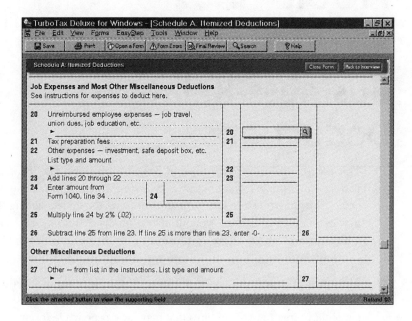

Unfortunately, miscellaneous deductions are subject to the "2% floor" rule. This means that they must exceed 2% of adjusted gross income before you are allowed to deduct any of them. This means, for example, that if you have adjusted gross income (as defined in Hour 5, "Introduction to Personal Income Tax Forms") of $40,000, your miscellaneous itemized deductions must exceed $800 before you are entitled to deduct them.

The good news is that for purposes of meeting the 2% floor, you can add all your different types of miscellaneous deductions together. Other types of miscellaneous deductions, as discussed in Hour 13, "Non-Business Deductions," include tax preparation fees, investment expenses, and so on.

 Schedule C is used to report your business income if you are a sole proprietorship. If your business is a corporation or partnership, you need to file a separate return to report its income.

Types of Employee Business Expenses

Employee business expenses are reported as either reimbursed or unreimbursed. Reimbursed expenses are amounts that you pay on your own and for which your employer reimburses you. Unreimbursed expenses are the ones that your company won't pick up but that are related to job responsibilities in one way or another.

Reimbursed Employee Business Expenses

If your employer reimbursed you for expenses that you incurred related to your employment, you are required to report both the expense and the reimbursement. This is the case even though it may seem like a sort of "wash" if your reimbursements equal the expenses that you incurred. Employee business expenses are reported using Form 2106, shown in Figure 14.2.

The amount that your employer pays you for reimbursements is reported on line 7 of the form. If the reimbursed amounts exceed your actual expenses, the excess amount is taxed as income. This issue arises often in the context of meal reimbursements, because you are allowed to take only half of your meal expenses as a deduction. If your employer reimburses you for the full amount of the meal, you are going to end up with some taxable income.

Unreimbursed Employee Business Expenses

Unreimbursed employee business expenses are also reported on Form 2106. They are amounts that you pay out-of-pocket without reimbursement and are entered like reimbursed expenses except that there are no reimbursement amounts reported on line 7.

You may be able to deduct unreimbursed employee expenses even if you don't have a job. Your job search expenses (resumes, travel, 50% of meals, and so on) constitute unreimbursed expenses if you are hunting for employment in your *present line of work*.

14

If you are looking for a job for the first time or changing fields, however, the IRS requires you to pick up these expenses without the benefit of a deduction to launch your new career.

FIGURE 14.2.

Use Form 2106 to report reimbursed employee expenses.

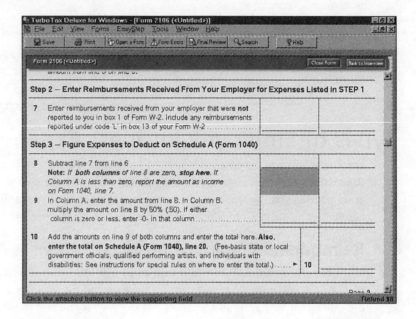

Examples of common types of unreimbursed employee business expenses include the following:

- Union and professional association dues
- Uniforms and special types of clothing that are required and not worn or suitable to be worn for other purposes
- Tools and supplies
- Publications, books, and manuals
- Cell phones
- Depreciation on your computer
- Medical examinations and license fees, if required
- Business related travel and entertainment
- Employment related education and training
- Home office expenses

TurboTax conveniently jogs your memory as to expenses you may have overlooked, using screens such as the one shown in Figure 14.3.

FIGURE 14.3.

TurboTax prompts you to take all the deductions to which you are entitled.

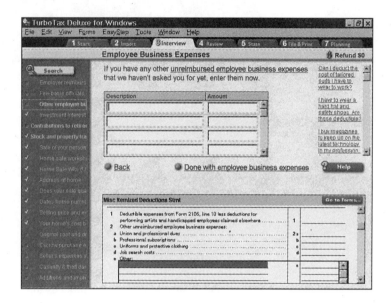

The last three types of business expenses appearing in the previous list—educational expenses, travel and entertainment, and home office deductions—are subject to special requirements. These types of deductions invite intense IRS scrutiny, whether reported on Schedule C or Schedule A, because of the potential for error in allocating business and personal use.

Home Office Deductions

The requirements for deducting a portion of your home as a business expense are the same whether you are an employee taking them on Schedule A or are a Schedule C filer. Employees report their home office deductions on Form 2106. Self-employed persons are required to file Form 8829, shown in Figure 14.4, to report home office expenses.

To take a home office deduction you must use a portion of your home "exclusively" and "regularly" for one of the following:

- A principal place of business for your Schedule C enterprise
- A place for meeting with patients or clients
- A separate structure adjacent to your home used in connection with your business

14

FIGURE 14.4.

Only sole proprietors complete this form to report home office expenses.

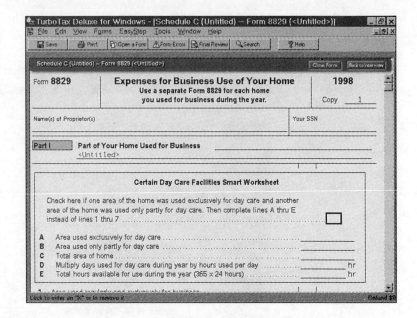

The exclusive use requirement is strictly imposed—it means that the portion of your home that is deducted cannot be used for personal purposes. For example, if you want to deduct your bedroom as an office, you can't do so if you have your waterbed in there.

There are two notable exceptions to the exclusive use rule. First, if your home is the only location from which you conduct business activities, you may deduct the portion of your home used to store inventory sold, wholesale, or retail. Second, if you maintain a licensed home day care center, you can deduct a room used regularly but not exclusively. For example, you can claim a deduction for a room used for naps or as a play area even though your family also used these rooms for other purposes.

You may claim a home office deduction for expenses such as the following:

- Mortgage interest
- Property tax
- Rent
- Utilities
- Repairs and cleaning
- Insurance
- Depreciation

Home office expenses are allocated based upon a formula that is the number of square feet used exclusively for business purposes divided by the total number of square feet in your home. This is referred to as your percentage of use. As an example, if you use 100 square feet of your 1,000 square foot home as an office, you are entitled to deduct 10% of the types of expenses listed above. Additionally, you are entitled to deduct in full expenses directly attributable to your business, such as rewiring to accommodate business equipment.

Refer to IRS publication number 587 for more information about determining percentage of use. Unfortunately, this publication is not included on the TurboTax CD.

If you are an employee, you must have yet another requirement to take a home office deduction. You must maintain the home office strictly for the convenience of your employer and not as a matter of your own personal preference as indicated to Figure 14.5.

FIGURE 14.5.

TurboTax cautions you to carefully consider whether you qualify for this deduction.

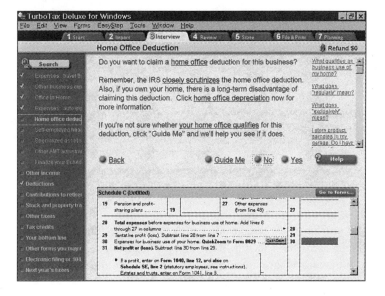

The Taxpayer Relief Act of 1997 has liberalized the rules for taking home office deductions. Beginning in 1999, these requirements are liberalized; you are permitted to deduct home office expenses if you perform administrative or management activities in your home and have *no other place* to perform such activities.

14

Finally, you may not take a home office deduction in excess of the income derived from your business after subtracting all other business expenses. For example, if you earned $2,400 from your business last year, this is the maximum amount of the home office deduction that you may take. TurboTax computes this for you automatically.

If you take a depreciation deduction for your home, the depreciation is subject to recapture upon the sale of the home. This means that you must pay tax on income equal to the amount of depreciation deductions previously taken.

Travel and Automobile Deductions

If you drive your vehicle for business purposes, you are permitted to take a tax deduction for related expenses. You are not permitted to take a deduction for driving from your home to your principle job site. However, the following types of commutes are deductible:

- Business related errands, sales calls, and customer visits
- Driving from one office or business location to another
- Driving from your home to another job site if your home is your principal place of business

Automobile expenses are calculated on page 2 of Form 2106, reproduced in Figure 14.6, using one of two methods: You can either deduct the actual costs of driving the vehicle or use the standard mileage rate. Actual expenses are listed on lines 23 through 29 of Form 2106. The standard mileage rate is 32.5 cents per mile for 1998. Under this method, you multiply the number of miles driven by the standard mileage rate.

If you are using the actual expense method, you must allocate your vehicle expenses based on the percentage of actual business use. TurboTax calculates your business use percentage using the information entered on the screen shown in Figure 14.7. Actual vehicle expenses include gas, oil, repairs, tires, garage rental, and other maintenance. You may also take a depreciation deduction for the vehicle as discussed in Hour 15, "Depreciation and Amortization."

FIGURE 14.6.

Calculate deductible automobile expenses using page 2 of Form 2106.

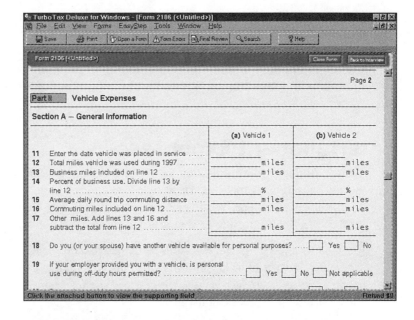

FIGURE 14.7.

You are entitled to claim a deduction only for the percentage of business usage.

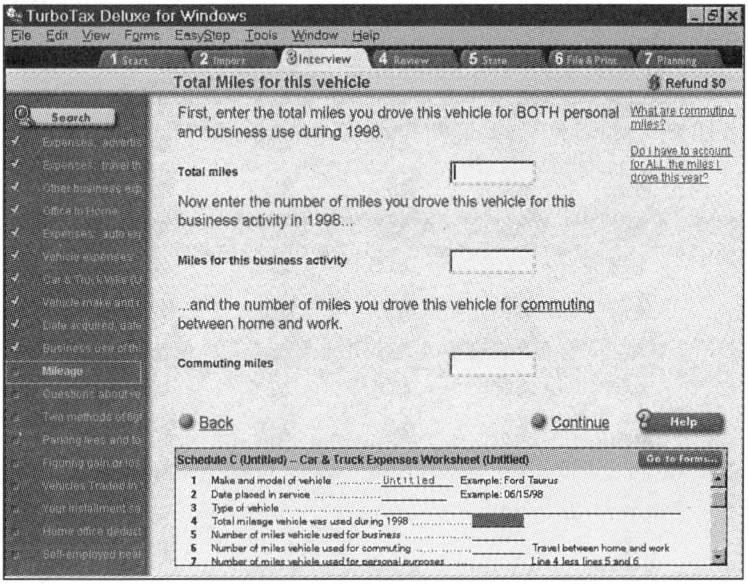

You may use either the actual expense method or take the standard deduction, depending upon which yields the best tax result. You may also deduct expenses for parking and tolls on line 2 of Form 2106, regardless of which method you opt to use. As with other types of business deductions, Schedule C filers may deduct automobile expenses in full. Employees must take them on Schedule A as miscellaneous deductions and contend with the required floor of 2% of AGI.

Entertainment Expenses

You are entitled to take a deduction for meals and entertainment for business purposes, including meals while traveling. Deductible entertainment expenses include restaurants, health club memberships, trips to attractive places, and so on. Deductions in this category are, however, limited to 50% of your actual expenses.

It is important to keep accurate records pertaining to these expenses; the IRS carefully scrutinizes this type of deduction. At a minimum, you need to keep dated receipts indicating who was entertained and the business purpose for incurring the expense (that is, what was discussed or accomplished).

Moving Expenses

You are entitled to take an adjustment, rather than a deduction, for moving expenses, regardless of whether your are an employee or Schedule C sole proprietor. The adjustment is reflected on line 26 of page 1 of the 1040, as opposed to Schedule C or Schedule A.

To be deductible, your move must meet the following tests:

- The move must be job related.
- The new job must be 50 miles farther from your house than the old job was.
- You must work full time in the same geographical area for at least 12 months subsequent to the move.

Deductible moving expenses are reported on Form 3903, shown in Figure 14.8. Allowable deductions include the costs of moving household goods and the costs of temporary travel and lodging.

FIGURE 14.8.

Moving expenses are carried from this form to line 7 of the Form 1040.

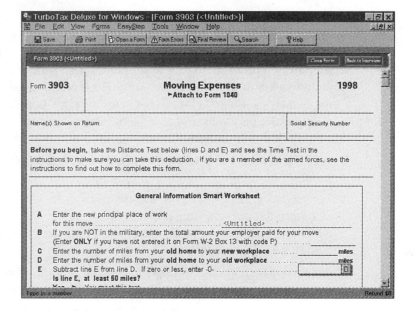

Education and Training Expenses

Educational expenses may be deducted if the training is required for you to keep your current job or to maintain and improve your job skills in your present field. Education expenses to qualify you for a new job or profession are not deductible.

Summary

The IRS recognizes that you have to spend money to make money, and deductions are allowed for a wide range of business related expenses. Generally, you can deduct these expenses whether you are self-employed or work for someone else. Employees, however, are required to claim job related expenses, other than moving costs as miscellaneous deductions, which are subject to a 2% of AGI floor. Additionally, the benefit of such deductions may be lost for taxpayers who do not itemize their deductions. Moving expenses may be taken as an adjustment on page 1 of the 1040 Form without regard to whether the employee itemizes.

Hour 15 discusses a type of deduction that is of great importance to many businesses and investment property owners.

14

Q&A

Q What are "hobby losses"?

A An activity is presumed to be a hobby, rather than a business, if it fails to show a profit for three of five consecutive years. (Horse breeding and horse-racing businesses must show a profit for two out of seven years). Generally, hobby expenses are deductible only to the extent of hobby income, rather than as a net operating loss, which may be taken against other income.

Q Is it true that the law is being liberalized with regard to home office deductions?

A Yes. Beginning in 1999, as a result of the Taxpayer Relief Act of 1997, your home office qualifies as your principal place of business if it is used to conduct administrative or management activities and you have *no other location* from which to conduct these activities.

Q Are there potential disadvantages to claiming a home office deduction?

A Yes. One potential disadvantage is heightened IRS scrutiny. Another issue is that you are *required* to take depreciation that is "allowed or allowable" on any portion of your home for which you claim the deduction. The gain attributable to the portion of your home used for business and the amount of the depreciation is taxed, even though after 1997 most other gains on the sale of a personal residence are excluded from income. This can be a tremendous disadvantage for highly appreciating homes. Proceed carefully before electing to take a home office deduction.

HOUR 15

Depreciation and Amortization

Everything discussed in this hour pertains to rules for business deductions. If you do not own your own business (this would include rental property and working at home as a consultant or graphic artist, for example), you can skip this chapter, unless you think you might start one up in the relatively near future.

Highlights of this hour include

- How TurboTax deals with depreciation
- What information TurboTax needs from you
- The tax forms used with depreciation

TurboTax Tackles Depreciation

When wading through documents that describe the depreciation process, many tax do-it-yourselfers have chosen that moment to look up from the books and say, "Honey, maybe we'd better call an accountant." And rightfully so. It's not that the depreciation and amortization process is that difficult, but it's hard to know which set of rules apply to you. How does one determine which depreciation *type*, or *method*, or *recovery period*, applies to your assets, and what percentage of those assets is eligible for depreciation? Of course, there are worksheets for everything, but is it necessary to fill out all of them? No. Then how does one decide which worksheets are important?

TurboTax brings all the tools for accurately depreciating and amortizing your assets within your reach. The program does a great job of determining when a particular worksheet or schedule is required and whips out the right forms when, and if, they are needed. If more documentation is beneficial, TurboTax asks for it and places the supportive data on the correct worksheet so that it can help you later. You can set up the depreciation and amortization of all your business assets, without having to leave the EasyStep Interview. If you do want to view the forms full-page, entering data yourself, TurboTax allows you to, providing warnings if you go too far astray. If you get a little generous in what can reasonably be called a business asset, TurboTax brings you back into the bounds of the credible (see Figure 15.1).

FIGURE 15.1.

TurboTax asks you whether you have evidence to back up a claim for business use of an asset.

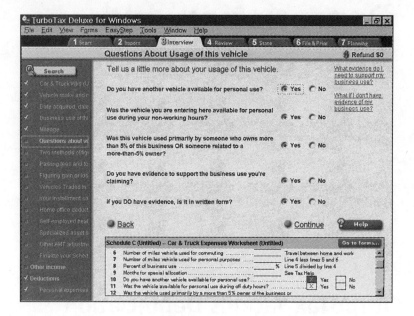

What Is Depreciation?

Depreciation is the act of deducting a business purchase over a number of years, rather than all at once. The IRS wants most business assets to be depreciated, rather than deducted from your taxable income in the same year. Business assets *types* are depreciated according to a depreciation schedule set by the IRS. We'd then say that each asset type (computers, heavy rental equipment, rental real estate) has its own depreciation *recovery period* (5 years, 7 years, 27.5 years). This recovery period is the number of years over which each asset type must be deducted. TurboTax calculates depreciation automatically based on the asset type you specift (see Figure 15.2).

When you depreciate your business assets over time, you're not necessarily deducting, for example, one-fifth of the value every year for five years. The IRS has set up *accelerated* depreciation systems that apply to most of your business assets. Happily, with TurboTax, you need not calculate these systems. TurboTax helps you determine the type of business asset you have, then suggests the most appropriate *depreciation method* (the rate at which you can depreciate your asset). If the method is *accelerated*, you can deduct a bit more in the early years. To set up the right depreciation system, TurboTax needs to know the year you placed this business asset into service. Try to have documentation that substantiates this claim.

Intangible assets (copyrights, patents, licenses and permits, and business records) are most often depreciated on a straight line, meaning you deduct an even amount every year for the duration. This process is called amortization, rather than depreciation. Most intangible assets are amortized (straight-line depreciated) over 15 years.

Factors Affecting Depreciation

When you deduct an asset, you do so according to the type of business activity it's used for (word processors for grant writing, for example, or lawn equipment for gardeners). If an asset is used for more than one business venture (if you have a home office and spend part of your time overseeing rental property and the rest of the time as a business consultant) you're expected to determine the percentage of that asset's time that is spent with each business venture, and divide your deduction of that asset accordingly (see Figure 15.3).

If a business asset is also used for non-business purposes (a car or computer, for example), you can depreciate only a percentage of that asset's cost. You need to show careful records justifying the business deduction of a "mixed use" asset. These assets are called *Listed Property*.

15

FIGURE 15.2.

TurboTax provides a drop-down list of asset types, making it easier to determine the asset life and recovery period.

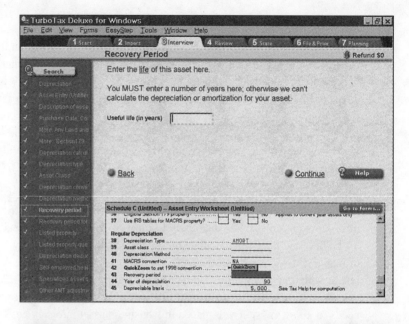

FIGURE 15.3.

If an asset is used for more than one business, enter the percentage for each.

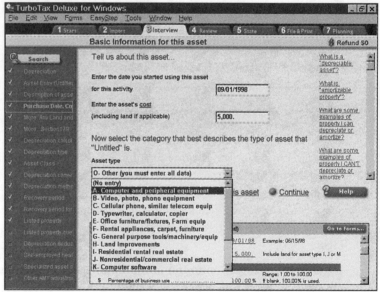

How much you can depreciate an asset *this year* depends greatly on the time of year it was *placed into service*. The date during the year in which you get to start depreciating your assets is called a convention. The following are some principles to remember when dealing with deciding what time of year to begin depreciating your asset:

- Most often, you get to start deducting your personal business property at mid-year, even if it was placed into service for your business a bit later. This is called the half-year convention and applies to most personal business property, such as video or photography equipment, or other machinery.

- Rental property (or portions of your house set aside for business) is depreciated according to the mid-month convention, which means that you must begin depreciating the property in the middle of the month you began using it for your business.

- Also, certain rules apply if you purchase more than 40% of your business property during the last quarter of the year. The mid-month rule stipulates that you have to start depreciating an asset from the middle of the first month you used this item for business (see Figure 15.4).

FIGURE 15.4.

TurboTax figures out the best approach to the convention, helping you to avoid the mid-quarter or mid-month rule if possible.

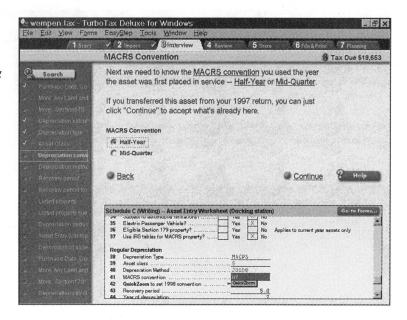

It's important to note that you do not have to remember these rules. At the right time, TurboTax asks you what it needs to know and applies the correct depreciation rules to your specific business assets.

The Section 179 Expense Deduction

To accommodate brand new businesses who need to make big-ticket purchases to get their business going, the IRS created the section 179 expense deduction (see Figure 15.5). You are allowed to directly deduct the cost of a business asset the first year you put it into use. You may deduct up to $18,500 for business items, if this is the first year they were put into use. Before you get too carried away applying it to your situation, read the following three common restrictions:

- Even when taking this deduction, you still have to follow the Luxury Auto Limit. That means you can only deduct up to $3,160 dollars per year for the use of a car for a business, even if the cost of the car exceeds that sum.

- Also, the section 179 expense deduction cannot be used for intangible property like licenses or patents.

- You cannot use the section 179 deduction on real estate property used 50% or less for business or trade.

FIGURE 15.5.

If applicable, the Interview leads you toward the Section 179 Expense Deduction, which lets you deduct many types of business purchases in the first year you use them.

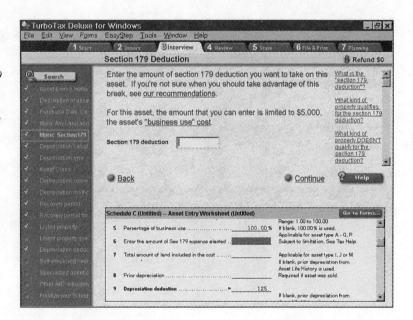

How Section 179 Can Help

Section 179 can be helpful to get around the mid-quarter rule for convention. Remember, the convention is when a business asset is first put to use. Generally, you can take the half-year convention, meaning that all equipment you put into use during that year can be depreciated as if it were placed into service at the half-year mark. However, if more than 40% of your business purchases were placed into service in the fourth quarter of the year, you must depreciate all your business assets from the midpoint of the quarter they were placed into service.

But some business purchases are unavoidable, and you may have to purchase a large part of your business assets in the year's fourth quarter, whether you like it or not. For example, if you bought $5,000 worth of start-up business equipment in June, you could deduct it according to the mid-year convention. However, if circumstances forced you to invest another $10,000 in October, you'd have to then use the mid-quarter convention, which would start your depreciation later in the year. ($10,000 is more than 40% of $15,000, thus, the mid-quarter rule applies to you.)

To offset the damage done to your entire business expense depreciation schedule, just apply your section 179 expense deduction to that late-year purchase, the one that threw you into the mid-quarter rule. (Deduct at least enough to bring the expense below the 40% mark.)

What TurboTax Needs from You

You need not remember all these rules. What TurboTax does require is an accurate picture of the following:

- The equipment you are depreciating. TurboTax suggests what *asset type* that equipment falls into and determines over how many years you are required to depreciate that asset.

- The cost of the equipment (or real property) you are depreciating and any money you've spent to improve its value.

- The year and month you placed that asset into service for your business.

- The nature of the business. Specifically, different rules apply to you if you rent *real property*, compared to other business ventures. Also, different rules apply if renting real property is your main business or something you do on the side.

- The level of your involvement with the business. Do you spend a good deal of time on this business venture, or are you simply investing the money and not involved in the day-to-day decisions?

- If you are taking the home office deduction, you need to specify what percentage of your home is used for this business (see Figure 15.6).

- You have to specify what accounting method your business uses (cash or accrual).

- If you deduct an asset for business, but also use it for recreation or other purpose, you are asked which percentage of this asset is used for business (see Figure 15.7).

- If you use an asset for more than one business, you are asked to break that asset into percentages used for each business.

FIGURE 15.6.

To take the Home Office Deduction, tell TurboTax what percentage of your home is used for business.

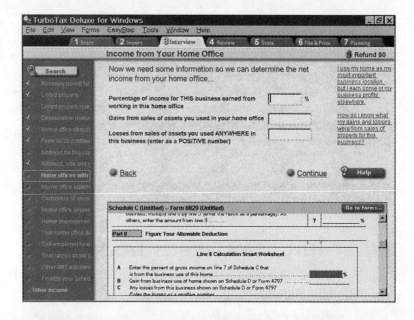

FIGURE 15.7.

If you have business assets that are used for other purposes besides your business, you must provide percentages.

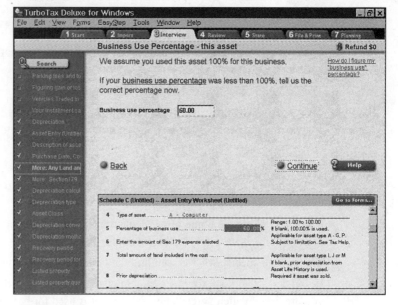

15

As well as keeping accurate records of how much you spend on each business asset (and when you spent it), it's a very good idea to have a bank account that you only use for business. If further documentation is ever requested to substantiate a business deduction claim, it's much easier if transactions can be followed clearly from one account.

The IRS does not demand that your business be profitable. If it does not turn a profit in three to five years or less, they want to see how you are going to fix that. What steps are you taking to make a profitable plan? They want to see your course of action altered. If not, the IRS might disallow later deductions, or even earlier ones.

Points to Keep in Mind

When your TurboTax EasyStep Interview starts discussing business property and depreciation, TurboTax also pulls out the correct form, schedule, and worksheet as needed. However, there are some points to keep in mind before you begin:

- You are depreciating the *cost basis* of your business asset. The cost basis refers to how much you paid for that asset, plus any improvements you made to it (see Figure 15.8), minus any devaluation it suffered between the time you bought the asset and the time you actually placed it into service for your business. Improvements you make to your rental property can be depreciated, as well as repairs. Improvements not only apply to rental or other real property, but to autos (a new paint job to take your clients around town) and computer equipment (a new hard drive to hold all your graphic design projects), to name only two examples.

When improving property, the TurboTax Interview asks you to differentiate between improvements and repairs, because the IRS applies different rules to each.

FIGURE 15.8.

TurboTax asks about improvements you've made to your asset that would increase its value.

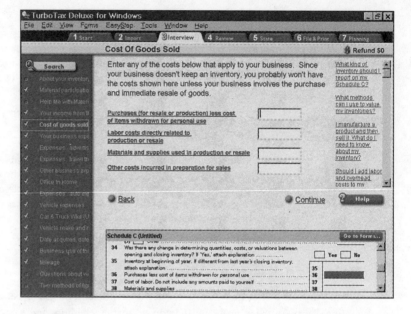

- If the business property you are depreciating is a car or truck, you may notice TurboTax opens a different form than other types of property. That's because the IRS requires a special worksheet for cars and trucks you use for your business.

- You cannot depreciate land. The IRS does not consider land to be reducing in value over time, only the *buildings* on it are said to depreciate (see Figure 15.9). Therefore, when depreciating a portion of your home for business use ("My office takes up 25% of my house, so I'm depreciating 25% of my home purchase as a business expense"), you need to look closely at your property tax and see how much of your tax is for the *land* and how much is for the *improvements*. Only the percentage of the total value that is based on improvements (buildings on the land), can be depreciated.

If you repair your roof, that repair was made to the house, and thus, you can deduct the roof repair (only according to the percentage of your home that you use for business). However, if you elaborately terrace your yard and make new retaining walls to stop the hill outside your home from sliding into the ocean, none of that may be deducted as a business expense, because it involves *land*, not the house itself.

FIGURE 15.9.

The IRS does not allow you to depreciate the land your property is on. Consult your property tax to determine the value of the land, which must be subtracted from your adjusted cost basis.

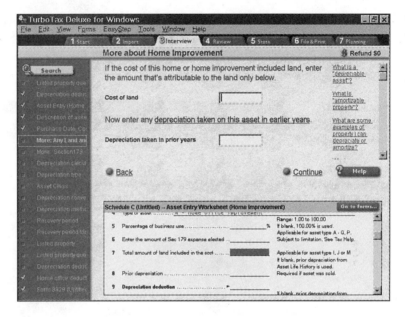

- The IRS looks at your assets in terms of *business activity*. So TurboTax conducts the interview by moving from business activity to business activity. ("Now that you are done with your underwriting business, let's move on and talk about your contracting business.") Therefore, if you use one business asset for various business activities ("Sometimes I *rent* my gardening tools, or sometimes I *garden* with them."), make sure you refer to that equipment again, in each business and accurately divide up the depreciation of that asset *among its various business uses*. Using the gardening tools example, if you do 60% gardening and 40% rental of those tools, then, when TurboTax interviews you about your gardening business, specify that 60% of the gardening tool cost should be depreciated. Then, when your rental business comes up in the interview, you can depreciate the other 40%.

Prior Year Issues

If you now realize that you put a piece of business equipment into service last year, you cannot "double up" your depreciation this year to compensate for the missed year. You have to call this current year the *second year* that this equipment was in service, and work from there. You can, however, file an amended return for last year and claim the first year of depreciation that way.

If this is the second year you are using TurboTax and you've entered depreciation schedules last year as well, all you need to do is transfer last year's TurboTax data. You'll find that the program has continued to properly account for your ongoing depreciations (see Figure 15.10).

FIGURE 15.10.

When calculating your current year's depreciation amounts, TurboTax takes into account previous year's numbers.

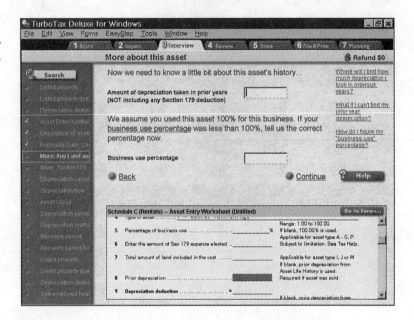

How TurboTax Approaches Depreciation and Amortization

Using the EasyStep Interview, the following is how TurboTax gathers depreciation and amortization information about your business expenses. The interview asks all the questions pertaining to one business activity and moves on to the next, if there are any:

- First, you are asked whether you want to depreciate your home or a home improvement as part of a home office deduction.
- TurboTax then asks about cars and trucks used for this business.
- Finally, TurboTax asks about other equipment and assets that are related to that particular business.

You'll find that TurboTax initially places your answers on the Asset Entry Worksheets (some of the home office deduction information goes on Form 8829) and are routed to the appropriate schedules. Depreciation and amortization questions related to real estate rental are ultimately entered onto Schedule E, whereas the same questions for other business depreciations end up on Schedule C. TurboTax asks enough questions to determine the correct asset type, depreciation or amortization type and amount, and recovery period, for each business asset.

The Forms You May See

As mentioned previously, you won't have to work directly with the worksheets and schedules. TurboTax walks you through them with the Interview. However, you may want to go back and make changes, and sometimes retracing your steps with the Interview Search feature or the Back button can be cumbersome. It's faster to just open the form and make your adjustment (see Figure 15.11). (Doing so simply supplements the information gathered with the Interview.) What follows are the names of some of the schedules, worksheets, and forms you come across when working with depreciating and amortizing your business assets.

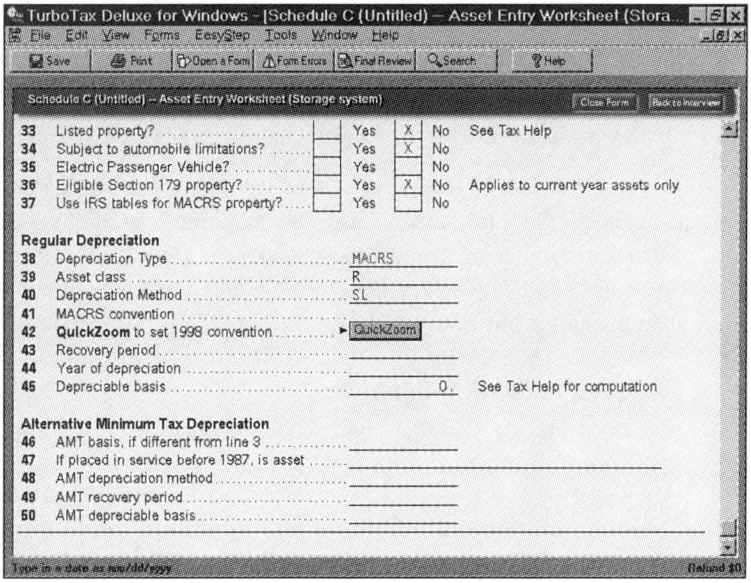

FIGURE 15.11.

Use the QuickZoom button to move between your schedule and the worksheets and forms that contribute to them.

Asset Entry Worksheet

Complete one of these for each depreciable or amortizable asset. Fill out this worksheet to determine an asset's deductibility and depreciation specifications.

Car and Truck Expense Worksheet

Enter depreciation information on any car or truck used in your business.

Form 4562: Depreciation and Amortization

Your Asset Entry Worksheets feed their information onto this form. In TurboTax, you need to enter very little data directly. To move from this form to the appropriate worksheets use the QuickZoom button, which you see on various lines where data *from* those worksheets is entered.

Some lines in this form deal directly with section 179 deductions. You are asked during the interview if you want to opt for a section 179 expense deduction. You are not required to enter anything directly on this form, but you might want to look over the 179 sections to see the totals. That's because, if you are approaching the limits of what you can deduct under section 179, you may want to take a depreciation on some of those assets instead and keep the section 179 limit open for·something else with more advantage. (TurboTax points out various advantages in the interview.)

Part II of Form 4562 is used to select the convention (what time of year you can begin depreciating your assets *from*) for your business assets. Look this area over to learn more about what TurboTax set up for you, and make changes, if you think some are necessary.

Part V of Form 4562 deals with Listed Property. That's property used partially for business and partially for personal use. The only time you might need to manually enter any data here is if you have a business-use vehicle not entered on a Car and Truck Expenses Worksheet, and you need to enter information that would allow you to take the deduction directly on this form.

Depreciation Report

This report lists and summarizes business assets you are deducting for the current year.

Asset Life History

Open this report if you want to view a year-by-year listing of allowable deductions for all your depreciating business assets.

Situations You May Be Faced with

Let's go over some of the depreciation and amortization-related questions that are likely to come your way, while walking through the EasyStep Interview. You notice that each question TurboTax asks has certain text elements written in blue. Those represent factors in each question that could use some detailed explanation. Click any blue text for a thorough description of that specific item.

As it comes time to choose a depreciation *type* (meaning how rapidly the asset is depreciated) for your asset, TurboTax selects one. Most often, your asset is depreciated according to the Modified Accelerated Cost Recovery System (MACRS, see Figure 15.12), but TurboTax lets you choose another type, if you happen to have a special reason to override the program's suggestion.

FIGURE 15.12.

There are several depreciation types, determining how fast you can depreciate your asset. MACRS is the most common.

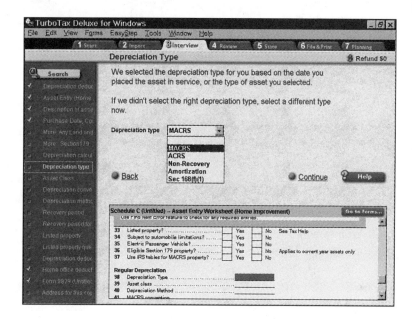

 When TurboTax asks to specify a depreciation type, the following is something to keep in mind: If your business asset was placed into service since 1987, select MACRS. If your asset was placed into service between or after 1980 but before 1987, select ACRS. You find TurboTax is pretty good about selecting the right depreciation type. If there's a question, TurboTax does not complete the field (it does not fill in a suggested depreciation type). If this happens, click the Help question mark at the upper right. You see a detailed discussion about choosing a correct depreciation type.

TurboTax helps you compute the useful life of an asset that you are amortizing, which greatly influences the length of the depreciation recovery period. As shown in the figure, click the word "life" for more information. The number determines how long depreciation takes, but the bulk of the depreciation may be accelerated and occur near the beginning (see Figure 15.13).

FIGURE 15.13.

You can accept what TurboTax has determined to be what the IRS would call the "useful life" of your asset, or type another.

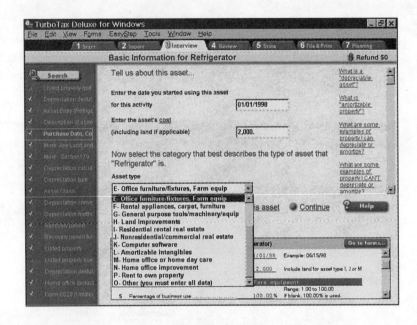

When you have entered all the needed information about an asset, TurboTax tells you so, as shown in Figure 15.14. Check Done with This Asset to move on.

FIGURE 15.14.

Click Done with This Asset to finalize the calculations.

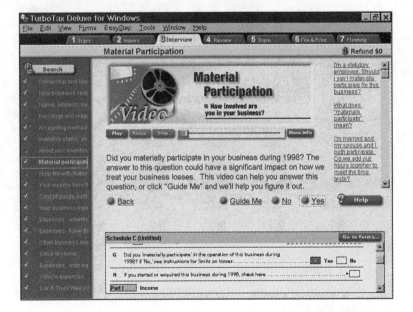

Summary

Although the rules for depreciating and amortizing business expenses can be daunting, TurboTax does not require you to tackle them head on. If you simply know some basic information about the assets you are depreciating, TurboTax walks you through the various depreciation schedules and worksheets and suggests choices based on IRS rules.

Q&A

Q **There's no way I'm going to be able to remember all the rules for depreciating and amortizing. After I start this path with TurboTax, I'm afraid I may end up quite lost. What do I really need to know?**

A You need to know the cost of your business assets when they were placed into service, and what percentage of these assets were actually used for business.

Q **Is there a way to guess how long the IRS wants to depreciate an asset?**

A No, not really. TurboTax selects a depreciation schedule based on the type of asset you are working with at the moment.

Q **I just bought this big-ticket item to start my business with, and now you're telling me I have to depreciate it over many years? What's a chemical company to do?**

A When you purchase an item for your new business, you can deduct it entirely during its first year of use, up to $18,500 dollars. This is called taking the section 179 deduction. Lots of restrictions apply, however, especially involving car and real estate purchases.

Q **I've been working my home business for a couple of years now, and I've yet to show a real profit. I'm rather sheepish about taking any further deductions. Am I inviting IRS scrutiny by giving it a go for a while longer?**

A If you make a serious effort to change course and modify your business plans in reasonable ways, the IRS does not fault you for not turning a profit. Also, consult experts, and show that you are trying to learn more about your business. Just don't keep beating the same path over and over again.

15

HOUR **16**

Tax Credits

This hour is devoted to a pleasant tax concept: the tax credit. A tax credit is even more beneficial to you than a deduction. The credit is a direct dollar-for-dollar reduction in your income tax liability, as opposed to deductions, which merely reduce a portion of your taxable income. For example, if you are in the 28% tax bracket, a $2,000 deduction reduces your tax bill by about $560. But $2,000 credit reduces your tax bill by the full $2,000. In the next 60 minutes, you learn to identify the different types of tax credits to which you may be entitled and what to do to avail yourself of them.

Highlights of this hour include

- Child and dependent care credit
- Credit for the elderly or disabled
- Earned income credit
- Education related credits
- Adoption tax credit
- Foreign and investment tax credits

Child and Dependent Care Credits

As women have entered the labor force in increasing numbers, the nation's tax returns have reflected this trend. The child and dependent care credit is now commonly included on tax returns.

This credit entitles you to a break for amounts paid for care of dependents while you or your spouse worked to earn taxable income. This credit, a direct dollar for dollar reduction of your income tax, is calculated and reported on Form 2441, shown in Figure 16.1.

FIGURE 16.1.

This form is used to provide the IRS with a range of information about your dependent care service providers and the amounts that you paid to them.

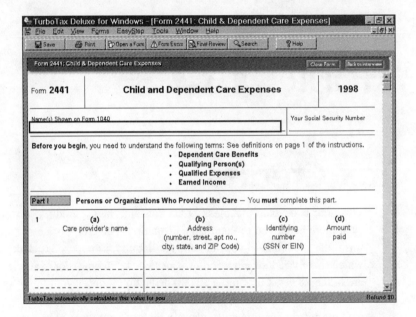

Determining Eligibility for the Dependent Care Credit

You are eligible to take the dependent care credit if you paid a third party to care for one or more of the following:

- Your dependent children under the age of 13.
- A spouse who requires care.
- Other persons in need of care for whom you are entitled to claim a dependency deduction, as discussed in Hour 2, "Preparation Options and Help Features." (The only exception is if the person had income exceeding the exemption amount.)

If you are divorced or separated—unless otherwise stipulated in a divorce decree—the parent who has custody of the children for a longer period of time during the year is entitled to claim the credit. If you are married but filing separately, you must meet these additional requirements:

- You must have lived apart from your spouse during the last six months of 1998.
- The dependent person for whom you are claiming the credit must have lived in your home for more than half of 1998.
- You have provided more than half the cost of keeping up your home.

Determining the Amount of the Credit

The amount of the child care credit that you are entitled to take is based on a percentage of costs that you pay for the child care up to a maximum of $2,400 for one child and $4,800 for two or more children. Your child care expenses cannot exceed the earned income of the spouse who earns the least amount. The criterion for determining earned income is discussed in the next section.

If you receive tax-free reimbursements from your employer to pay dependent care expenses, you must reduce the amount of your dependent care credit by the amount of the reimbursements. TurboTax asks you to enter the amount of tax-free child care reimbursements you receive from your employer in field number 10 of the screen shown in Figure 16.2, where you enter your W-2 information.

FIGURE 16.2.

Employer paid child care benefits reduce the credit that you may claim for such expenses.

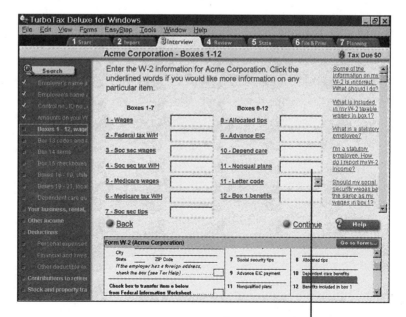

Enter tax-free dependent care benefits here

16

Qualifying Dependent Care Expenses

The following types of expenses paid to third-party providers are qualified child care expenses:

- Cost of an in-home care provider (including incidental housekeeping expenses)

 The in-home care provider can be your own child if your child is at least 19 years of age and not claimed as a dependent on your return.

- Cost of daycare facility
- Cost of kindergarten, nursery school, or summer camp, if care is provided and cannot be separated from the educational components of the program

Calculating the Credit

Earned income is income that comes from work or employment. Generally both spouses must have earned income in order to qualify for the credit. However, if one spouse is a full-time student, the IRS treats $200 of the income of the couple as earned income of the student spouse, regardless of the actual source or nature of the income.

The amount of the dependent care credit that you are permitted to take is based upon the earned income of the lesser-earning spouse. If you are married but file separately, you cannot take the credit unless *both* spouses have earned income.

The amount of the credit that you may take is based upon the percentage chart that appears in Part II of Form 2441. Depending upon your adjusted gross income, you are permitted to take a deduction of between 20% and 30% of the first $2,400 of qualified child care expenses ($4,800 for two or more children) provided your earned income equals or exceeds these amounts. The amount calculated on line 9 of Form 2441 is reported on line 41 of the Form 1040.

 You may lose your dependent care credit if you are subject to alternative minimum tax, as discussed in Hour 21, "Additional Types of Taxes Imposed."

Earned Income Credit

The earned income is a credit available to certain low-income taxpayers to supplement their income. Many of the requirements for taking the earned income and child care credits are similar. However, the benefit of the child care credit is lost if you do not have taxable income for the year. In contrast, the earned income credit is a "refundable credit," which means that you actually receive money back if you do not have a tax liability for the year. It is analogous to receiving a refund for overpayment of tax.

TurboTax uses personal and income information entered during the EasyStep Interview to automatically determine whether you are eligible for the earned income credit. You are prompted to enter any information that the program is missing to make the determination, as illustrated in Figure 16.3.

FIGURE 16.3.

TurboTax prompts you to supply all information necessary to qualify for the Earned Income Credit.

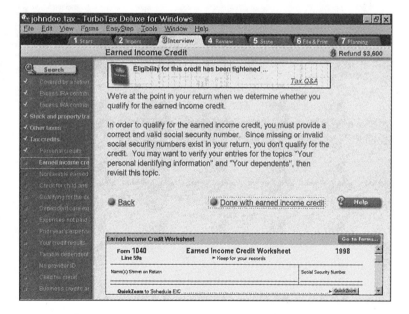

If TurboTax determines you are eligible to take the Earned Income Credit, it completes Schedule EIC shown in Figure 16.4. This amount is carried to line 59a of the Form 1040.

To benefit from the earned income credit, you must have earned income and meet the following additional requirements:

- You must have at least one qualifying, dependent child in your household under the age of 19 (24 if a full-time student) or you must be between the ages of 25 and 65 and claimed on someone else's tax return.

FIGURE 16.4.

The credit computed on this schedule may be refunded to you even if you don't owe any tax.

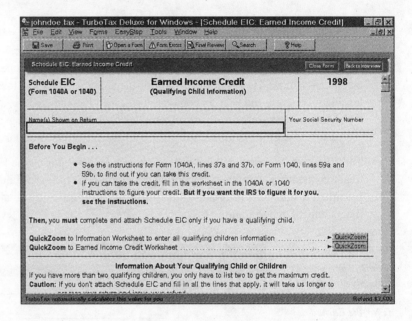

- You must have earned income and adjusted gross income of less than the levels reflected as follows:

Income Limitations for Earned Income Credit

One qualifying child	$26,473
More than one qualifying child	$30,095
No qualifying children	$10,030

Maximum Earned Income Credit for 1998

One qualifying child	$2,271
Two qualifying children	$3,756
No qualifying children	$341

A taxpayer may also elect to receive advance earned income credits through his or her paychecks by requesting a Form W-5 from his or her employer.

Credit for the Elderly and Disabled

There are advantages to aging, and one of them is that you may be permitted to take an additional tax credit using Schedule R that appears in Figure 16.5. TurboTax determines whether you are eligible to take the credit based on various personal and income information you provide during the EasyStep Interview and then it completes Schedule R. The amount computed on Schedule R is then carried forward to line 42 of the Form 1040.

FIGURE 16.5.

Schedule R is for elderly and disabled taxpayers who meet certain income requirements.

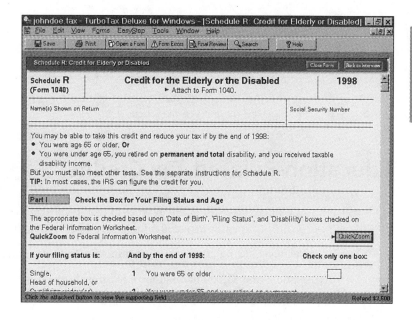

The maximum amount of the credit is $1,125 for a married couple or $750 for a single person, but you must meet the income requirements in Table 16.1 to qualify for the credit. Additionally, you must turn 65 on or before January 1, 1999. Alternatively, if you are under the age of 65, you may claim the credit if you are retired because of a permanent and total disability and have received taxable disability income in 1998 from a disability plan sponsored by a former employee.

TABLE 16.1. LIMITATIONS ON INCOME CREDIT FOR THE ELDERLY DISABLED.

Filing Status	Adjusted Gross Income Limit	Base Amount for Computing Credit
Married Filing Jointly; one spouse eligible for credit	$20,000	$5,000
Married Filing Jointly; both spouses eligible for credit	$25,000	$7,500

continues

TABLE 16.1. CONTINUED

Filing Status	Adjusted Gross Income Limit	Base Amount for Computing Credit
Married Filing Separately	$12,500	$3,750
Single*	$17,500	$5,000

No credit is available to a single individual who has an adjusted gross income of $1,750 or more, or if the individual receives more than $5,000 in non-taxable Social Security, pension annuity, railroad retirement, or Veteran's benefits.

 You may be subject to additional limitations for purposes of the elderly and disabled credit if you file Schedule C, D, E, or F.

Education-Related Tax Credits

The Taxpayer Relief Act of 1997 added Section 25A to the Internal Revenue Code, which permits you to take two different types of credits for qualified tuition and related expenses. Qualified expenses included tuition, fees, books, room, and board.

The Hope Scholarship Credit allows you to take a credit for the following:

- 100% of the first $1,000 of qualified educational expenses
- 50% of qualified educational expenses for the next $1,000, subject to a maximum credit limitation of $1,500

A Lifetime Learning Credit (for qualified expenses paid after June 28, 1998) allows for 20% of the first $5,000 qualified tuition payments to institutions attended to acquire or improve job skills. This credit has a maximum amount of $1,000, and you can claim only one student per tax return—even if you have two or more students.

Both the Hope Scholarship Credit and Lifetime Learning Credit are reduced for taxpayers having modified adjusted gross income in excess of certain amounts. This amount is between $40,000 and $50,000 for single taxpayers and $80,000 to $100,000 for married taxpayers filing jointly. Refer to the online Help option within TurboTax for other stipulations with these credits.

Child Tax Credit

In 1998 taxpayers are permitted to take a child credit of $400 for each qualifying child that is under the age of 17 as of the last day of the tax year. This credit is phased out (that is, reduced) by $50 for each $1,000 of "modified" adjusted gross income for tax-payers exceeding the following amounts:

Married, Filing Jointly	$110,000
Single or Head of Household	$75,000
Married, Filing Separately	$55,000

16

Other Types of Tax Credits

In addition to the most common types of credits previously discussed this hour, there are a number of credits that apply to special situations. It is certainly to your economic advantage to take them if you qualify.

Adoption Credits

An adoption credit of $5,000 is available for reasonable and necessary costs associated with adoption, such as legal fees. This credit amount is increased to $6,000 if the child is disabled. This credit is reduced for taxpayers having adjusted gross income of $75,000 or more; no credit is allowed for taxpayers with adjusted gross incomes in excess of $115,000. Unused adoption credits can be carried forward for up to five years. The adoption credit is claimed on Form 8839, shown in Figure 16.6.

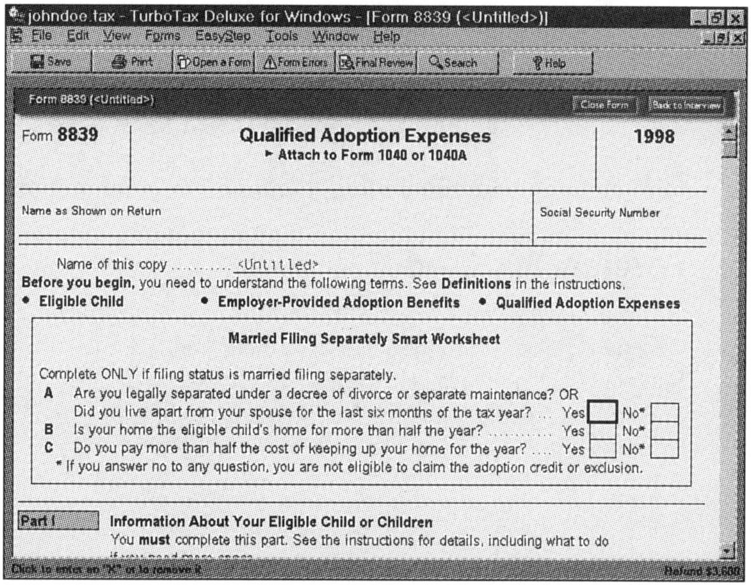

FIGURE 16.6.

The amount computed using this form is carried forward to line 42 of Form 1040.

Investment, Energy, Reforestation, and Rehabilitation Tax Credits

These types of credits are available for special types of investments in real property. The rules for claiming these types of credits and the methods for computing them are extremely complicated. TurboTax asks you a series of interview questions that help you determine whether your property qualifies. If you do qualify, TurboTax automatically prepares Schedule 3468 and carries the amount computed on the Schedule to line 47 of your Form 1040. Form 3468, shown in Figure 16.7, is also used to claim reforestation, energy, and rehabilitation credits.

FIGURE 16.7.

Amounts computed on this form are carried forward to line 47 of the Form 1040.

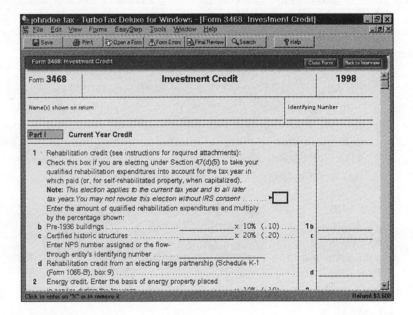

Foreign Tax Credit

You may claim either a deduction or a credit for foreign income taxes paid—not both. Generally, it is to your advantage to take the credit. If you indicate, during the EasyStep Interview, that you have paid these taxes, TurboTax automatically prepares Form 1116. The amount reported on Form 1116 is carried to line 46 of the Form 1040. Form 1116 is reproduced in Figure 16.8.

FIGURE 16.8.

Amounts computed on this form are carried forward to line 46 of the Form 1040.

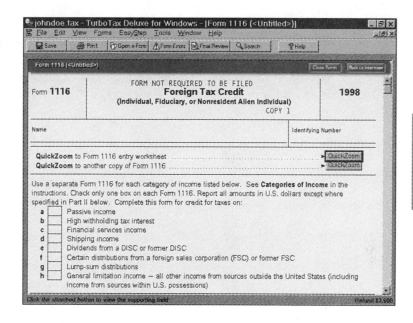

16

Summary

This hour covered the various types of tax credits that may be claimed on Form 1040. Credits may be claimed for child care expenses, limited educational expenses, adoption costs, certain types of investments, and foreign income taxes paid during the year. Additionally, low-income taxpayers may claim the earned income tax credit, and elderly and disabled taxpayers may claim a special credit using Schedule R. Additionally, beginning this year, parents are allowed a $400 child tax credit for each qualifying child.

Credits are the final section of the EasyStep Interview. Hour 17, "TurboTax Review Features," assists you in evaluating all the information you have entered into the system.

Q&A

Q I am adopting my spouse's children. Can I claim the adoption credit for our legal expenses?

A No. The adoption credit is not available for expenses attributable to adopting a spouse's child.

Q Is there an available credit for student loan interest paid?

A No. But beginning in 1998, a certain amount of student loan interest is *deductible*.
A deduction is allowed for the first 60 months in which interest payments are
required. The maximum allowable deduction for taxpayers with less than $40,000
of adjusted gross income ($60,000 for married filing jointly) is $1,000.

PART V
Reviewing and Filing a Return

Hour

Hour 17

TurboTax Review Features

After you type your last tax entry and get up to put away your pencils and papers, wouldn't it be nice to have someone go through and double-check things? Look over the math, see if there are deductions you didn't take, or check for things that would raise a red flag with the IRS and invite an audit. TurboTax has such a feature.

Highlights of this hour include

- TurboTax's tax form review
- Error check
- Checking overrides
- The deduction finder
- The personalized tax report

TurboTax's Tax Form Review

After the EasyStep Interview displays the dollar amount you owe, and brings up the possibility of filing a deadline extension, TurboTax starts the review. This review ensures that your return is accurate, checks the math, and looks for inconsistencies and potential problems.

During the review, each problem is presented point-by-point. Changes are made on the spot. The process is as friendly and non-intimidating as the rest of the EasyStep Interview. Most often, the process takes only a few minutes. As shown in Figure 17.1, the following are the steps you walk through in the review:

- Error Check
- Deduction Finder
- Audit Alerts
- U.S. Averages
- Tax Report

FIGURE 17.1.

The five TurboTax Review steps. The review starts automatically as you finish filling out your tax form.

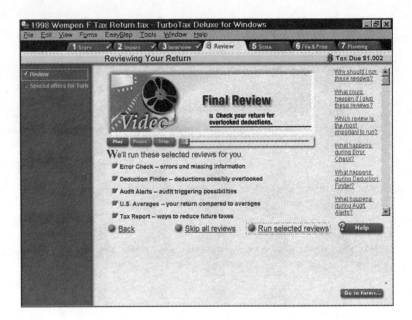

In this hour, we walk through each step of the TurboTax Review and see what's in store. If you've not yet completed a tax return, understanding the review now helps you avoid some of the problems that TurboTax is likely to catch and wants you to fix later anyway. It's nice to know that TurboTax takes every precaution to make sure your tax return is accurate and to your advantage.

TurboTax takes this review process one step at a time. Most often, TurboTax can handle any changes that need to be made without requiring you to leave the review. Just move through the steps, and you emerge on the other side with a tax return that has all the bases covered.

You need not worry about which step appears first. Simply click Next, all the way through the interview, and TurboTax walks you through each step as necessary. How long each step takes depends entirely on your tax return. For some users, Error Check takes much longer than Deduction Finder. For others, the reverse is true. In any case, as soon as TurboTax has finished searching your form, it moves on to the next step.

17

Even if you're not done calculating your taxes, you can always preview the review process by clicking the Review tab at the top of the TurboTax Screen. In following along with this chapter, you may want to do so now. Jumping ahead through the review before it comes up in the Interview does not adversely affect calculations.

If you are following along by clicking the Review tab at the top of the TurboTax screen, remember that the questions and points that TurboTax flags on your tax return are unique to your situation. Not everything we review in this chapter is going to appear on your screen. Also, items you come across in your review process may not be covered here.

To skip a review step, check the step you want to skip. With the check removed, TurboTax leaves that option out of the review. To skip the entire review, click Skip. This is not advisable unless you've already walked through the review, and you simply needed to go back into the Interview to make a change and are now racing toward the finish line. Otherwise, please make sure you at least allow TurboTax to check for errors, before sending in your return.

Finding an Entry You Made

During this review process, there may be times you need to open a form yourself and check the numbers there. Most often, you do not have to leave the review. Just click the View Current Form tab at the bottom of the screen, and change the number TurboTax has highlighted for you.

However, if you do have to search for a number from a particular form, follow the steps outlined in the following To Do section.

To Do: Locate a Specific Entry

1. From the Tools menu, choose My Tax Data. A window appears listing every line on any form that you placed an entry on.

2. Next to the name of the form, you see what information you entered as well as its source (see Figure 17.2).

3. Double-click the desired topic to go directly to a particular line on a tax form or worksheet. The form then appears with that specific line highlighted.

FIGURE 17.2.

Use the My Tax Data dialog box to locate any line of any form you've filled out in your tax return.

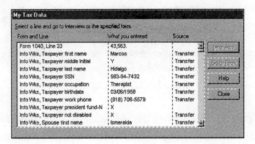

If you are asked to leave the review for a moment and open a certain form, simply save your tax form after typing data in the form by clicking File at the upper-left of the screen. Select Save, and then click the Review tab again. These steps return you to the Review process.

Remember that you can click the Back button at any time during the review to change an answer, review what you've done, or go back and take care of something you've skipped. TurboTax is very good about letting you go back and make adjustments to your return.

Beginning the TurboTax Review

When you first start your review, you are prompted to obtain a TurboTax Update (see Figure 17.3). Because tax laws are always in flux, TurboTax continues to make changes to its software *even after you've bought it.* Intuit, the software manufacturer, then makes those changes available to you as updates. The TurboTax software automatically installs updates as soon as you put them on your computer.

FIGURE 17.3.

To keep computations current, download a TurboTax Update, when prompted.

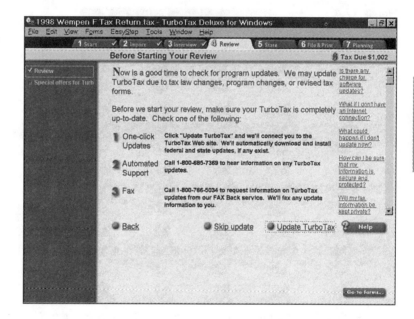

Obtain TurboTax Update information by fax, phone, or through the Internet. However, it's best to download the actual software updates from the Internet, because, as soon as the file is downloaded, the program simply makes the changes to the software (and to your return) as needed, without bothering you about it. If you obtain update information by fax or phone, you have to employ workarounds that can be a bit cumbersome.

To Do: Download an Update

To obtain a TurboTax Update online, first open your Internet connection, and then do the following:

1. Click the Update TurboTax link on the very first screen you see when you start the Tax Review, as shown in Figure 17.3. (If this opening screen does not appear, use the Back or Next button to locate it.) If prompted to save your file, click Yes.

▼ 2. The program then checks the TurboTax Web site to see whether new updates are available. If a TurboTax Update is found, you are prompted to download it. An Update panel appears. (If no update is found, TurboTax moves you to the first step in the review process.)

3. To begin, click the Update button. TurboTax begins downloading. A blue bar indicates the download progress (see Figure 17.4).

FIGURE 17.4.

The blue bar fills to the right as the download progresses.

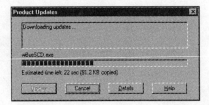

▲ 4. When the downloading is finished, the Update panel tells you the nature of the update, and you are prompted to restart TurboTax, and perhaps to restart your PC as well. After doing so, the update installed, and you do not have to think about it again.

If you do not have an Internet account, any online connection will work, including America Online or Prodigy. The TurboTax CD includes an America Online free trial offer.

Now you'll get acquainted with each TurboTax Review step. We'll start with Error Check.

Error Check

After reading the screen listing the five Review Steps (as shown earlier in Figure 17.1), click the Run Selected Reviews link. TurboTax moves you to the first step that we have selected in our example: Error Check (see Figure 17.5).

Error Check searches your tax return and forms for the following:

- Figures that just don't seem right, whether they are either too high or two low compared to the rest of the return.
- Excluded information of any type, perhaps dates left off, or income figures you forgot to type.

FIGURE 17.5.

The Error Check opening screen. This features reviews and prompts you to fix tax form mistakes.

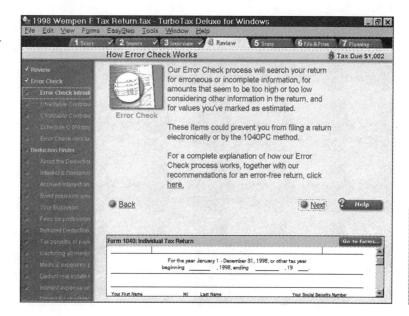

- Any number you marked as estimate. Now is the time you must firm up those estimates and type a "hard and fast" number.

After reading the introduction to Error Checking, as shown in Figure 17.5, click Next. TurboTax explains a little more about how the process works, reminding you that you can always jump to the Forms Method at any time, if need be. Click Next again, and finally, each error that TurboTax identifies is brought to your attention, one by one. The following are some examples of errors you may see:

- *Omitted Entry Errors.* If you forgot to make a required entry on a form, TurboTax brings it to your attention (Figure 17.6 is an example).

- *Making an Entry in an Automatic Entry Field.* Many lines on TurboTax forms are filled in automatically. TurboTax fills in these lines with data drawn from other forms and computations. Still, if you leave the interview and cruise the tax forms on your own, it's easy to erroneously think that these lines might need your individual attention. They don't. If TurboTax sees that you've typed in a form that should remain blank, you are prompted to remove it (see Figure 17.7).

17

FIGURE 17.6.

*Error Check prompts
you to fill in missing
required material.*

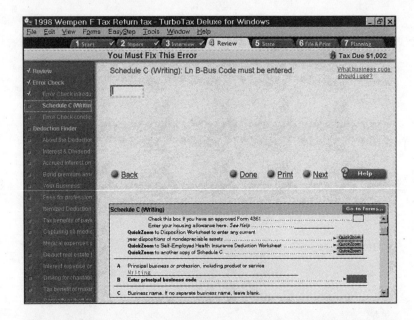

FIGURE 17.7.

*Error Check prompts
you to remove data
from a form TurboTax
fills in automatically.*

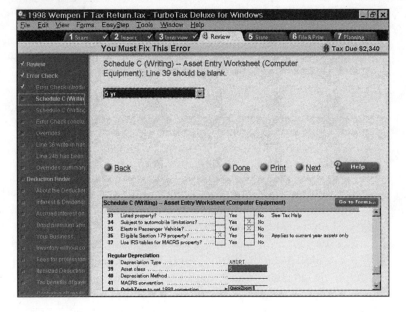

- *Entries That Require Separate Worksheets.* Often, the IRS requires that two similar deductions, allowances, and assets be entered on separate worksheets, as shown in Figure 17.8.

FIGURE 17.8.

Error Check tells you when you've used one form for data that requires two different forms.

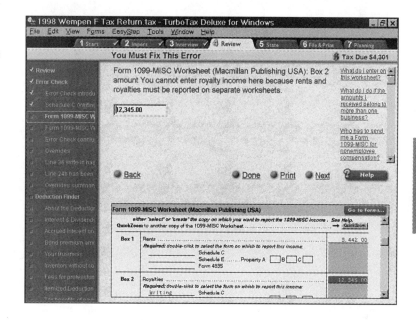

When TurboTax points this out, you can't simply click "Fix This Problem," and type new data. You actually have to return to that part of the interview where you should have begun using two forms.

To Do: Momentarily Leave the Tax Review

If Error Check requires you to go back to a prior section of the EasyStep Interview and you don't want to lose your place in the Error Check process, do the following:

1. Click the Navigation bar on the left side of the screen.

2. Scroll up on the list on the left to locate the interview segment right before where this error is mentioned (or, click Tools, then My Tax Data, as mentioned earlier in this chapter).

3. In Figure 17.9, you can see a user scrolling up and reopening the Your Home Office Deduction segment of the interview. That's because the error referred to in Figure 17.8 involved *dividing Rental and Royalty Income* onto two different forms.

17

To Do

FIGURE 17.9.

View the list of previous Interview steps and scroll up to locate an area that needs fixing.

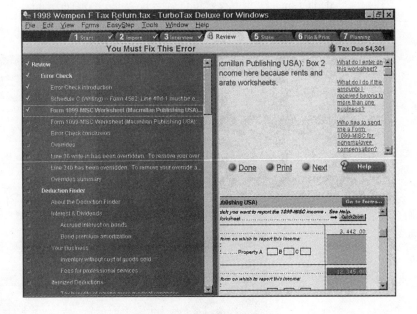

4. Scroll right before that segment of the EasyStep Interview, click there, and proceed to where you are prompted to create that second form, or otherwise fix the error. Just click Next to move forward, as usual.

5. Correct the error as instructed. After doing so, click the Review tab at the top of the screen, and click Next twice.

6. Look at the list that appears on the lower half of the screen. This list shows all the steps of the Error Check Review that you've completed.

7. Locate where you were in the review, before you jumped back to fix this error.

8. Click that line in the list to resume the review.

Let's get back to discussing what Error Check is likely to bring to your attention.

- *Entries Marked As Estimated.* If, while conducting the EasyStep Interview, you've marked a value as estimated, TurboTax gives you an opportunity to firm up that number. By now, you should have done the required research, and you should know exactly what to type in that estimated field. When Error Check opens the estimated number, just right-click the number as it appears in the Interview (no need to open the form in question). Select the Unmark Estimated option, and then click the Fix This Problem button.

- *Invalid Entries.* If you entered an invalid code, account number, or another type of data that TurboTax knows to be incorrect, you'll be prompted to fix it (see Figure 17.10).

FIGURE 17.10.

Error Check scans your tax form for invalid entries.

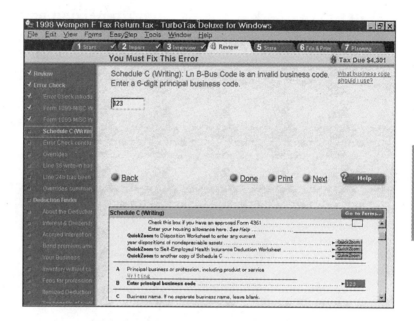

- *Inconsistent Entries.* If you typed one number on a particular form and later typed a different number when prompted for the same information, TurboTax makes it easy to choose which entry was correct, and fix the other one.

- *Entries That Just Seem Wrong.* If you provide data that simply seems "out of whack" when compared to other taxpayers in similar situations, TurboTax prompts you to review that entry and fix it, if necessary.

The above are just examples of possible errors. TurboTax can locate and help correct mistakes of all types.

How to Fix an Error

When an error is identified, TurboTax presents you with a brief description of it. You can click one of two option buttons: fix it or skip it.

TurboTax automatically displays the field containing the error. Just type a correction in the field or make a change on the form below it, and then click Next. Or, to skip the error, click Next without making a correction.

Sometimes fixing an error requires several steps, and it's easy to lose your place in the review. To return to the Error Check Review after you've been sidetracked fixing a particular mistake, follow the steps in the following To Do section.

To Do: Get Back to the Review After Fixing an Error

1. After you've made your final adjustment and fixed your error, click the Review tab at the top of the screen. The Update screen appears. Click Skip Update.

2. Click Run Selected Reviews. The opening Error Check screen appears.

3. To continue checking for errors, click Next again, and resume your check.

4. A list of errors to be reviewed appears in the Navigation bar (see Figure 17.11). To skip ahead to where you were, locate the error you were last working on and double-click its name. TurboTax opens to that location.

FIGURE 17.11.

To jump back into Error Check after fixing a line in a form, open up this list and click your prior location.

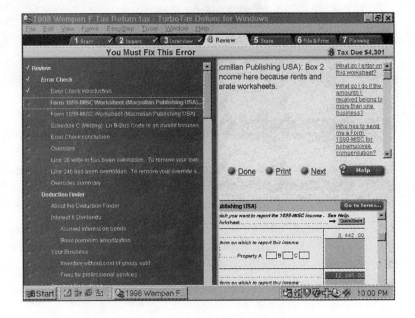

If TurboTax reports that an error must be fixed, TurboTax continues to issue more warnings if you try to fill out your form without correcting this problem.

Skipping a Problem

If you need more information before an error can be fixed, you can click Next to skip it. Later, return to the review and locate your prior position by doing one of two things:

- Start at the beginning of the review section and click Next until you find the problem in question.

- Return to the review, and click the error you skipped in the list of errors that appears in the Navigation bar.

When the final error has been checked, you see the screen shown in Figure 17.12, indicating you are moving on to the next phase in TurboTax.

FIGURE 17.12.

TurboTax wraps up Error Check.

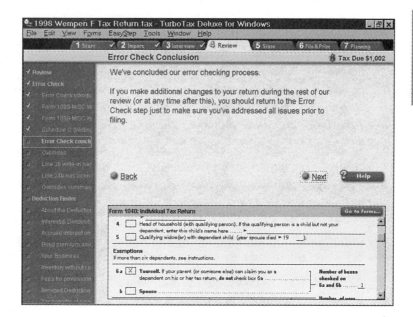

 After fixing errors, it's a good idea to save your TurboTax file. To do so, select File and choose Save.

Checking Overrides

Next, TurboTax takes a look at your overrides. Overrides are not considered to be errors, so the program begins reviewing overrides after closing the Error Check section.

In reviewing overrides, TurboTax wants to make sure you truly intended to include numbers that TurboTax cannot validate or double-check. When you use an override, TurboTax's "checks and balances" can't be applied to what you've typed. Unlike an error, TurboTax allows you to leave an override value in place, after you confirm you really want it there.

Review of Overrides

To review what an override is, remember that TurboTax lets you type information into a form that is contrary to TurboTax's calculations. Overrides don't only include numbers, though. If you rename an asset, or change the name of a dependent without doing so through the proper forms, you have to use override to do this. Later, during the review process (which we are learning now), TurboTax reminds you of the changes you made and points out the best way to include your new information in a way that doesn't disrupt TurboTax's checks and balances.

To override a value TurboTax has placed on a tax line, just right-click it and select Override. Then, type the new number. TurboTax makes note of this overridden value, and, when you review your tax return, it again is brought to your attention.

Restoring an Override Value

During the review, TurboTax encourages you to restore override values to what they were before, or, go and make the change on the intended form.

Figure 17.13 shows how TurboTax deals with a typical override. When the TurboTax Review presents you with an override, you have three choices:

- Click the field TurboTax highlights in the form, and then select Cancel Override from the Edit menu, or right-click and choose Cancel Override. This restores the original value to that field.

- Click Next to retain your override.

- Type yet another value into that field. TurboTax continues to mark this name or number as an override and includes it on your tax form if you insist. If you walk through the review again later, TurboTax again prompts you to restore the program's original calculation. Typing a new value always "trips" the override alert.

Let's move to the next review feature: The Deduction Finder.

FIGURE 17.13.

TurboTax encourages you to restore an override's original value, or change the value using the correct method.

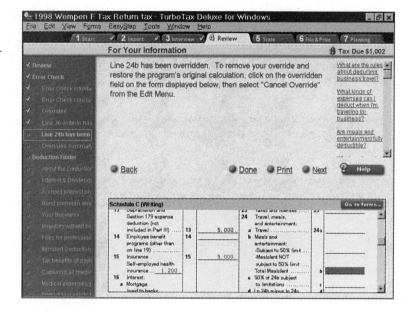

The Deduction Finder

The Deduction Finder appears as soon as TurboTax finishes looking at your overrides (see Figure 17.14). The main screen explains that your tax return is scoured for missed opportunities, looking over your entries and making you aware of potential deductions that could very well apply to you. Please note that some of Deduction Finder's suggestions you may have already explored. Also, a suggestion by TurboTax to investigate a deduction is not a guarantee that you can take that deduction.

Looking Up Deduction Facts

When Deduction Finder makes a suggestion, click any blue underlined text you see in the deduction's description. Remember, in TurboTax, click any blue underlined writing to open an article elaborating on the topic at hand. Also, to read more supportive information about the stipulations of a certain deduction, click the Help button at the upper-right of the screen.

Typical Deduction Finder Suggestions

Some Deduction Finder suggestions are applicable to a large number of people. For example, the program asks if you live in a state with mandatory deductions for State Disability Insurance, or something similar. If so, you can often deduct from your federal tax the amount you pay toward that state tax.

FIGURE 17.14.

The Deduction Finder scours your tax return for more possible deductions.

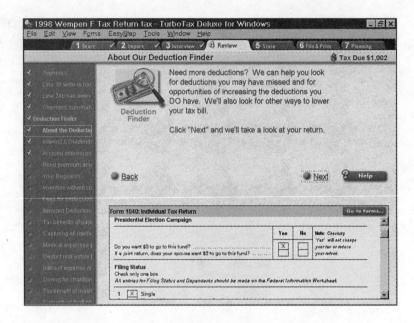

Depending on your situation, you are asked different questions, such as whether you are in the Armed Forces, are setting up a home office for a business, or carrying over deductions from the previous tax year (as shown in Figure 17.15), to name a few examples.

FIGURE 17.15.

Deduction Finder begins by asking broadly about deductions that could apply to many people.

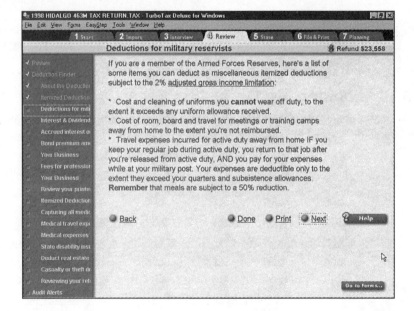

Next, the Deduction Finder zeroes in specifically on your tax return, pointing out areas where you may have a deduction coming. Figure 17.16 shows an inquiry about a bond purchase. Certain types of interest accrued from bonds can be tax deductible. In this manner, Deduction Finder reviews your return to make sure you're taking advantage of all the deductions available to you. TurboTax is especially good at making sure you've deducted appropriate start-up business costs and stock that's essentially of no value, if you own any. Special attention is paid to setting up retirement plans that have a strong tax advantage. If you've not yet investigated Simplified Employee Pensions or Keogh Accounts, TurboTax brings them to your attention while running Deduction Finder.

FIGURE 17.16.

Deduction Finder thoroughly examines your return for any opportunity that might be missed.

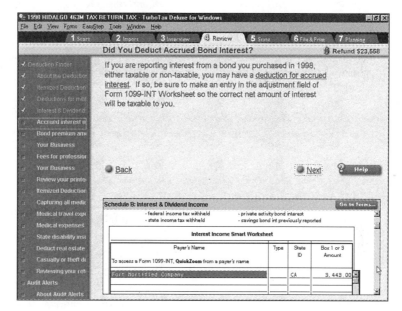

17

Locating the Right Form for the Deduction

As you can see in Figure 17.15, when Deduction Finder suggests a deduction, you can click a Go To Forms button to open the related form. At times, however, you have to open the form yourself and read the associated Help files. (Just click the Help icon at the upper right.) Don't forget that if you do have to locate the form on your own, just scroll up through the Interview history, at the lower-half of the screen. This shows a list of all the entries you've made on forms. Click any reference to the form containing information about your potential deduction.

In TurboTax, a form's Help file contains detailed information about whom this form applies to and specific rules regarding each line. So any time you are not sure whether a particular law or rule applies to you, open the related form and click Help. Rules regarding deductions are discussed as well.

Besides TurboTax Help entries, you can click the Government Instructions tab that appears behind any TurboTax Help article. Government Instructions simply replicates the *"Tear off and retain for your records"* portion of an IRS form, as well as related documents.

The Deduction Finder is quite thorough and can take longer to complete than most of the other review steps.

As TurboTax wraps up hunting down deductions, clicking Next opens Audit Alert. Audit Alert reviews your return for potential "red flags" that might cause you unwanted attention from the IRS.

Audit Alert

As explained on Audit Alert's opening screen (see Figure 17.17), TurboTax scours your tax return for the types of inconsistencies and liberties that have caused taxpayers to be audited in the past. TurboTax might point out a potential problem on your form, and you very well may not get audited. What TurboTax brings to the table, though, is its knowledge of what is likely to bring you under the scrutiny of the IRS. TurboTax thoroughly examines this likelihood, showing you the statistical national "breakdown" of who gets singled out. Audit Alert is here to tell you how to avoid that hot seat.

You could also follow TurboTax's advice here and end up getting audited anyway. However, because so few tax returns get audited, if you do little to draw negative attention to yourself, it's most likely that you will be left alone.

How Audit Alert Works

Like Error Check, Audit Alert searches your tax form for inconsistencies, such as sums on different forms that should be identical, but are not. However, Audit Alert analyzes your return with an eye for more detail. For example, Audit Alert looks for gaps in income reporting that might raise an eyebrow or two, or situations in which taxes were withheld as part of a penalty (see Figure 17.18).

FIGURE 17.17.

Audit Alert points out tax form irregularities that could create problems with the IRS.

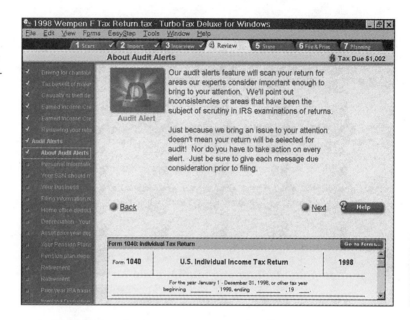

FIGURE 17.18.

If taxes are levied that appear to be a penalty for past underpayment, the IRS is encouraged to examine this further.

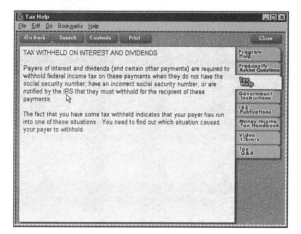

17

Audit Alert points out sums you report that the IRS is likely to have access to from other sources. If an agency or individual you work with is going to be reporting income that's been paid to you (including interest or dividends), make sure your numbers are the same as theirs. Also, make sure you report all income sources, no matter how small.

Other occurrences that Audit Alert (and the IRS) are likely to flag are as follows:

- Claiming many more itemized deductions than other people in your income bracket
- Sudden increases in income
- Businesses that never produce a profit
- Home office deductions that seem too large compared to the *potential* income generated by your business
- Prior year depreciation of assets that are not in keeping with what you depreciate this year
- Assets assigned to both business and personal use

 Please note that when Audit Alert flags a situation as inviting scrutiny, that's not to say you should abandon the deduction altogether or change your entire strategy. You should, however, make sure you have more than enough documentation to support your claim.

When Audit Alert Makes a Suggestion

As with Error Checking, Audit Alert attempts to present the means to correct an error right on the EasyStep Interview screen. Most often, you do not need to hunt down a form. If, at times, you do have to change location and leave the Interview format, remember the tools you have at your disposal. They are as follows:

- Click Take Me To at the lower-left and scroll through the list of entries and double-click the form as it appears in that list.
- Select My Tax Data from the Tools menu, scroll through the list, and double-click the desired form name to open the document in question.

Wrapping Up Audit Alert

Audit Alert finishes by providing a host of resources outlining your chances of getting audited (see Figure 17.19). If you enjoy comparing statistics and averages, Audit Alert's last few screens give you a good deal to contemplate. Although Audit Alert makes no promises, if you follow its advice, you stand a better chance of keeping out of harm's way.

FIGURE 17.19.

The final Audit Alert page provides links to articles arming you with information for avoiding an audit.

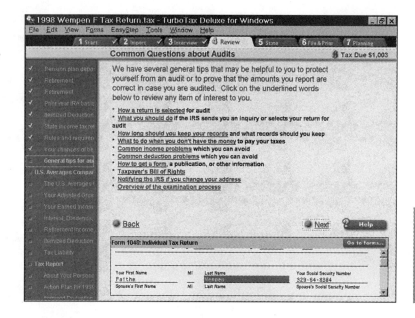

Next up, the TurboTax Review compares your tax return to other American households in your income bracket. Click Next after reading the final Audit Alert screen, and the U.S. Averages Comparison begins. We explore that feature now.

The U.S. Averages Comparison

This feature compares your form to those from the rest of American taxpayers in your income bracket. This is how the U.S. Averages Comparison works.

After viewing the opening screen (shown in Figure 17.20), the program presents statistics about other U.S. taxpayers in paragraph form. This feature will include discussion about how your income or tax return compares to the others.

Figure 17.21 shows an Adjusted Gross Income Report, followed by a national average comparison. Figure 17.22 shows how this same individual's *tax liability* compares to average tax liability in that income bracket.

As you click Next and read the comparisons, TurboTax breaks down each of the highlights of your tax return and reveals comparisons to the rest. Your goal as a taxpayer is to find yourself squarely in the middle of these numbers. Use this standard to determine whether you've paid too much in taxes, compared to others who earn as much as you, or even paid too little, which would increase the likelihood of an audit.

FIGURE 17.20.

*U.S. Averages
Comparison presents
taxpayer statistics for
others in your income
bracket.*

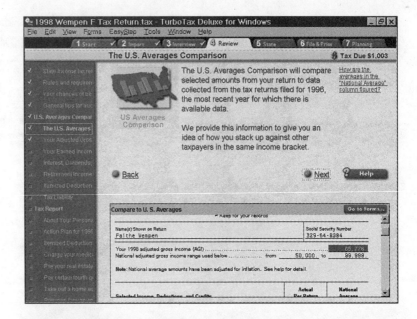

FIGURE 17.21.

*Your own adjusted
gross income is pre-
sented along with a
comparison to the
national average.*

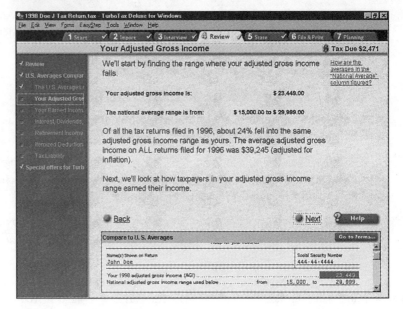

FIGURE 17.22.

An individual's tax liability is compared to the national average.

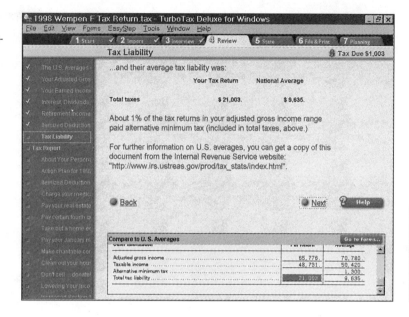

This information helps determine the following:

- If your taxes are above the national average rate, you need to check out better tax shelters for the following year.
- If you've paid too little, it is likely that "someone is watching," so make sure you save every little receipt or document that helps justify this fortunate niche you've found yourself in.

The Personalized Tax Report

The U.S. Averages Comparison breezily segues into the review's final feature: The Personalized Tax Report. Just click Next, and the opening screen shown in Figure 17.23 appears, after the Comparison makes its final comment.

Having had a good glance at your current tax return, TurboTax's Personal Tax Report provides acres of useful information on how to decrease your tax liability next year. Oh, and don't wait until the end of the year to review this information. There are plenty of steps you can take right now.

FIGURE 17.23.

The Personalized Tax Report compiles tips and suggestions for preparing next year's return.

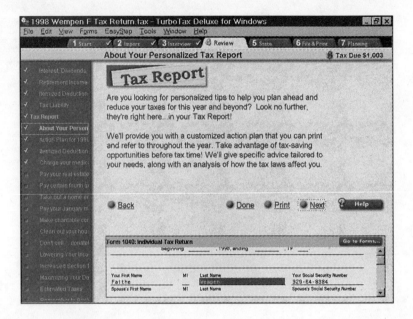

How the Tax Report Works

The Tax Report looks at current taxation trends, including bills that Congress just passed, and sees how you can stay ahead of the game. The Report pays special attention to instances in which the conventional wisdom of the day may no longer apply. The following are two examples:

- If certain tax income breaks are due to be effective next year, TurboTax might advise you to not take all the deductions you can, allowing your adjusted gross income to be a bit higher than you normally would.

- By the same token, if TurboTax sees you are headed for a particularly punitive income bracket (some tax deductions won't be available to you if your income is too high), you are advised to avoid crossing that income threshold at all costs.

TurboTax is excellent about keeping abreast of what Congress has in store for us and what sort of special tips and tricks apply specifically to the coming year, and to you, as a specific taxpayer.

Applying Tax Report to Your Situation

The Tax Report begins by advising you to "run the numbers" for next year using the "What-if Worksheet," available from the Forms menu. This way, you can plan ahead, and make any adjustments in your income, withholdings, Pension Plan withholding, and so forth. Then you won't be caught off guard in the following tax season. Some of the strategies are quite clever, such as paying medical expenses with a credit card (see Figure 17.24).

FIGURE 17.24.

After reviewing your tax return, the Tax Report offers concrete suggestions to reduce your tax bill next year.

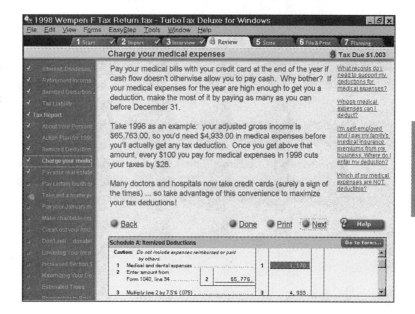

It's important to make sure you are using the newest version of TurboTax with the most current updates. That's because so much of TurboTax information is timely (some deduction and income brackets change from year-to-year). You could lose out if you are not reading from the latest information sources.

The bottom line: Before making big financial decisions, such as buying or selling stock or real estate, taking out tuition loans, or starting a home business, read through the Tax Report.

Summary

TurboTax Review features give you the assurance that your tax form has been reviewed under the eye of experts. TurboTax not only looks over your tax return for errors, but locates deductions you may not have thought of, and points out "red flags" in your return that increase the likelihood of being audited.

Q&A

Q After the TurboTax Review points out a mistake, is it a lot of trouble to fix?

A No. The review is part of the TurboTax Interview, so you are still working in the same familiar format in which TurboTax presents you with data you need, without having to go searching for a form.

Q Okay, so TurboTax lets me keep my overrides, but I'm always reminded that I should try to fix them. If I need to alter numbers that TurboTax does not agree with, what alternative do I have?

A Most overrides occur not as a result from typing numbers that TurboTax disagrees with, but from trying to place them on the wrong form. See if the form you are trying to "force" these numbers into is actually filled with numbers from a different form. Open that form, and type your numbers there, instead.

Q Can I really skip the review all together, if I'm quite confident in the accuracy of my tax return?

A You can skip most segments, if you must, except certain errors must be corrected. At a minimum, TurboTax requires you walk through the Error Check Review feature.

Q Why should I be concerned about next year's taxes now?

A TurboTax makes it easy to project changes in your earnings, and thus, changes in your tax liability. TurboTax strives to keep abreast of time-limited or income-limited deductions. To make sure you take full advantage of all the tax relief that's available to you, TurboTax helps you plan ahead with full knowledge of these time-limited factors.

HOUR **18**

Filing a Printed Return

In this hour, we talk about the process of filing a printed return and walk through the options TurboTax presents you, after you decide to file on paper. For starters, you learn the reasons why you might want to file a printed return, rather than electronic, and the different filing strategies and choices TurboTax and the IRS make available to you. When it's time to actually print the forms, we take a brief look at Printer Setup and troubleshooting issues and let you know where to go for help with TurboTax and your specific model of printer, if needed.

Highlights of this hour include

- Deciding how to file
- Filing with the 1040PC
- Filing a printed return
- Printing the forms
- Assembling and mailing your return

Deciding How to File

The TurboTax EasyStep Interview walks you through filing your return and actually asks you very early in the interview if you intend to file electronically. However, you can change your mind at any time. Even if you've already had TurboTax prepare your return as if you were filing online, you can still file a paper return if you choose to.

Reasons for filing a paper return would include the following:

- No available modem.
- No available credit card.
- An objection to having financial data transmitted via modem.
- An objection to the $9.95 fee TurboTax requires for electronic filing.
- You've always filed a paper return before, without any problems. Therefore, if it works, don't fix it.

Filing with the 1040PC

If you opt to file a paper return, don't think that you are stuck on the slowest track and get your refund long after everyone else. TurboTax uses the Internal Revenue Service's 1040PC Form, a special provision made for filers who use tax-preparation software—that would be you. This form condenses your return to about two pages and is greatly favored by the IRS over the conventional paper form. You often get your refund (if you are due one) in about three weeks after filing. If the refund has not yet arrived, you are invited to call the IRS to expedite it. Also, the IRS has an easier time depositing your refund directly into your bank account if you use the 1040PC Form.

Filing for an Extension

When you file, you may consider whether or not to file an extension. Extending the time to file a return is covered in Hour 20, "Special Filing Issues," but there are some related points worth looking at now.

To begin with, don't file for an extension because you lack the money to pay all your tax debt. Let's clarify what filing for an extension is: You're asking to delay submitting your tax return, not asking to delay payment.

You should file for an extension if you are awaiting a document required to file an accurate return, not because you don't have enough money to pay your tax bill.

Sometimes hardship and lack of necessary filing documents go hand-in-hand. For example, if your house burned down, you probably need to file an extension because you lost important tax-related documents in the fire. Or, if you live in a disaster area, you may file for an extension because FEMA hasn't quite sorted out how much value your home has lost as a result of the disaster.

A Word on Automatic Extensions

If you live outside the United States, or are in the armed forces and your post of duty is outside the U.S. or Puerto Rico, you receive an automatic June 15 extension for filing your return and paying taxes. In fact, if you walked through the TurboTax Interview and indicated your home or main place of business is outside the U.S., you were already told this. However, this is one of the very few instances in which the IRS doesn't expect to hear from you by April 15.

What If I'm a Bit Short of Cash?

If you don't have enough money to pay your entire tax bill, it's more imperative than ever to file on time (in fact, early is even better). Send whatever money you can, and ask the IRS to work out a payment plan. You are charged interest and fees for such service, but it will be better for you if you file on time, or early.

The point is that the IRS sometimes regards filing your tax return and paying your tax bill as two different processes. If things are not looking good for you and your current tax bill, the worst thing you can do is avoid filing. If you owe lots of money in taxes, 'fess up as soon as possible. The IRS appreciates that and generally works with you to find a way for you to pay it.

As an example, all my Vietnam War-era tax resister friends that filed tax returns and refused to pay taxes certainly got into trouble. But the ones who flat-out did not file a return went to jail for tax evasion, a far more serious offense.

Filing a Printed Return

After reviewing your return and filling out state tax forms, TurboTax proceeds immediately to the filing process. If you just want to follow along now and are not ready to file your tax return, jump right in by clicking the Filing tab (Tab 6) at the upper right of the screen. If you are "just practicing," all the steps are not available to you. But you can at least get a feel for what's in store by clicking through the steps that are available.

18

If you are doing a practice run for now, when TurboTax asks whether you want to save your file, click No.

Whether you click the Filing tab or have completed your return and are now ready to file, the first screen you see is shown in Figure 18.1.

FIGURE 18.1.

When you're ready to file, TurboTax lets you again choose which method to use.

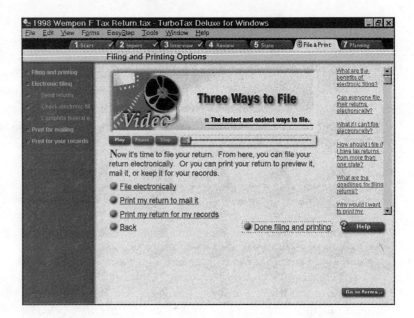

The following are the filing method options. You see four buttons in the main part of the screen:

- To file electronically, click the button labeled File Electronically. This is covered in Hour 19, "Filing an Electronic Return.".
- To print your return for mailing, click Print My Return to mail it. Only the forms you must mail will print.
- To get a copy for your files, click Print My Return For My Records. All forms and worksheets you have used will print.
- If you are finished filing and printing, click Done Filing and Printing.

The 1040PC: Why or Why Not?

If you are going to file a printed return, it's best to try to use the 1040PC Form. This form prints only the lines of your tax forms that have amounts identified by a code. When viewing a 1040PC Form, you are looking at a cryptic list of sums identified by codes. This list moves from column to column and spreads out across approximately two pages.

You can receive refunds sooner, paper use is reduced, the IRS likes the streamlined format, and you can get your refund direct deposited.

The following are some reasons for not using the 1040PC Form:

- The 1040PC does not look like a tax return. If you were hoping to be able to take a glance at the numbers one more time before mailing it in, the 1040PC does not look like anything you've seen before, if you've ever worked with one.
- You cannot file electronically with a 1040PC Form.
- The 1040PC cannot accommodate many complex tax situations. For example, most instances of filing a Schedule C Form would rule out filing with a 1040PC Form.

Nonetheless, filing a 1040PC Form represents a nice middle ground between the drudgery of mailing a paper return and near-instantaneous electronic filing. In fact, TurboTax does try to steer you in that direction, if at all possible.

Determining If You Are 1040PC Eligible

That said, if you've decided to file a paper return, click Print My Return to Mail it and then mark the 1040PC Format check box and click Print (see Figure 18.2). See what happens. If it turns out you're eligible for filing with a 1040PC Form, life is more convenient if you do so. If you're not eligible, a message to that effect appears. After you've determined whether to print a 1040PC Form, click Print.

You may be told there are kinks to work out before filing with 1040PC (see Figure 18.3).

TurboTax applies more stringent error checking and simplifies some results before allowing you to print out the form. You have two choices:

- If you want to allow TurboTax to whittle away at your tax form and get it into shape for 1040PC filing, Cancel the print job for now, and click the Back button, allowing further inspection.
- If you'd just as soon take your lumps with the longer, conventional tax form, return to the Print for Mailing screen (refer to Figure 18.2) and deselect the 1040PC Format check box.

18

FIGURE 18.2.

After you decide to file with the 1040PC Form, TurboTax offers to print information about the form and how it works.

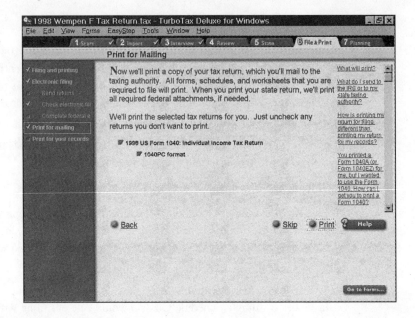

Streamlining Your Tax Return for 1040PC

Selecting Review My Return allows TurboTax Error Checking to once again have free roam. TurboTax now attempts to streamline your results, making your tax return eligible for 1040PC filing. You may find that, after Error Check completes, you click Next, thinking you're now ready to print.

Instead, Error Check may want one more "go" at it, finding even more changes that need to be made. In fact, you may have to let TurboTax run through Error Check an additional three or four more times (very few changes are made with each pass), before you are finally allowed to print the form.

Each time Error Check completes a pass through your form, you are prompted to either allow TurboTax to make more changes or give up on 1040PC all together and just print out the conventional form.

If you've chosen to print out the conventional form, you are allowed to print without much ado. If errors still exist in your return, you receive a warning, but if you click past it and print your form anyway, you are not warned again.

After Your Return Is Printed

Next, you learn what needs to be done after your form is printed.

To Do: Getting Your Forms Ready to Mail

1. Make sure your tax return and schedules are signed and dated. Staple Copy B of your W-2, W-2G, and any other required forms to the front of your tax form, where indicated.

2. As you see later in this hour, you can print out supportive statements and Smart Worksheets for your own records, but you need not include them with your return unless explicitly directed to do so.

3. Don't forget to include the payment, if any, and make out the check to the Internal Revenue Service, not IRS.

4. When TurboTax prints out a tax return, the first page is for your own information. It summarizes what you owe and have paid and provides the address where you are to mail your return. You should, however, use the preprinted envelope and label that the IRS sent you.

Other issues regarding filing, printing, assembling, and direct deposit of a refund are covered later in this hour.

A Quick Direct Deposit Review

Before we get into the nuts and bolts of printing and mailing your return, let's look at how to make sure your directly deposited refund goes smoothly, if you have one coming.

Near the beginning of the EasyStep Interview, TurboTax asks you whether you want to use the 1040PC Form for filing. This choice facilitates easy direct depositing. Please note that you do not need to file electronically to obtain a direct deposit refund.

Although TurboTax walks you through setting up direct deposit as part of the interview, you can open the form yourself and make sure all the needed information is provided. The Direct Deposit segment of Form 8453 only pertains to electronic filing, so that won't help you here.

To Do: Setting Up Direct Deposit Using a Printed Return

1. Open your tax return form by clicking Forms and then choosing Show My Return.

2. Double-click Form 1040: Individual Tax Return, and scroll down to the Refund section (lines 65-67).

3. Go to the Refund section, and enter the nine-digit Routing Number (RTN) for your bank or credit union. Check with your institution for this information. This number appears at the bottom left of most checks. Include any hyphens, but do not include spaces or special characters.

▼ 4. Check either Checking or Savings, depending on which account you want the funds deposited into.

5. Make sure you enter your account number where indicated (the Depositor Account Number, or DAN, as its called). This number also appears at the bottom of your check. Again, include hyphens, but not spaces or special characters.

6. If filing with a conventional printed return, attach proof of this account with your return. If you are filing a 1040PC Form, you need not do so.

▲ 7. Close the form and continue to go about filing your return.

If the IRS finds problems with your account or account numbers, or determines you are not eligible for direct deposit refunds, you receive the refund in the mail, which may result in a delay of two weeks.

Getting It All on Paper

In this section, we discuss printing a test page, setting up your printer, and determining which files and forms you are required to print for your return.

Printing a Test Page

Before printing any forms, you may want to print out a "test" copy just to make sure all is well between TurboTax and your printer. Just click File and then choose Print Test Page.

Printing a test reveals any printer setup issues that need to be taken care of before you print the actual forms. Look for text quality and alignment. The data must be easily legible.

When you print a test page, TurboTax prints valuable information about your printer: the printer driver and version, the port being used, and print margin information. If you ever have to call Intuit's technical support line to obtain help with your printer, having this page of information handy makes it easier for the technician who takes your call to help you.

Setting Up Your Printer for TurboTax

To begin with, TurboTax tax forms can be printed out on standard computer printer paper. TurboTax recommends paper that is cream-colored, $8^1/_2$ by 11 inches, and at least 18 pounds in weight (standard printer paper is 20 to 24 pounds). Adjust your printer to produce good quality printed text, and make sure your alignment is accurate. (Most printers have a print head alignment program that is worth running before printing your forms.)

Getting Better Print Results

TurboTax has a handful of recommended settings for certain types of printers. If you have problems printing out your forms, see if TurboTax's help files have something to say about your model of printer.

To Do: Locate Printer Help

1. Click the Help menu and choose Tax Help.

2. When the Help dialog box appears, click Search. Type `Printing` and click the Display button. The Topics Found box appears.

3. Scroll down and double-click Checking Printer Settings. You'll see an article: "Checking Your Printer Settings in TurboTax." This article outlines tips for various printers on how to maximize your tax return's printed quality.

4. These entries can be of some help even if your exact printer is not found in the list. Just locate tips for a printer similar to yours, and see if the advice offered seems applicable to your printer.

Also, for more specific troubleshooting tips for various popular printers, open TurboTax Help as indicated in the preceding steps, click the Search button, type `Printing`, and then select Troubleshooting Printing Problems. You see a list of tips for many typical printing problems.

Let TurboTax Do the Collating

Because printing your tax forms and related documents may run into several pages, let TurboTax do the collating for you. When you are actually ready to print your forms (click Print from the File menu), TurboTax lets you choose a *page printing direction* to facilitate your printer's option. If paper comes out of your printer face down, select Front to Back in the Print Order drop-down menu of the Print dialog box. If your printed pages come out face up, select Back to Front. (We explore the Print dialog box momentarily.)

Printing the Forms

Now that your printer is set up, you can get ready to actually print some forms, specifying which forms you want to print, and how much supportive information should be printed out as well. You may have already printed using the steps earlier in this chapter; if so, you can skip this.

18

Choosing What to Print

After you've allowed TurboTax to review your return and determine your eligibility for filing with the 1040PC Form, set up your printer, set up your printer paper, and printed a test page, click Print from the File menu. You see the Printing dialog box shown in Figure 18.3.

FIGURE 18.3.

The Printing dialog box lets you choose which forms to print and how much supportive detail you should include at this time.

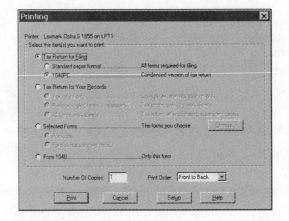

You are choosing the items you want to print, the number of copies, and the order in which the pages should be printed.

- To print the return you actually send to the IRS or a copy to your State Tax Board, click the Tax Return for Filing option, and choose either Standard Paper Format or 1040PC. Clicking the 1040PC option prints out the fewest number of forms possible, for a streamlined return.

- To print and file away a tax form of your own, click Tax Return for Your Records. You see options to print the recommended forms and worksheets as well. Because the purpose of this copy is to be able to retrace your steps later, if this return is ever called into account, it's advisable to go ahead and print out all files associated with the return.

- To take more control over what forms get printed and mailed out, click the Selected Forms option. Then click Choose to choose the forms (see Figure 18.4). Scroll through the list and pick a form to print, or, to print more than one, hold down the Ctrl key while clicking as many forms in the list as you like. There's also an option to print the form currently visible on your screen.

FIGURE 18.4.

Choose which form to print by clicking one, or select several by holding down the Ctrl button while you select.

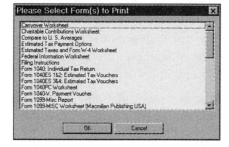

Overriding the Default Form TurboTax Chooses

TurboTax may determine that you can be accommodated very well by having your return printed on a 1040EZ or 1040A. However, perhaps you want to provide more detail or take deductions that are not allowed if the 1040EZ or 1040A is used.

To Do: Forcing TurboTax to Print a 1040 Return

1. Open the Federal Information Worksheet by selecting Open a Form from the Forms menu and double-clicking the Federal Information Worksheet.

2. Scroll down to the lower half of page 2 of the worksheet.

3. Click the box labeled Calculate Form 1040 Regardless.

Choosing the Number of Copies and Collating Settings

To print more than one copy of each form, type a number in the Number of Copies field. And, as mentioned earlier, save yourself the chore of having to collate the forms after you've printed them by selecting an option in the Print Order drop-down menu: If printed paper from your printer emerges face down, choose Front to Back. If it comes out face up, choose Back to Front.

Printing Extra Copies of Your Return

You can return to the Printing dialog box at any time to print more copies.

TurboTax prints one copy for your records as part of the EasyStep Interview, just by you clicking Next and walking through the steps. For your copy, TurboTax prints out all related forms, Supportive Detail documents and Smart Worksheets. Remember that you need not send all these forms to the IRS, but do keep them for your own records.

TurboTax also offers to print a form for your State Tax Board. Most states require a copy of your Federal Tax Form, as part of your state tax filing procedure. The state would only require the form itself, not supportive documents.

18

Assembling and Mailing Your Return

The 1040 indicates where and how W-2s and other required paperwork should be attached. Attention to this type of detail helps facilitate smooth handling of your return. The following are some points to remember:

- If you are required to submit other specifically requested paperwork, the IRS that prompted this extra submission also indicates where to attach it.
- If you submit the 1040PC Form, you find that very little, if any, extra paperwork needs to be included.
- Please don't go out of your way to include extra documents that are not asked for. If you've completed your tax return using the EasyStep Interview, TurboTax automatically prints any schedules and forms you need to send along. You don't need to over-explain this story! If the IRS determines they want more documentation from you about something, they do not hesitate to ask.
- If you owe a payment, attach your check where indicated, and make it out to the Internal Revenue Service, not IRS.

Just as a reminder, you received a special labeled envelope from the IRS indicating where your form should be sent. If you cannot find that envelope, the first page of your printed TurboTax form or Appendix B of this book includes the IRS address for your state.

Quarterly Payments and Payment Vouchers

If your tax payment is very large (meaning you vastly underwithheld last year), TurboTax may have computed quarterly installments or voucher payments that you need to begin paying. This prevents your next tax bill from growing so precipitously. While printing your tax return, TurboTax also prints forms to attach to each quarterly payment. The forms indicate when each payment is due.

Set these aside and make a note of when the first payment needs to be mailed. Keeping up with these quarterly payments helps minimize the risk of further scrutiny from the IRS about past underwithholding.

Getting a Running Start for Next Year

If you print your final tax forms while walking through the EasyStep Interview, click Next after printing, and TurboTax offers to display the Tax Planner and IRA Planner (see Figure 18.5). These forms help reduce tax liability for the coming year and help you plan your investing strategies.

FIGURE 18.5.

Yes, you're almost fin-ished but there's always next year to prepare for. Make sure to review TurboTax's Tax Plan for your fol-lowing year.

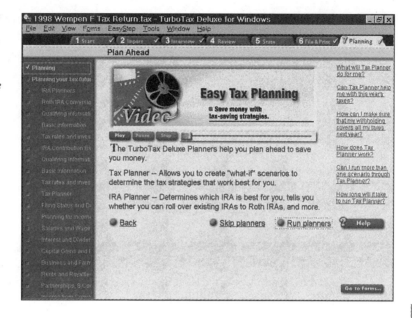

Summary

In this hour, you learned how to send the IRS all the wonderful information you've gath-ered. No longer do you have an excuse to stand in line at the post office at 11:55 p.m. on April 15. TurboTax allows you to neatly print and collate all your tax information in one easy step.

If you have objections to killing trees for the sake of the government, or if you want your refund back even faster, then TurboTax enables you to use an even faster option for filing your taxes: filing electronically. It may sound scary, but TurboTax makes it very simple and pain-free, as you'll see in the next hour.

Q&A

Q If I don't file electronically, I won't be able to have my refund direct deposit-ed, right?

A Wrong. The IRS can direct deposit your refund if you indicate such on your print-ed tax form. Make sure your routing number and account number are correct. Using the 1040PC Form especially facilities rapid deposit of your refund.

Q **If I don't file electronically, my tax return generally proceeds at a snail's pace, while all the electronic returns are processed first, right?**

A Wrong. The IRS has facilitated rapid processing of your written return by setting up Form 1040PC. Recognizing the advantages of using this variation on the 1040, TurboTax tries to steer you in that direction, if you are eligible.

Q **I don't have enough money right now to pay my tax bill. Should I file for an extension?**

A No. Not having enough money on hand to pay your tax bill is not a reason to file an extension. File your return well ahead of time, include what payment you can, and request a payment plan. Do not delay filing in such a case.

Q **Why did TurboTax print so much more paperwork for my personal copy of my tax return?**

A TurboTax encourages you to keep hard copies of all worksheets and supportive details for your tax return. However, when it prints a form to send to the IRS, TurboTax prints only the required forms specifically requested by the IRS.

HOUR 19

Filing an Electronic Return

In this hour you learn how to file your return electronically. We explore how the process works and learn its advantages and requirements. Some issues covered in the previous chapter are worth taking a look at because they won't be repeated here. If you skipped the previous chapter because you knew you'd be filing electronically, take the time to read the sections "Filing for an Extension," and "What If I'm a Bit Short?"

Highlights of this hour include

- How TurboTax deals with depreciation
- What information TurboTax needs from you
- The tax forms used with depreciation
- Special electronic filing deadlines
- Who cannot file electronically
- How to file electronically
- The electronic submission process
- Walking through electronic filing's own Error Check
- Submitting your eligible return

A Glance at What's Ahead

The idea of filing electronically raises a few questions. When you send an electronic return, is no paperwork exchanged? Does that mean if you owe money, the IRS comes raiding your bank account after you authorize some sort of transfer?

To briefly cut to the chase, the following are several phases to filing an electronic tax return:

- After submitting your return online, wait for a day or two, then go online and check the status of your return.
- If the IRS has accepted your electronic return, you are assigned a Declaration Control Number (DSN) and are instructed to send in a form (Form 8453-OL) with W-2s and other pertinent documents attached.
- If you owe payment, you send in a check, along with a 1040V Form (a small voucher-like coupon).
- All this must occur within one business day of receiving news that your electronic tax return has been accepted.

This is said up front to dispel any notions that all your tax business can be banished with a couple mouse-clicks. As with everything else around tax-time, electronic filing involves paperwork, deadlines, and strict imperatives that must be followed to the letter.

Special Electronic Filing Deadlines

Speaking of deadlines, they're a little different when you file electronically. TurboTax wants you to file electronically by April 10. That allows time for the IRS to process your electronic return, get back to you with your DSN number, and give you a day or two to mail in your money and documents.

If you do file electronically, and the IRS rejects your tax return, you receive a few days grace period to send it in via mail. (Intuit takes care of this for you, if you file through TurboTax, but they want your corrected return by April 18 for things to go smoothly with the IRS).

If you file for an automatic extension, you can still use TurboTax to submit an electronic tax return as late as the final date for filing.

To read more about TurboTax's electronic filing deadlines, select Tax Help from the TurboTax Help menu. Click the Search button and type Electronic. Double-click Electronic Filing, and from the resulting list, double-click the topic Deadlines.

The Ups and Downs of Electronic Filing

Well, then, what good is electronic filing? If you are owed money, you get paid faster. The IRS likes it, and your return is less apt to get bogged down in delays. Not everybody gets to file electronically, though. Part of this chapter is spent pointing out the types of tax situations and errors that can disqualify you from electronic filing. Also, Intuit charges $9.95 to file electronically, and the only method of payment allowed is credit card.

Both Intuit and the Internal Revenue Service say that filing electronically does not increase the likelihood of an audit.

Who Cannot File Electronically

Just to save some people extra reading, let's identify some situations that out-and-out disqualify you from electronic filing. If you recognize yourself in one of these, you can, without further ado, retreat to the previous hour: "Filing a Printed Return."

While you're at it, check out a few typical entries on tax forms that are not compatible with electronic filing. These entries can be easy to change. In fact, TurboTax does so, as part of its prefiling review, as you prepare to send your form across the wire. Please note that the list below is not exhaustive. If you attempt to file electronically and TurboTax finds something amiss, you are given an opportunity to read the entire list of electronic filing disqualifications (see Figure 19.1).

FIGURE 19.1.

You might not care about all the situations that can disqualify you from filing electronically, until TurboTax says that one of them applies to your form.

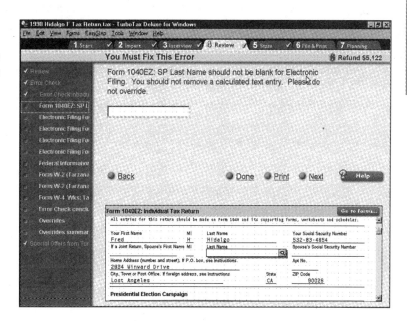

19

The following are some situations that disqualify you from filing electronically:

- Descendent or survivor returns, such as joint returns filed by the surviving spouse.
- Amended or corrected returns.
- Most situations in which a return is filed on behalf of another person.
- Taxpayers with a foreign address. Please note that Armed Forces Post Offices are not considered foreign addresses.
- Some types of Married Filing Separately returns are not eligible.
- "Special Consideration" returns, such as those involving waivers or changes of accounting methods for a business.
- Returns that include Medical Spending Account Forms (1099-MSA).

Situations that TurboTax is "on the lookout for," and must be changed if you file electronically, include the following types of tax returns:

- Returns with sums broken down to cents (for example, $25.15, rather than $25). The IRS encourages you to round out sums to dollar amounts regardless.
- Only one Schedule A, B, or D is allowed per electronic return. Likewise, a maximum of five Schedule C Forms and two Schedule F Forms may be included.
- You are limited to 20 W-2s, and tax returns that include more than 30 statements cannot be submitted electronically.
- Regarding Schedule B and D, the number 97 seems to be a common cut-off. To file electronically, your Schedule B can have no more than 97 interest or dividend payers, and your Schedule D can have no more than 97 long- or short-term transactions.

The above lists are only a small sampling of situations that can disqualify you from electronic filing. However, after you've indicated that you are planning to file electronically, TurboTax takes great pains to steer you clear of such problems.

How to File Electronically

Leaving nothing to chance, TurboTax asks you during the EasyStep Interview whether you plan to file electronically (see Figure 19.2). Also, during the interview, TurboTax asks you if you'd like to pay or be refunded by the IRS electronically, or via a check in the mail (see Figure 19.3). Direct deposit moves very quickly if you choose to file electronically.

FIGURE 19.2.

Very early in the EasyStep Interview, TurboTax asks you whether you plan to file electronically.

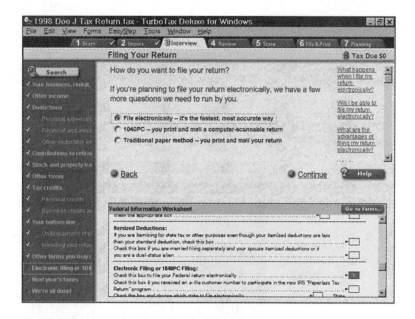

FIGURE 19.3.

TurboTax also asks you whether you plan to pay the IRS electronically, or by mailing a check.

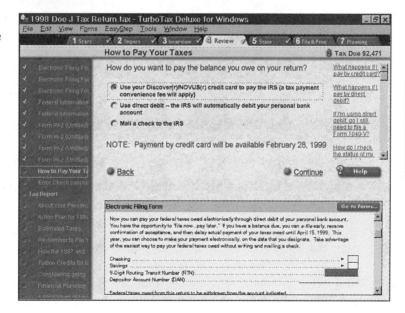

19

After letting TurboTax know you intend to file electronically, you may not hear another thing about it until you enter the filing phase of the EasyStep Interview. You can preview this area by clicking Tab 6 (File & Print) at the upper right of the TurboTax screen. Late in the game, after the end is in sight, you are again prompted to indicate your intention to file electronically.

During the EasyStep Interview, you see the screen in Figure 19.4, outlining the steps discussed briefly at the beginning of this chapter.

FIGURE 19.4.

When you reach the filing stage of the Interview, and you indicated a preference for electronic filing, you see this screen, explaining the steps.

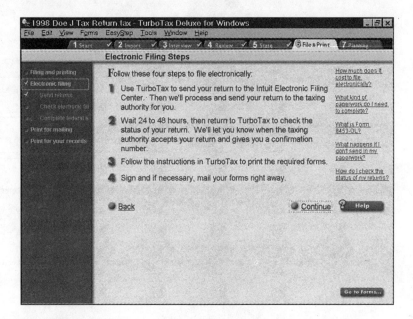

Understanding the Electronic Filing Process

As we move through this chapter, you learn all the steps involved in filing an electronic tax return. While you are looking at the four steps outlined in TurboTax's introductory screen, there are some things you should keep in mind:

- When you submit your tax file online, it is not sent across the World Wide Web. Rather, you are using a private, secure Internet connection.

- When you file your electronic return with TurboTax, it is not sent to the IRS. Rather, it goes directly to the Intuit Electronic Filing Center, and the return is automatically processed and forwarded to the tax agency.

- When you file an electronic return with TurboTax, you are granting Intuit certain rights. They act as a go-between, sending your return to the IRS, then funneling back to you news of its acceptance, or rejection, by the powers that be. Intuit is empowered to work with you to correct the reasons for rejection and aid you in resubmitting a return, printed this time.

- Upon hearing that your electronic tax return has been accepted by the IRS, you mail two forms (both prepared and explained by TurboTax in due course). On one form, the 8453-OL, you're required to attach W-2 Forms and other necessary documents. On the other form, the 1040V, fill it out and attach your payment, if any is required.

- Although TurboTax fills out and prints these forms for you, providing directions about how they are to be mailed, you mail them to the IRS, not to the Intuit Electronic Filing Center.

Data Entry Tips

Before we jump into the nuts and bolts of sending your return electronically, the following are some data entry tips that help ensure that TurboTax can submit your return with a minimum risk of rejection by the IRS. TurboTax urges the following:

- Use the Override feature very sparingly. Intuit says "many problems" with electronic filings are the result of indiscriminate use of overrides.

- Many TurboTax forms do not require you to enter data directly into them, because the program fills those forms with computations derived from other forms. If you do enter data yourself onto these lines, you increase the risk of entering faulty data. If you plan to file electronically, don't stray too far from the Interview unless you are sure of what you are doing.

- When you enter lists of numbers (such as amounts that are added into a sum at the bottom of a page), do not skip lines. Try not to leave blank lines between numbers that are going to be added together.

- Do not enter zeros in lines that do not have amounts.

- Amounts with cents (such as $18.93) should be rounded to the nearest dollar.

Now let's proceed to getting your tax file submitted online.

Determining Electronic Filing Eligibility

After reading those introductory four points on the Electronic Filing Steps screen, click Next, and you probably see the Consent to Disclosure screen. Read this and the

19

following screen to empower Intuit and its employees to acknowledge the receipt and acceptance of your tax form by the IRS and report to you the reason for its rejection, if it is rejected. Clicking past these screens indicates your consent to those terms.

After clicking Next, if TurboTax sees nothing amiss with your return, you are prompted to print a copy of it first, just to review before filing (see Figure 19.5). If you'd like one final look at the document before sending it, click Print. If not, click Next.

FIGURE 19.5.

It's a good idea to print a copy of your return before filing it online.

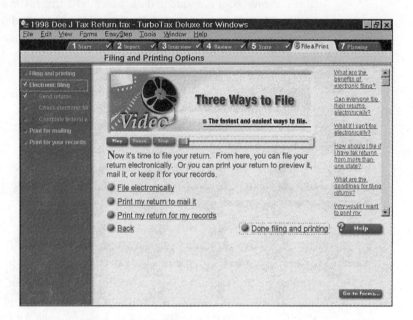

 It's a very good idea to print a copy of your tax return, and all supportive documents, for your own records. After finally reviewing your tax form, select Print from the File menu and explore the options, or review the Printing segment of Hour 18.

The Electronic Submission Process

Because TurboTax has found nothing objectionable in your forms, TurboTax prompts you to save your form before sending. This means you are finally ready to electronically submit your tax return (see Figure 19.6). Before you click Next again, make sure your Internet connection is open. Log on to your Dial-Up ISP, AOL, or whatever method you use to access the Internet. When you are ready to send your return online, click Next.

FIGURE 19.6.

TurboTax prompts you to save your form, indicating you have made the grade and are ready to submit your electronic tax return.

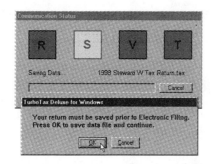

After clicking Next, a Communication Status appears (see Figure 19.7). This box stays on the screen for as long as it takes to submit your return. The online submission process could take up to 15 minutes.

FIGURE 19.7.

While your return is being sent across the wire, this confirmation box is onscreen, indicating the return is still being sent.

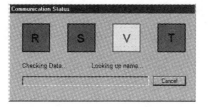

Checking Your Return's Status

While your form is being submitted, a blue bar indicates upload progress, as shown in Figure 19.8. Remember that your tax return is not being sent to the IRS, but rather, to the Intuit Electronic Filing Center. From here, it is sent to the IRS, and you are to check back for confirmation between 24 and 48 hours.

19

FIGURE 19.8.

A blue bar indicates TurboTax is uploading your form.

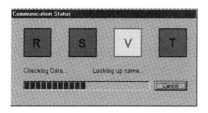

Notice the Check Status button in Figure 19.8. Return to this screen again, in the time indicated, and click this button to find out whether your return has been accepted by the IRS. If you have trouble locating this screen again and are trying to remember where the

Check Status button can be found, don't worry. Just select Electronic Filing from the File menu, and choose Check Electronic Filing Status from the menu that appears (see Figure 19.9).

FIGURE 19.9.

You don't need to hunt down the Check Status button to find out how it's going with your return. Just use the menu command, instead.

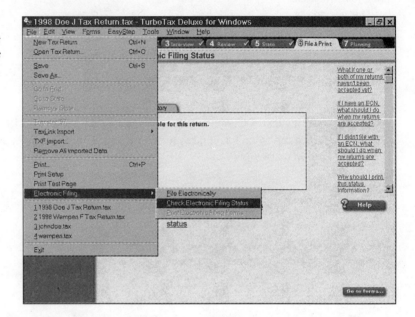

Walking Through Electronic Filing's Own Error Check

You've just learned what to expect when TurboTax is happy with your tax return. After reading the Disclosure Agreement, you are prompted to make a copy for yourself and transmit the tax return. You are told to check the status of your return in a day or two.

However, TurboTax does review your return one more time before filing. In this review, it keeps an eye out for problems related specifically to electronic filing. If you told TurboTax early in the EasyStep Interview that you want to file an electronic return, there are very few, if any, adjustments to make before uploading your return. However, if you just made this decision when filing popped up in the Interview, TurboTax may have a little work to do.

> TurboTax requires you submit your electronic tax return before April 10. This
> is to ensure that you have adequate time to mail in the necessary supportive
> documents before April 15.

Review or Retreat

After you read the Electronic Filing Disclosure Agreement, TurboTax scours your form
again for errors, and you may see an error or two to fix. You have a choice here to correct the errors or abandon the airwaves all together and go load up the printer with more
paper (click the File & Print tab and choose a different filing method). It may be that
only one or two adjustments need to be made (review Hour 17, "TurboTax Review
Features," for a reminder on how Error Checking works).

FIGURE 19.10.

*If TurboTax has found
a problem with your
electronic filing, an
error message
appears.*

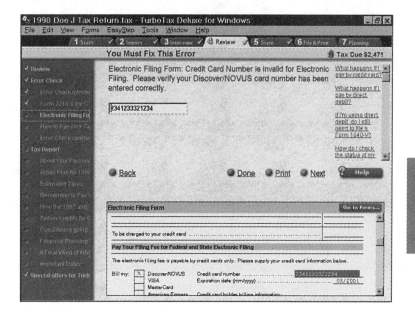

It is not uncommon, though, for Error Checking to require several passes before
TurboTax gives you a clean bill of health and lets you file electronically. TurboTax
announces its success by simply offering to print a copy of your return for yourself, as
shown earlier in Figure 19.5. You are then on the "good track" and see the screen for
transmitting your return electronically.

Not Taking No for an Answer

If TurboTax finds errors in your form that it deems unsolvable in the EasyStep Interview format, you see the Not Yet Eligible to File Federal Return screen (see Figure 19.11). All is not lost, though. Click the Review Federal Return option, as indicated, and edit the problem described in the previous screen, as shown in the figure. The TurboTax Interview never encourages you to begin making corrections to forms that require you to dig too deeply.

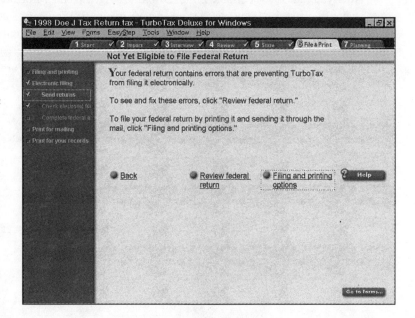

Again, as soon as you've removed the form entry that caused problems for you, TurboTax welcomes you into the family of electronic filers by offering to print a form for your copies first. It must be emphasized because one might assume that because you are seeing the word Print, you've been defeated, when in fact, the opposite is true.

Submitting Your Eligible Return

Now that your return has finally been deemed acceptable for electronic transfer, after printing your own copy, open your Internet connection. Click Next to upload your tax return. Transferring your form online may take up to 15 minutes, so be patient. After your return has been transferred, wait 24 to 48 hours, as mentioned above, and then check your return's status. (Select Electronic Filing from the File menu, and choose Check Electronic Filing Status. Your Internet connection must be open to do this.)

Getting IRS News About Your Return

TurboTax informs you online that your tax return has been received and reviewed. If it was accepted, you can move to the next step and mail the 8453-OL, with important documents attached. If you owe money, you must also mail a check as well as a 1040V Form.

If your electronic tax return was not accepted, TurboTax at this time, explains why. You cannot, however, resubmit an electronic tax return. It now has to be mailed in. If this happens to you, review Hour 18 of this book. The IRS gives you a few extra days beyond April 15 to submit a printed return, after an electronic one has been rejected. Because you are still creating all your documents with TurboTax, it's important to note that Intuit gives you until April 18 to submit a corrected, printed return.

Mailing Your 8453-OL and 1040V Forms

If, when you check your tax return status, TurboTax informs you that it was accepted by the IRS, you have only one business day to get it together. It's important to point out that this step of the filing process, mailing in the additional forms, must take place before April 15. Just like all the modem-less little people, you, too, can be caught in the mad rush of passing off envelopes to harried postal workers in the late hours of the preceding day.

> If you cannot get online to obtain your DCN number and verify your electronic return's acceptance, call 520-901-3271. If you can get to a computer with a modem, but cannot open TurboTax for some reason, complete tax return status is available at www.turbotax.com/efstatus.

19

After your return has been accepted, TurboTax walks you through the remaining steps. Your Declaration Control Number (DCN) appears on the screen. This information is recorded by TurboTax on the appropriate forms. Still, write it down, in case you need to pursue issues regarding your return by phone or by regular correspondence.

After noting this number, simply follow the onscreen steps TurboTax outlines for printing and mailing the following two forms.

Form 8453-OL needs to be signed and mailed within one day of receiving your DCN from TurboTax. Attach to it the following forms, and any others specifically requested of you by the IRS:

- Copy B of your W-2, and W-2G
- Any 1099R Forms

- Form 2120, 8283, and 8332
- Statements verifying permanent disability or blindness, if applicable

If you owe taxes, send your check, made out to the Internal Revenue Service and attach it as directed to Form 1040V, which TurboTax prints for you as you complete the EasyStep Interview. Write your Social Security number in the memo area of the check.

Getting a Running Start for Next Year

After you've mailed your paperwork, and clicked the final Next, TurboTax offers tax and IRA planning help, as shown in Figure 19.12. Use these planners to help get your finances in shape for next year. See chapters 22 and 23 for additional help.

FIGURE 19.12.

The Tax Planner offers to help prepare you for next year. To open the forms mentioned here, click Open a Form from the Forms menu.

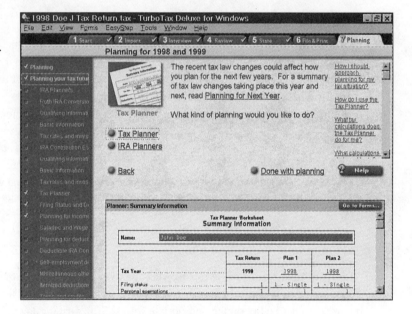

Summary

In this hour, you learned how to file your return electronically. You learned who is eligible to file electronically, how the process works, and about its advantages and requirements.

Hour 20, "Special Filing Issues," addresses filing extensions, making changes to a return that you already sent in, and filing issues that arise for divorced taxpayers.

Q&A

Q **Because I've decided to file electronically, does that mean I don't have to submit paperwork?**

A You still have to send in paper forms. After your electronic tax return is accepted, you have one business day to mail in the necessary items.

Q **Can anyone file his or her taxes electronically?**

A No. There are several situations that disallow you from electronic filing. In TurboTax, after you indicate your desire to do so, you are steered clear of making decisions that rule out filing electronically.

Q **I don't have a credit card, but I'd still like to file electronically through TurboTax. Is there another way to pay?**

A TurboTax requires that you pay your fee for electronic filing with a credit card.

Q **I'm going to file for an extension, and I'd still like to do so electronically. Will TurboTax still be accepting electronic tax forms later in the year?**

A Yes. TurboTax handles electronically submitted tax forms through October 15.

19

Hour **20**

Special Filing Issues

This hour covers issues beyond the four corners of the Form 1040. For starters, it addresses that all-too-common April 14 issue of extending the time for filing a return. You also learn how to make changes to a return that you sent in on a timely basis but that you subsequently find contains errors. You are apprised of the estimated tax filing requirements and the underpayment penalties that are assessed if you fail to pay enough money by year-end.

Finally, this hour addresses some of those sticky filing issues that arise for divorced taxpayers. Decisions must be made by you and your "ex" as to who is to claim dependency exemptions. You also need to be sure you correctly report alimony and child support that you pay or receive.

Highlights of this hour include

- Filing for an extension
- Amending a return
- Requesting installment payments
- Estimated payments and underpayment penalties
- **Tax** treatment of alimony and child support
- Special dependency exemption forms

Extending the Time to File Your Return

Running late? You can obtain an automatic extension of time for filing your tax return by filing Form 4868 on or before the April 15 deadline. A copy of Form 4868 appears in Figure 20.1.

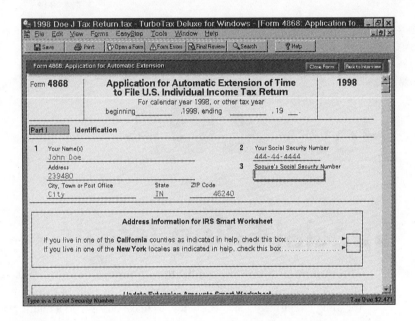

The form is simple enough to complete without the assistance of the EasyStep Interview, but the user-friendly screens *do* simplify and expedite the process. The program allows you to transfer information from the "draft" return that you are preparing directly onto the extension form using the screen that appears in Figure 20.2. You can initiate this section of the interview by clicking the section of the outline that references the topic.

Filing of Form 4868 automatically extends the time for filing your return by four months. If you use this form to extend your 1998 return, your new due date is August 17. But Form 4868 does *not* extend the time for paying your taxes. Because presumably you are filing an extension because you do not have all the information you need to file your 1040, you need to estimate the amount that you need to file with your form to avoid the underpayment penalties discussed later this hour.

FIGURE 20.2.

The EasyStep Interview can be used to expedite the completion of Form 4868.

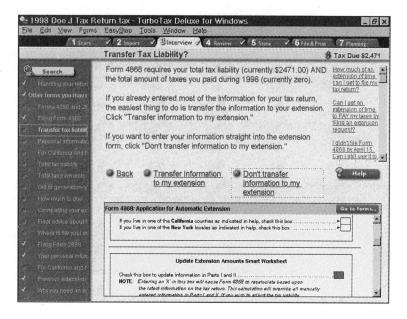

If you are close to having all the information that you need, you may want to go ahead and file your 1040 with a few estimated amounts for the items you don't have. You can amend the return later, as discussed in the following section.

What if you filed an extension and procrastinate to the extent that you still don't have your return done on August 17, 1999? In that case, you need to file Form 2688, shown in Figure 20.3. The two-month extension requested by Form 2688 is *not automatic*, as with the Form 4868. You must state a reason for the request and complete the mailing label at the bottom of the form. The IRS uses this label to respond to your request and notify you as to whether it is accepted.

20

Do not be intimidated by the requirement that you must state a reason for requesting an additional two-month extension on Form 2688. The IRS generally grants these extensions for any valid reason, such as inability to compile required information.

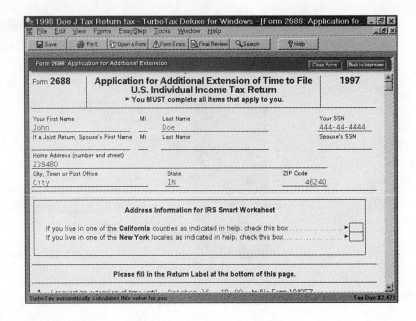

FIGURE 20.3.

File Form 2688 if you have not completed your return by the extended filing deadline.

Amending a Tax Return

After you have filed your return, if you believe that the tax that you have reported on your return is incorrect, you can file Form 1040X, reproduced in Figure 20.4. You may pay additional tax with the Form 1040X or allow the form to serve as your claim for a refund due to you. You must file a separate Form 1040X for each year being amended. If you are amending a state return, you must follow the requirements of your state. (See Hour 8, "Completing Your State Tax Return," for more information.)

Generally, the statute of limitations for filing a claim for a refund is three years from the time the return was filed or two years from the date the tax was paid, whichever is later. For purposes of this standard, a return filed before the due date is treated as filed on the due date. This means, for example, that if you filed your return on April 1, it is treated as having been filed on April 15 for purposes of calculating the amount of time that you have to file a refund.

If a claim for a refund relates to worthless securities or bad debts, the time for amending the original return is seven years. If the refund relates to a net operating loss or capital loss carryback, the time for filing the 1040X is six years after the due date of the return reporting the loss that was carried back.

FIGURE 20.4.

Form 1040X is used to amend your return or file a claim for an additional refund.

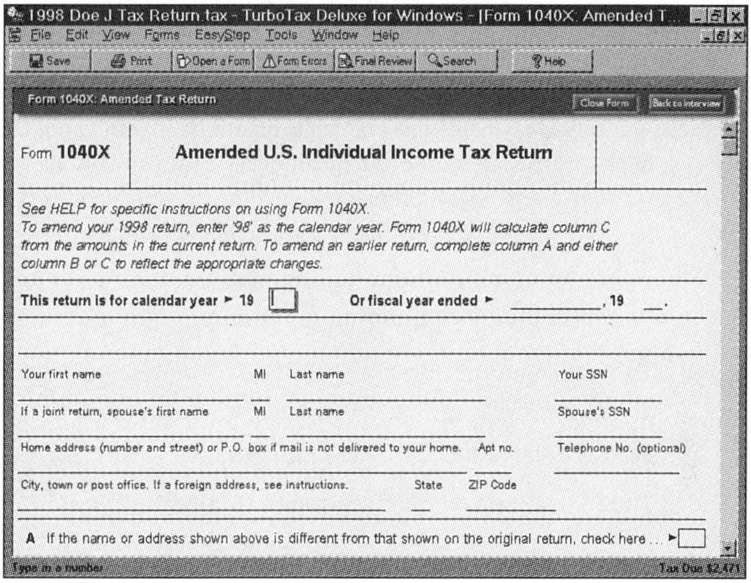

Application for Installment Payments

If you cannot pay the tax that is due with your return, go to the TurboTax Forms menu, and open Form 9465. This is an Installment Agreement Request. The form is reproduced, in part, in Figure 20.5. This form cannot be accessed through the EasyStep Interview.

FIGURE 20.5.

If you cannot pay the additional tax due with Form 1040X, consider filing a request to make installment payments.

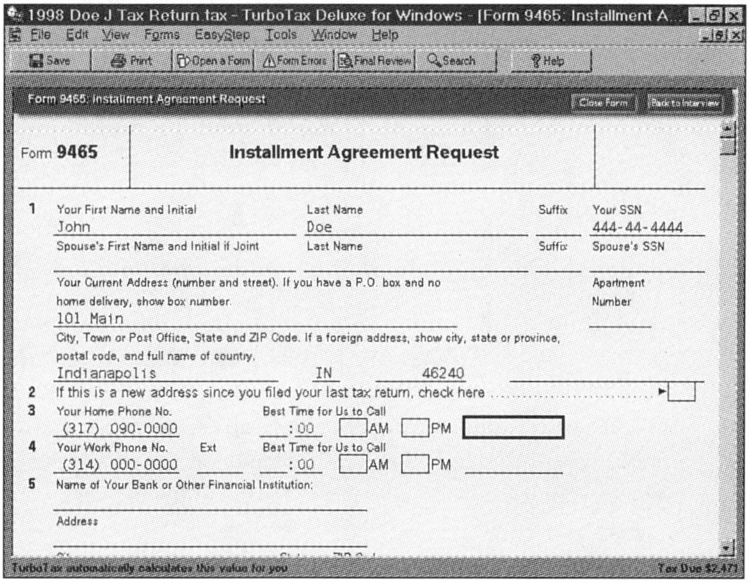

20

Estimated Payments and Underpayment Penalties

Estimated tax payments must be made quarterly, if you do not have sufficient amounts withheld from other sources. Generally, you must pay 90% of your final income tax liability by year-end either through withholding or estimated tax payments. Estimated taxes include the total of your income and self-employment tax liability.

You must use the Form 1040-ES payment voucher, shown in Figure 20.6, to submit your estimated tax payments. Estimated tax payments are made quarterly. The 1999 due dates are as follows:

First Installment	April 15, 1999
Second Installment	June 15, 1999
Third Installment	September 15, 1999
Fourth Installment	January 15, 2000

FIGURE 20.6.

This form must be submitted quarterly with your estimated tax payments.

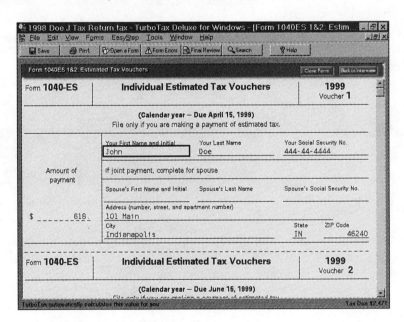

TurboTax offers you the option of preparing estimated tax vouchers using the EasyStep Interview, as shown in Figure 20.7. Based upon your tax liability for the year, TurboTax prepares your estimated tax vouchers for the following year.

FIGURE 20.7.

TurboTax prepares vouchers for the next year based upon this year's tax liability.

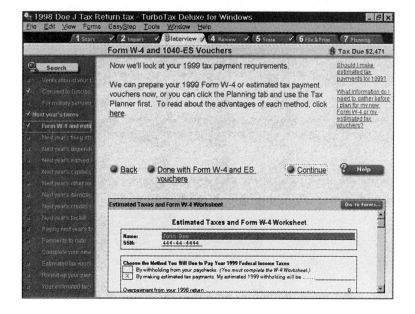

Generally, you are required to pay 25% of your liability with each quarterly voucher. (Paying it all with the last voucher would negate the effect of the law.) If you do not pay the full amount of your tax liability by January 15, 1999, you can escape the underpayment penalty if you have done the following:

- Paid at least 90% of the tax shown on your 1998 return.
- Paid 100% of the tax reflected on your current year's return.
- Monitored your income during the year and made payments based on when your income is actually earned. (This is useful for taxpayers engaged in seasonal occupations or businesses, or who have income that is subject to fluctuation.)

Taxpayers who owe less than $1,000 of tax for the year are not required to make estimated payments. Also, you are not required to make estimated tax payments if you had no tax liability for 1998.

If you underpay your estimated taxes, the IRS computes the applicable penalty for you and notifies you accordingly. You can also compute the penalty on your own using Form 2210, shown in Figure 20.8. The additional amount due is the amount of interest that is attributable to the amount of the underpayment and the length of time of the underpayment. The IRS adjusts its interest rates quarterly to reflect market factors, so you have to make sure you are working with the current rate if you decide to compute the penalty on your own.

20

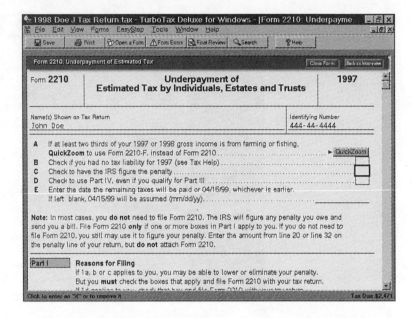

FIGURE 20.8.

You can verify the penalty assessed by the IRS by computing it on your own, using this form.

Tax Treatment of Alimony and Child Support

Most people do not think to have their accountants review their divorce decree or the final judgment of the court fixing the rights and payment obligations of both parties at the time of the divorce. However, it would probably be a good idea.

The Importance of Classifying Payments

Alimony payments are deductible to the ex-spouse who is making payments. They are reported as taxable income on Form 1040, line 11 by the spouse receiving them. In contrast, child support payments are *not* deductible by the payer and neither are any payments made as part of a division of the couple's assets. The IRS maintains specific criteria as to how payments are to be classified for tax purposes and specifically, when they constitute alimony.

When Are Payments Deductible as Alimony?

Alimony is cash payment made to a former spouse pursuant to a divorce decree or separation instrument. (It is not necessary that a couple be legally divorced for payments to be classified as deductible alimony.) For payments to be considered alimony, they must cease upon the death of the recipient.

The following types of payments are *not* considered alimony:

- Child support

- Cash payments made as part of a property settlement

- Payment taxes, insurance, and monthly mortgage payments made to maintain property used by either spouse

- Payments that are not required by the legal divorce or separation instrument or decree

What if the spouses agree that they do not want to designate a payment as alimony, and the paying spouse agrees to forgo the deduction? This can be accomplished by including a provision in the divorce or separation agreement stating that the payments are not deductible by the payer and are excludable from the recipient's income.

> Alimony and child support should be clearly designated as such in your divorce decree.

Special Dependency Exemption Forms

Another issue that frequently arises in a divorce situation is who gets to claim the dependency exemption for the children. Generally, the dependency exemption goes to the parent who has custody of the children for the greater part of the tax year. However, this rule applies only if the child receives over one-half of his or her support from parents who are divorced, legally separated, or who have lived apart for the last six months of the calendar year.

There are two widely relied upon exceptions to the general rule that the custodial parent is entitled the dependency exemption. The first exception exists if there is a multiple support agreement in effect that allows a child to be claimed as a dependent by someone other than the custodial parent. A multiple support agreement is a legally binding agreement reached in connection with the divorce settlement.

Alternatively, the custodial parent may release his or her right to claim the dependency exemption by filing Form 8332 with the IRS. This form is available from the TurboTax forms menu, and is reproduced in Figure 20.9.

20

> Form 2210 is filed when two or more taxpayers who provided over 50% of the support of another individual (for example, an elderly parent). The form states one of the payers is waiving the right to claim the exemption. This form is available in TurboTax.

FIGURE 20.9.

A parent entitled to claim a dependency exemption might legally waive the right.

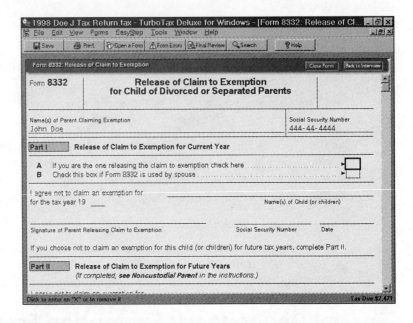

The EasyStep Interview covers both the filing of the multiple support agreement and the alternative of filing Form 8332. You can get some assistance from TurboTax as to the legal requirements for claiming a dependent using this form as illustrated by the screen shown in Figure 2.10.

FIGURE 20.10.

The EasyStep Interview reminds you of pertinent legal requirements for filing this declaration.

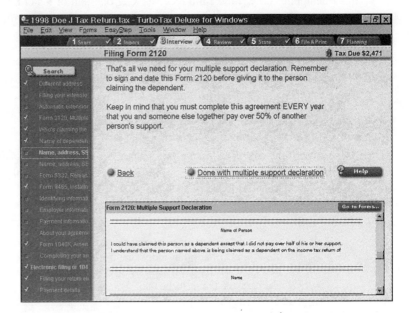

Summary

This hour dealt with issues beyond the scope of what appears on your 1040 Form. You learned how to file an extension and how to amend an individual tax return. You also became familiar with the estimated tax reporting requirements and the penalties resulting from underpayment.

Finally, this hour provided some insight as to the tax consequences and elections that must be made in the event of a divorce.

Hour 21, "Additional Types of Taxes Imposed," continues to address tax issues that extend beyond the information entered on the Form 1040.

Q&A

Q Can you amend an amended return?

A Yes, you can. Fill in the leftmost column of the Form 1040X from the *last* version of the 1040 that was filed or the most recent Form 1040X.

Q Can you file a Form 1040X changing your filing status?

A Yes, you can do so for any filing status change, with one exception. If you are making a change from Married Filing Jointly to Married Filing Separately, this change cannot be made after the due date for filing your original return has passed.

Q Can the divorced spouses agree to change the tax treatment of payments made under a divorce decree?

A Generally, yes. Most states allow amendment of divorce decrees. The procedure and requirements for doing so vary from state to state.

20

PART VI

Advanced Tax Return Preparation Topics

Hour

Hour **21**

Additional Types of Taxes Imposed

In this hour, we cover the Alternative Minimum Tax, a fate that befalls taxpayers if they reduce their tax bill below a certain level, and the kiddie tax, by which the IRS puts the brakes on certain tax advantages in transferring assets to your children. We also cover the nanny tax, a set of tax rules that apply to all household employees.

Highlights of this hour include

- Learn about the Alternative Minimum Tax
- Learn whether you're subject to the Alternative Minimum Tax and how to calculate it
- Learn what qualifies for "kiddie tax"
- Learn what form to use for "kiddie tax"
- Learn how to use "nanny tax" for household employees

The Alternative Minimum Tax

Some people are so good at reducing their adjusted gross income that they end up paying little or no taxes at all. To prevent this, the IRS set up an Alternative Minimum Tax that is applied to any taxpayer whose AGI falls below a certain level. When the Alternative Minimum Tax is "triggered" by a taxpayer's use of excessive miscellaneous deductions, for example, the taxpayer must then recalculate their tax debt according to the Alternative Minimum Tax and pay the amount computed therein, which would invariably be more than paying the regular tax.

How does the Alternative Minimum Tax Work?

The Alternative Minimum Tax is really a second tax system that runs parallel to the regular tax system and kicks in if a taxpayer whittles his tax debt below a certain minimum, using pet deductions and other calculations. The AMT is calculated alongside your normal tax burden. If it appears that you owe more taxes under this Alternative Minimum Tax than you would normally (meaning, you've been too smart for your own good), the Alternative Minimum Tax is applied to you, and you have to recalculate your tax debt using this alternate system. You've therefore "triggered" the AMT. Thus your adjusted gross income (AGI) that you've so carefully whittled down to a pittance has been replaced by the more robust Alternative Minimum Taxable Income (AMTI).

After you've triggered it, the Alternative Minimum Tax begins stripping away most tax preferences (favorite deductions and tax shelters), applying a new set of adjustments that are unfamiliar to the average taxpayer, and granting a single, simple exemption.

Do not pass go; do not collect $200.

How Is the AMT Calculated?

The Alternative Minimum Tax is calculated on Form 6251, one of the IRS's most complicated forms, and it is in your interest to avoid walking into this lion's den if at all possible. Just so you know, the Alternative Minimum Tax is imposed at a rate of 26% on the first $175,000 of Alternative Minimum Taxable Income and 28% on any amount above $175,000. It is sometimes referred to as a flat tax because there are fewer categories and brackets. There is no simplicity to be found in this flatness, though. Form 6251 is very complex.

You do get an exemption. Currently, it's $45,000 in the case of married individuals filing a joint return and surviving spouses (these figures may change, so let TurboTax provide the calculations for you), $33,750 for single taxpayers and head of households, and $22,500 for married individuals filing separate returns.

Please note that these exemption figures are reduced (phased out) by one-fourth of the amount that an individual's income exceeds a certain threshold. If your income is particularly high, you don't get to hold on to your entire personal exemption. In other words, the exemption is reduced by $1 for every $4 your income exceeds the income threshold. There is no inflation indexing of these amounts or thresholds.

Although the Alternative Minimum Tax was particularly designed to make sure the wealthy and the "too-clever-by-half" among us did pay their fair share, the rules were designed back when the dollar was worth more. The income thresholds that trigger the Alternative Minimum Tax are not as high as they were meant to be. Therefore, more and more "average Joes" are getting caught in its clutches. Congress is indeed looking at big changes to the Alternative Minimum Tax, because some tax experts predict that by 2005, more than six million people could be subject to this alternative tax, up from 414,000 in 1995.

How Is the AMT Avoided?

Your goal is to never ever have to deal with the AMT, if at all possible, and avoid the following behaviors that trigger it:

- Reliance on too many miscellaneous deductions. For example, lots of deductions for work-related expenses. Try to see if you can get the boss to reimburse you for some of these "extras," rather than reflexively deducting them from your income tax.

- Investments in lots of tax-free bonds. The interest on some bonds is not taxable under regular tax law but is taxable under the Alternative Minimum Tax. (This may very well be printed on your bond.) If you rely on such bonds for a large source of your income, the IRS might indeed calculate that you owe more money under the Alternative Minimum Tax than under regular tax law and start the whole show, making you recalculate your tax under AMT. Be careful with using incentive stock options to lower your Adjusted Gross Income.

- Using lots of accelerated depreciation of certain types of real property and leased personal property.

- Reducing your AGI by deducting state and local income taxes.

- Farm losses that are obviously a tax shelter.

You Pay Whichever Is Higher

21

The above (not at all complete) list of Alternative Minimum Tax "triggers" are called triggers not because the IRS thinks they are bad, but because, if you were to calculate your income tax using the AMT, you would not be able to implement these advantages (called tax preferences) to reduce your declared income, at least not to the normal extent.

Now, the IRS is going to get you with whichever tax method brings them the most money. Each time you deploy any of the above advantages, you can be sure that your adjusted gross income under AMT is not reduced to the extent that it is under normal tax law. Like a game of hangman, when the final hand or foot finally gets drawn in, after your taxes under AMT rise above what you would normally have to pay, AMT is "triggered."

The prudent rule: Be careful deploying these methods to reduce your taxable income. Some is okay, too much is not. Over-dependence on the above AGI reducing techniques trigger the AMT, which does not make you happy.

The AMT and TurboTax

TurboTax works with you to avoid the AMT, calculating the 6251 Form in the background, and issues plenty of alerts, if you near a trigger threshold. You can also open Form 6251 yourself and run the numbers. (As soon as you open the form, you find that TurboTax has filled in many of the fields from other worksheets.)

To Do: Taking a Sneak Preview of the 6251 Form

If you think you are getting close to invoking the AMT, run your numbers beforehand to see what TurboTax says.

1. Select Open a Form from the Forms menu, and when the list of forms appears, scroll down to locate Form 6251, as shown in Figure 21.1.

FIGURE 21.1.

Use Open Form to locate and view a form, even before the EasyStep Interview brings it up.

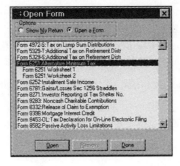

2. Double-click the name Form 6251: Alternative Minimum Tax and the form appears. If you'd rather review it in the Interview form, click the Take Me To tab at the lower left, and then click Interview Search.

3. In the top field, next to the Find Topics button, type Form 6251.

4. Click the Find Topics button. You then see what calculating the Alternative Minimum Tax looks like, in the Interview format (Figure 21.2).

FIGURE 21.2.

Form 6251 is the Alternative Minimum Tax form. You can open it up for a dry run, just to see whether you are edging too close to the AMT.

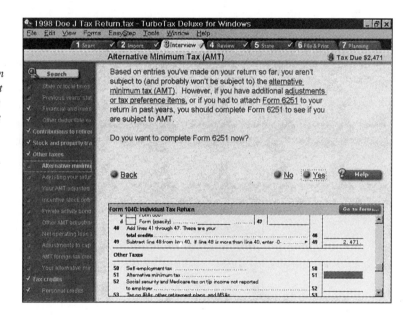

If TurboTax leads you to the Alternative Minimum Tax form (Form 6251), simply answer the questions as they arise, clicking Next just like you'd normally do.

If you've opened Form 6251 on your own to see how close you are to the edge, after answering everything you are asked, TurboTax tells you whether you are liable for the Alternative Minimum Tax (see Figures 21.3 and 21.4). Do not save your file if you are just getting a sneak preview.

TurboTax Says I'm Subject to AMT!

If you trigger the AMT, TurboTax does not abandon you. TurboTax continues to help you whittle down what you owe.

Review the portion of this chapter "Avoiding the Alternative Minimum Tax," rework your return (press the Back button many times), and see whether you can create a scenario that does not trigger the AMT, by not taking so many tax preferences.

21

For example, consider stretching out certain deductions and depreciations over a number of years, rather than choosing the accelerated options. It's better to go without a few deductions than to have to deal with the Alternative Minimum Tax.

If you trigger the Alternative Minimum Tax, you can still work though the EasyStep Interview, though the questions asked of you may be more complicated than other portions of the interview. For example, regular tax law allows you to spend a certain amount of money you borrow against your mortgage for items not related to fixing up your home, and it can still be tax deductible. The Alternative Minimum Tax has stricter provisions for how such money is spent. TurboTax walks you through the steps, points out the issues as they arise, and helps you make the right decisions.

That's all for the Alternative Minimum Tax. Now we discuss the so-called kiddie tax.

FIGURE 21.3.

TurboTax announces you are subject to AMT.

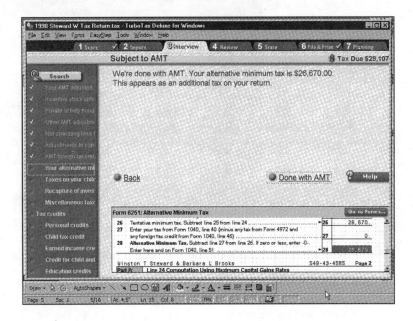

FIGURE 21.4.

TurboTax tells you not to worry this year.

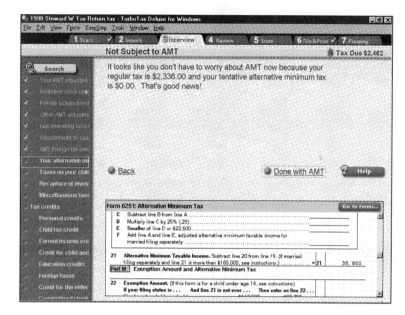

The Kiddie Tax

A popular tax planning technique for parents has been to transfer assets to children so that these assets are taxed at the child's lower rate. This allows parents to build a tuition nest-egg, for example. They could invest in mutual funds in the child's name. That way, the child could hang on to more of the dividends and capital gains than the parents would be able to, and thus, have a little something tucked away for college.

However, the kiddie tax places limits on how much of this unearned income can be taxed at the lower, child's rate. The following is how it reads:

> "Children who have not reached the age of 14 by the end of the tax year will not enjoy the children's tax rate for unearned income in excess of $1,400. Instead, all such income above $1,400 will be taxed at the parents' highest tax rate."

Assessing the Effects of the Kiddie Tax

The kiddie tax is not as much of a killjoy as it may seem at first glance. Please note the following:

21

- The kiddie tax applies to unearned income, such as interest, dividends, and capital gains. If your child works for you in your unincorporated business, lower tax rates and other advantages (such as no Social Security and Medicare taxes if your child is under 18) still apply.

- Also note that the kiddie tax leaves untouched earnings less than $1,400 per year, which can be substantial. You can still give an annual "gift" of $10,000 to your child, and as long as investment income accrued from this gift does not exceed $1,400, you do not trigger the kiddie tax.

- The tax applies to income *in excess* of $1,400. Triggering the kiddie tax does not cause the sum below $1,400 to be taxed at the parent's rate.

- Finally, this tax applies to children under the age of 14. Transferring assets to children over the age of 14 does not trigger it.

Income Shifting Still Works

Kiddie tax or not, income shifting is still a good method to maximize what is available for children as they reach college age. You can purchase stock in growth-oriented companies, committing yourself not to sell them until the child reaches 14. (Remember that mutual funds are required to pay out dividends and capital gains annually, which is what you want to avoid here.) You can also invest in Series EE savings bonds, electing that the interest on the bonds not be available for withdrawal until after the child turns 14.

TurboTax brings up the issue of your child's unearned income as part of the EasyStep Interview (see Figure 21.5). The program asks many detailed questions about that income, so have any source documents such as interest and dividend statements handy.

Which Form to Use?

One decision you have to make is whether to use Form 8615 (you file a separate return on behalf of the child) or Form 8814 (you report the child's unearned income on your return). Generally speaking, it's better to use Form 8615. However, TurboTax lets you read a brief article "Advantages/disadvantages of using Form 8814" as part of the EasyStep Interview (see Figure 21.6), if your child's unearned income becomes an issue. Just click the link to it shown in Figure 21.5

After answering the questions, TurboTax informs you of any extra kiddie tax you have to pay (see Figure 21.7).

We finish up by going over the nanny tax, which is the tax you are required to pay on behalf of any household employee.

FIGURE 21.5.

The EasyStep Interview asks you in due course about a child's unearned income.

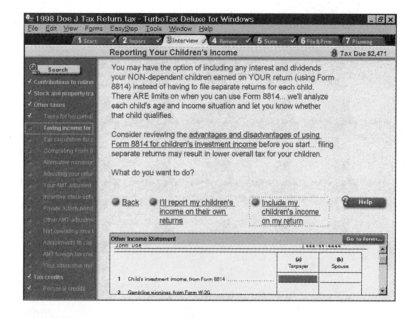

FIGURE 21.6.

Before determining how to file your child's unearned income, read and figure out which form is best.

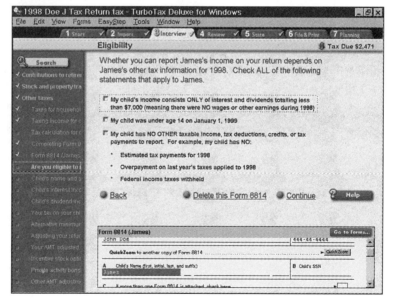

21

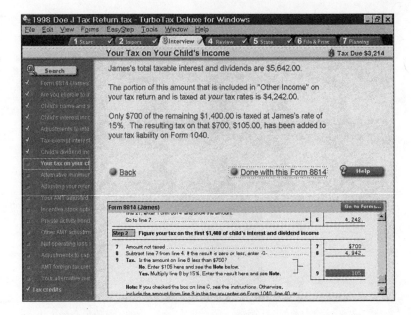

FIGURE 21.7.

*TurboTax calculates
your kiddie tax, if any.*

The Nanny Tax: Paying Taxes for Household Employees

The so-called nanny tax is a term covering your obligation to pay various taxes on household employees and to see to it that they pay these particular taxes as well. Before you read any further, it may be that your household employee is not one at all. In which case, you can skip this section entirely. Or, if you pay your household employee less than $1,100 per year, the following tax rules do not apply to you either. So, let's clarify who is a household employee.

Who Is a Household Employee?

A household employee is someone in your employ who does household work. This work could include, for example, drivers, caretakers, housekeepers, yard workers, and baby-sitters. They need not work for you full time to be called a household employee. By the IRS's definition, a household employee could be paid hourly, by the job, salaried, or as often is agreed upon. You are not subject to the nanny tax unless you pay this worker more than $1,100 dollars per year.

People who work for you through an agency, or self-employed individuals who perform services for you, are not considered household employees. A household employee need not be a live-in.

The Nanny Tax and Federal Income Tax

In dealing with household employees, there are two types of tax obligations that need to be clarified. One is the Federal income tax that your household employee must pay. You are not obligated to withhold Federal income tax from a household employee. You need to give them a W-2 Form, but they need to fill out their own W-4 Form, just as any other employee of an institution, and work out how many dependents they want to claim, determining the best way to pay their taxes.

You, as their employer, can withhold and regularly pay their Federal income tax, if you both agree that it's a good idea.

The so-called nanny tax on household employees is different. It is a combined Social Security and Medicare tax (FICA) that both you and your household employee are obligated to pay. As an employer, you also pay FUTA, or unemployment tax. The nanny tax holds you responsible for two tasks:

- Paying your share of the FICA and FUTA tax. You may either make regular payments to the IRS for this amount, or simply increase your regular deductions from your own paycheck. Either way, the IRS gets paid. It doesn't have to get mailed anyplace special.

- Seeing to it that your household employee's share also gets paid to the IRS.

Paying Unemployment Tax

You, as the employer, must also pay Federal unemployment tax (FUTA tax) on behalf of your household employee. TurboTax walks you through questions regarding this responsibility as part of the EasyStep Interview. You, as the employer, pay this tax. The employee does not.

Federal unemployment tax applies to only the first $7,000 of your household employee's income.

You probably pay a state unemployment tax as well, which can be deducted from your Federal unemployment tax. You need not send money to a special location or make quarterly arrangements to pay this tax. TurboTax simply calculates the FUTA tax you owe, combines this amount with other Schedule H sums (household employee taxes), and places them on the appropriate line of your 1040 Form. Thus, covering FUTA tax for a household employee is usually just a matter of making sure you are having enough withheld from your own paycheck.

21

It is illegal not to pay unemployment tax. If an employer evades unemployment tax, this becomes evident as soon as a former employee tries to collect unemployment.

Deducting the Employee's Share

The employees must pay their share of the nanny tax. However, this can be difficult to manage because if you agree to pay household employees, say, $300 per week, they probably are not, in their mind, factoring in their share of FICA tax on that amount. After such a deduction, their share would be in the neighborhood of $277 dollars weekly. For such a reason, you may want to clarify net pay issues with employees while initially discussing salary.

Perhaps you can simply pay the employees' entire nanny tax and not worry about arranging withholding from their check. The amount you pay in nanny tax is recorded on its own line on your 1040 Form, so if you simply make sure you deduct enough to cover your household employee's tax by adjusting the withholding you've arranged on the paycheck from your employer, the IRS is happy.

> The only portion of the nanny tax that employees are obligated to pay is FICA, a combined Social Security and Medicare tax. They need to understand, however, that this tax is not in lieu of their Federal income tax.

If you do pay your employees' share of the nanny tax, using an example of $300 per week, you'd actually be paying them about $25 dollar more per week. Please note that, when calculating their own Federal income tax, your employees have to include this extra bonus as if it were wages, which would slightly increase their tax liability.

TurboTax and the Nanny Tax

Nanny tax is calculated on Schedule H, and is covered in due course during the EasyStep Interview. You know you're headed in that direction when TurboTax asks you whether you have any household employees (see Figure 21.8). TurboTax asks you all Schedule H related questions as they arise (see Figure 21.9).

To get an idea of what you are asked, you can view this form before it comes up in the interview.

FIGURE 21.8.

As TurboTax asks about household employees, you know you are going to be discussing nanny tax issues such as FICA and FUTA taxes.

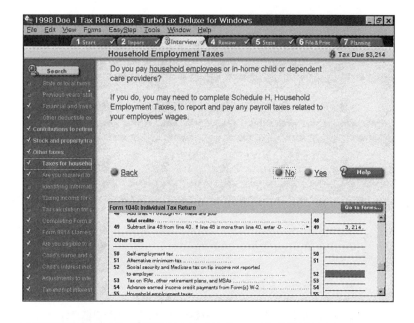

FIGURE 21.9.

Nanny tax questions are dealt with on Schedule H.

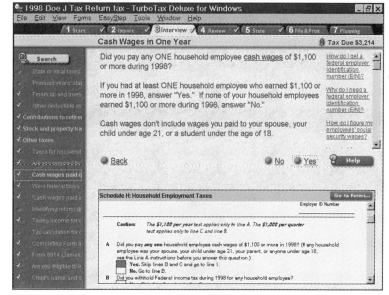

21

To Do: Preview What the Nanny Tax Is All About

1. Click the Search button on the Navigation bar.

2. When the Search window appears, type Household and click the Search button.

3. A list of forms appears. Double-click "Are you required to pay household taxes?" The Interview jumps to Schedule H questions.

Calculating Your Nanny Tax

Although TurboTax calculates taxes with regard to your household employee, it may be nice to have a rough idea of this tax liability in the back of your mind, especially when you are determining how much to pay a domestic employee. This additional tax burden should be calculated in as part of your true cost of hiring a household employee. The NaniPay Web page (www.4nannytaxes.com) has a calculator just for this purpose. Just answer a few questions about what you intend to pay this employee, and the calculator displays your approximate nanny tax.

Obtaining an Employer ID Number

While completing Schedule H, TurboTax asks for your employer identification number (also called EIN, see Figure 21.10). Fill out a mail Form SS4 to obtain one, although you are free to use the same EIN you used for a previous household employee. To obtain Form SS4, also called the Social Security Administration Form, call 800-829-3767. Take care of this well before your taxes are due.

FIGURE 21.10.

You need to have an employer identification number before you can complete Schedule H.

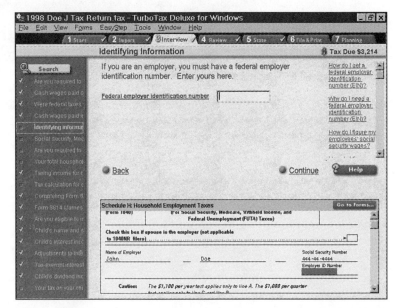

If Your Employee Has No Social Security Number

While filling out Schedule H, you notice TurboTax requests your household employee's Social Security number. Not everybody has one. The IRS has implemented a new procedure for tax processing that allows workers without Social Security numbers to file a tax return. (The IRS does not provide information about undocumented workers to the INS. The IRS simply would prefer that undocumented workers pay taxes.)

Your employee without a SSN needs to obtain an Individual Taxpayer Identification Number (ITIN) so that you can file your Schedule H. The employee needs to complete Form W-7 to obtain an ITIN number. It takes 4–6 weeks for the IRS to process this form, so leave plenty of time to do it.

The following are a few things you need to know about your employee's ITIN number:

- Holding an Individual Taxpayer Identification Number does not constitute a legal right to work in the United States. It only means you get to pay taxes.

- The ITIN does not set you up to receive Social Security benefits. It does not take the place of a Social Security number, nor is it some sort of temporary SSN that somehow ensures that a permanent SSN is on its way.

- Again, the IRS does not disclose confidential tax information to immigration authorities.

Summary

TurboTax is always on the lookout to make sure you steer clear of additional taxes or taxes triggered by applying too many deductions, such as the Alternative Minimum Tax. If you think you may be veering too close to the taxes discussed in this hour, take a sneak preview at the forms involved, run the numbers, and see whether you are teetering too close to the edge.

Q&A

Q What is the Alternative Minimum Tax?

A The Alternative Minimum Tax is a tax system that a taxpayer falls into if he whittles his tax burden to a very low amount. Designed to make sure that those who are able to amass a myriad of tax preferences at least pay *some* tax, falling into this tax system is both expensive and complicated.

21

Q What is the kiddie tax?

A Designed to limit the effects of minimizing adjusted gross income by transferring assets to children, the kiddie tax places a ceiling on how much unearned income a child can amass and be taxed at a low, child's rate.

Q What is the nanny tax?

A The nanny tax is really a collection of taxes and rules for their application, relating to household employees. Basically, when you have a household employee, both you and the employee must pay Social Security and Medicare tax, whereas you, as the employer, must also pay a Federal unemployment tax as well.

Q When you fall into the clutches of these extra taxes, how can TurboTax help?

A TurboTax walks you through questions regarding these taxes, using the EasyStep Interview. If at all possible, TurboTax helps you steer clear of them entirely.

Hour 22

IRAs, Pension Plans, and Annuities

This hour explores the popular IRA (Individual Retirement Account) and some other types of retirement plans that are available to self-employed individuals. Traditionally, taxpayers have been able to make deductible contributions of $2,000 per year, which are allowed to grow tax-free until withdrawal. The Taxpayer Relief Act of 1997 introduced new variations of the IRA. Other retirement plans such as the SIMPLE, Keogh, and SEP may also involve establishment or IRA accounts for self-employed persons and their employees.

Highlights of this hour include

- Individual Retirement Accounts (IRAs)
- Simple plans
- Keogh accounts
- Self-Employment Plans (SEPs)

Individual Retirement Accounts

The Individual Retirement Account (IRA) is an account that you set up during your working years to save for your retirement. IRAs are afforded generous tax treatment. Contributions to the traditional IRA accounts are subtracted from gross income to arrive at taxable income. In general, adjustments to income are better than deductions because you may benefit from them even if you do not itemize. Alternatively, you may elect to establish a non-deductible IRA, called a Roth IRA. Contributions to a Roth IRA are not deductible when made, but they are allowed to grow tax-free and are not taxed upon withdrawal.

You must make your contribution before the due date of your return, generally April 15. Beginning in 1998, taxpayers must choose among the three different types of IRAs: the traditional type of IRA that has been around for many years, the new Roth IRA, and the educational IRA, listed on the TurboTax screen shown in Figure 22.1.

FIGURE 22.1.

Taxpayers now have several choices in addition to the traditional IRA.

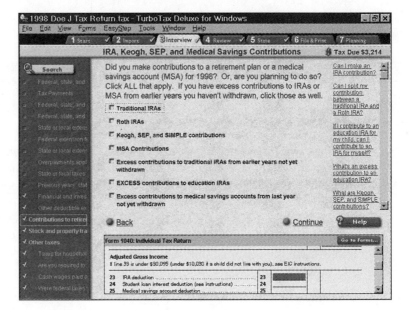

The Traditional IRA

Eligible taxpayers are permitted to make deductible IRA contributions equal to the lessor of $2,000 (single filer) or $2,250 (combined regular and spousal IRA) of your earned income for the tax year. You are eligible to make contributions to a traditional IRA account if you do not turn age 70$\frac{1}{2}$ during the tax year and if you have earned income (that is, you must be working). TurboTax automatically determines your eligibility to make contributions, based on information you have entered into the system.

If you withdraw the funds before turning age 59½, a 10% early withdrawal penalty generally applies. Alternatively, if you fail to make minimum distributions from your IRA after you turn age 70½, you are subject to additional penalties.

> You may make taxable withdrawals from your IRA prior to age 59½ if the proceeds are used to purchase a first time home or for qualified educational expenses.

Many taxpayers are unable to deduct contributions to IRA's because they participate in retirement plans sponsored by their employers. You cannot take an IRA deduction if you are covered by another retirement plan and your modified adjusted gross income is over $40,000 to $50,000 (married filing jointly) or $25,000 to $35,000 for single persons. This limit will increase annually until the year 2007.

> If you are not covered by a plan, but your spouse is, you may make deductible IRA contributions unless you and your spouse have a combined adjusted gross income in excess of $160,000.

The Roth IRA

The Taxpayer Relief Act of 1997 introduced a popular new form of IRA account aptly named for one of its congressional sponsors. The Roth IRA is a *non-deductible* IRA (see Figure 22.2). This means that contributions to it are not deductible. However, the Roth IRA has a distinct advantage over the traditional IRA, which allows for deductible contributions. If you retire after age 59½ and begin making withdrawals from your Roth IRA, distributions you make from it are tax free. In contrast, distributions from a traditional IRA are taxed at regular income tax rates.

Unlike a regular IRA account, you can continue making contributions to your Roth IRA after you turn 70½, regardless of whether you have earned income. In other words, you can continue to put money in the account and allow it to grow tax-free even if you have retired. This benefit is enhanced by the fact that there are no minimum distribution requirements at age 70½ with a Roth IRA.

Unfortunately, the benefits of the Roth IRA are not fully available to all taxpayers. The benefit is reduced for single taxpayers with more than $95,000 of adjusted gross income and for married taxpayers with more than $150,000 of adjusted gross income. The Roth IRA is completely unavailable for taxpayers with income of more than $160,000.

FIGURE 22.2.

Enter contributions made to a Roth IRA using this screen.

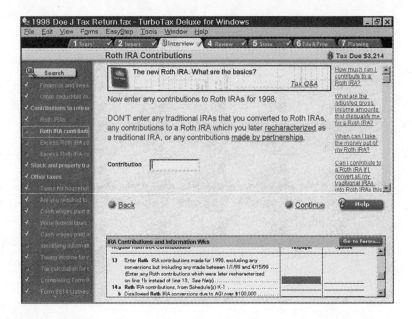

The Education IRA

The educational IRA is a distant cousin to the traditional IRA and the Roth IRA, but the fundamental purpose of the accounts is dramatically different. Whereas the other IRAs are intended to provide for retirement, the education IRA is designed to provide a tax break to families trying to save for their children's college education.

The maximum contribution that you can make is $500 per year for *each* beneficiary. Withdrawals for tuition, fees, room and board, and other educational expenses are tax-free.

The educational IRA is unavailable for individual taxpayers with adjusted gross income of $95,000 or more and married taxpayers with joint adjusted gross income in excess of $150,000.

SIMPLE Retirement Plans

The acronym SIMPLE stands for Savings Incentive Match Plan for Employees. This type of retirement plan first became available in 1997. It can either be established as an IRA or as a 401(k) plan, which is a type of plan that involves pooling of the investments held in employee accounts.

The SIMPLE is available for the benefit of self-employed individuals and employees that work for businesses having fewer than 100 employees. The SIMPLE is not available if

22

the employer maintains another type of qualified retirement plan for the benefit of its employees.

The primary advantage of the SIMPLE is that it allows larger contributions to an IRA than the other options for such accounts permit. The maximum amount that can be contributed to a SIMPLE IRA is $6,000 per year.

Employees (that is, people who are not self-employed individuals) contribute to the SIMPLE through a salary reduction plan. The employer makes the SIMPLE contribution directly to the IRA or 401(k) plan, rather than to the employee. If you are self-employed, you make your contribution directly to your IRA account.

Contributions to a SIMPLE are not subject to federal income tax or any type of withholding. If you are an employee, SIMPLE contributions are not included as taxable wages on your W-2 Form. No entry is required on Form 1040 for your contribution, and therefore, you won't find SIMPLE contributions addressed in the EasyStep Interview. Self-employed persons enter their contributions on the Keogh/SEP/SIMPLE worksheet, shown in Figure 22.3.

FIGURE 22.3.

Self-employed individuals should enter their SIMPLE contributions on this worksheet.

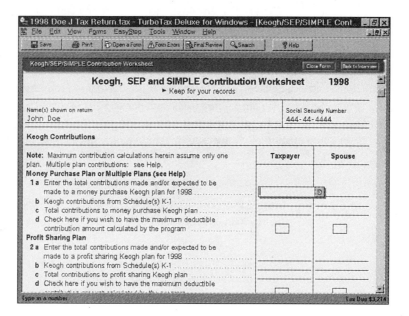

Distributions from SIMPLE plans are taxed much like distributions from other types of IRAs. Earnings accumulate tax-free until they are distributed.

The early withdrawal penalty that applies for distributions made prior to age 59½ is more stringent and punitive than the penalty imposed on distributions from traditional IRA accounts: 25% instead of 10%.

Keogh Plans

A Keogh plan is a pension or profit-sharing plan that is available to self-employed individuals. If you participate in a Keogh plan, you can contribute up to $30,000 or 20% of your net earnings from self-employment for the year (reduced by the amount of the Keogh contribution). If your plan is a profit-sharing plan, contributions are limited to 13.0435% up to a maximum of $24,000. A Keogh must also fulfill certain annual reporting requirements.

You may set up the plan as either a defined benefit or a defined contribution plan. A defined benefit plan is one that pays a specific (defined) amount upon your retirement at a designated age. For example, a plan that provides that you receive $3,000 a year at age 75 for a 10-year period is a defined benefit plan. Generally, you need the help of a trained financial advisor or an actuary to calculate the contributions that you need to make to a defined benefit plan and help you set it up.

Defined contribution plans are more common. Your account balance for this type of plan depends upon your contributions to the plan and the performance of the investments. You don't know in advance *exactly* what you'll receive upon retirement. Annual contributions to this type of plan are limited to the smaller of $30,000 or 20% of net earnings after subtracting your Keogh contributions and one-half of any self-employment tax paid. The maximum amount of compensation upon which you can base this percentage is $160,000.

> TurboTax Help provides an extensive explanation and many examples to assist you in understanding how to compute your Keogh contribution.

You can have TurboTax calculate the maximum Keogh contribution that you can make. The program assumes that you want to claim the maximum deduction regardless of the amount that you contribute. Enter your Keogh contributions using the screen shown in Figure 22.4.

FIGURE 22.4.

Enter your Keogh contribution on this screen, or check the appropriate box to have TurboTax calculate your maximum contribution.

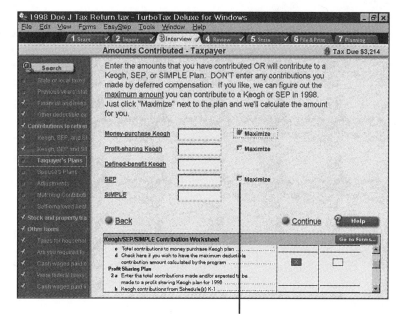

22

Check here to have TurboTax
calculate maximum contribution

You can still make tax deductible contributions to an IRA even though you have a Keogh account.

The Simplified Employee Pension Plan (SEP)

A Simplified Employee Pension Plan (SEP) is a retirement plan for self-employed individuals and their employees. These plans are simpler to maintain than Keoghs because SEPs do not have an annual reporting requirement. You just have to make sure that every employee gets a copy of the plan agreement. A SEP plan provides a separate IRA account for each employee.

The SEP is, however, stricter with respect to the requirements for covering your employees. Generally, you must cover all employees who are 21 years old, have worked for the employer for three of the last five years, and have earned $400. Additionally, you are not permitted to make hardship withdrawals or loans from a SEP for home purchases or educational expenses like you can from IRAs.

If you are self-employed, you may make a contribution to the SEP on your own behalf of the lessor of 15% of your earned income or $22,500 to a SEP. For the self-employed person, the maximum percentage is actually 13.0435% because it is figured on your business's income *after* the contribution is deducted. The maximum contribution you can make to an employee's account is 15% of wages up to a maximum of $24,000. As with Keogh contributions, TurboTax determines your maximum deductible amount.

Which Plan Should You Select?

Your choice of retirement plan is based on the make-up of your business, the amount you can afford to contribute, and your personal priorities. The differing requirements and contribution limits of the various IRA, SIMPLE, Keogh, and SEP plans attract different types of taxpayers.

If, for example, you were looking to maximize your deductible contribution, you would be advised to look into the Simple, Keogh, or SEP plan as opposed to a traditional IRA. The traditional IRA permits a maximum deduction of $2,000. In contrast, you can contribute as much as $10,000 to a Simple plan. Keogh and SEP plans, with contribution limits based on a percentage of income, also afford you the opportunity to make larger deductions.

Similarly, if you have a lot of employees, you might not want to be obligated to make contributions to cover all of them. If this is the case, the SIMPLE, Keogh, and SEP plans might be less attractive to you despite the relatively high contribution limits. These plans require minimum contributions on behalf of employees, whereas the IRA does not.

Summary

Deductions for contributions to retirement accounts are taken as adjustments to income, which means that there is no tax paid on such amounts and you get to subtract them from your income if you can not itemize. The Internal Revenue Code offers you the option of several types of retirement plans with varying limits on deductibility and contribution requirements. The Taxpayer Relief Act of 1997 introduced several new opportunities, such as the Roth and education IRA accounts, which provide greater flexibility and enhanced savings opportunities to eligible taxpayers.

Hour 23, "Some Advanced Planning," acquaints you with additional opportunities to reduce your taxable income and provide for your future.

Q&A

22

Q Can I take money out of my regular IRA and put it in a Roth IRA?

A Yes, but you must pay tax on withdrawals from a traditional IRA. However, you can elect to pay the tax over a four-year period if your transfer from a tradition IRA to a Roth IRA was made in 1998. Additionally, to avail yourself of this option, your adjusted gross income must be more than $100,000.

Q Can I take money out of my regular IRA and put it into an educational IRA?

A There are no provisions in the Taxpayer Relief Act of 1997 specifically contemplating this. However, the 10% early withdrawal penalty is waived for qualified educational expenses (such as college tuition, fees, and books) beginning in 1998.

Q What is rollover?

A Taxpayers are sometimes permitted to transfer funds from an IRA, SIMPLE, or SEP account to another one without paying income taxes or early withdrawal penalties. This type of transaction is known as a "rollover."

Q When is a Roth IRA a more attractive alternative than a traditional IRA?

A A Roth IRA is attractive to taxpayers who expect to be in a high tax bracket after retirement, and expect to enjoy a long post-retirement life expectancy. Alternatively, taxpayers that expect to be in a lower tax bracket after retirement may benefit more from a current deduction.

HOUR 23

Some Advanced Planning

In this hour you are introduced to some interesting tax animals. The medical savings account is a hybrid creature, a cross between a medical expense deduction and an IRA account. This hour also addresses the peculiar tax issues associated with taxation of Social Security benefits, an odd type of arrangement whereby the federal government pays you money and then takes some of it back each year. Finally, this hour provides some tips for small business and insights as to some basic year-end tax planning strategies commonly used by tax accountants.

Highlights of this hour include

- Medical savings accounts
- Taxation of Social Security benefits
- Special tips for small businesses
- Year-end tax planning ideas

Medical Savings Accounts

The medical savings account (MSA) was introduced in 1997 for a trial period that is to extend to the year 2000. A medical savings account resembles an IRA, except you are permitted to take money out of it for medical expenses that aren't covered by health insurance.

The MSA is available to self-employed individuals and to businesses having fewer than 50 employees. It is designed to operate in conjunction with a high-deductible health insurance plan. To be considered a high-deductible plan, the policy must have a deductible of at least $1,500 for a single person and $3,000 for a married individual.

The MSA is generally established as a tax-exempt trust or a custodial account. You can either make tax-free contributions to the MSA maintained by your health insurance provider, or your employer can make them for you.

The maximum contribution that you can make is based on the deductible required under the health insurance plan. For an individual, the contribution amount is 65% of the plan's deductible. For a married person, the contribution limit is 75% of the plan's deductible.

Because the amounts contributed to the MSA are not taxable to you, they do not appear on your W-2 Form and need not be reported on your tax return. Distributions from the account for qualified medical expenses are reported on Form 1099-MSA, depicted in Figure 23.1.

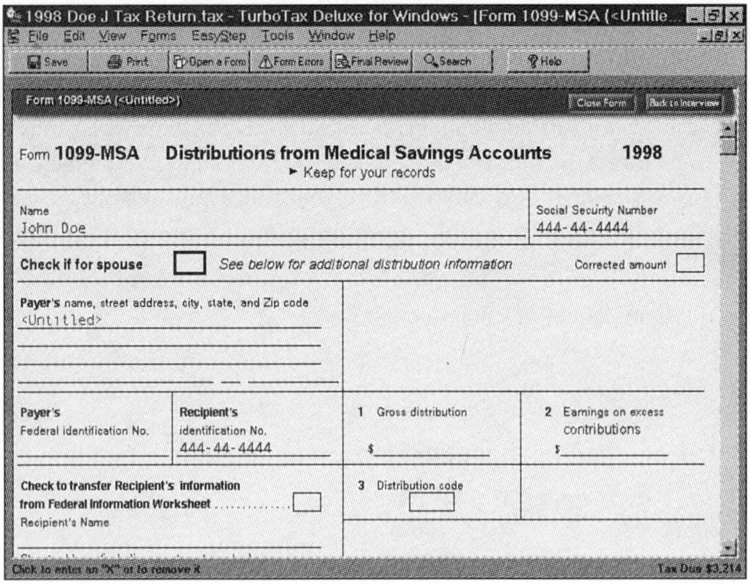

FIGURE 23.1.

Taxable distributions from an MSA account are reflected on this form.

Qualified medical expenses, for purposes of MSA account distributions, include just about any type of medical expense that you could deduct on Schedule A (except insurance premiums). The qualified medical expense must have been incurred *after* you were eligible to begin making contributions to your MSA account. For example, you cannot make a tax-free distribution to pay medical expenses incurred before January 1, 1998. If you withdraw the money other than to pay qualified medical expenses, the money is taxable to you and a hefty 15% penalty applies. The EasyStep Interview assists you in determining the tax treatment of distributions from your MSA account, as shown in Figure 23.2.

FIGURE 23.2.

TurboTax helps you determine the tax treatment of various types of MSA distribution based upon the code reflected on the Form 1099-MSA.

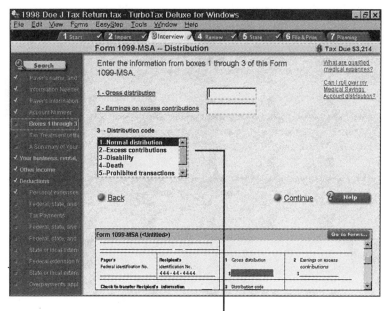

Distribution code

What happens if you don't use all the money in your MSA? All the money left at the end of the plan year carries over to the next plan year. The money is your money, which you can let grow tax-free until you are age 65. Upon reaching this age, you can withdraw the money and use it for any purpose tax-free.

Beware of a trap for the unwary! If you cease to maintain a high deductible health insurance plan, any undistributed MSA funds are immediately taxed to you and subject to a hefty 15% penalty.

Taxation of Social Security Benefits

Social Security benefits are a strange tax animal indeed. Each month you receive money from the government, only to have a portion of it taken back from you in the form of income tax. The amount of Social Security benefits that you received during the year is reported on your Form SSA-1099.

Also shown on the Form SSA-1099 are any Medicare premium payments made on your behalf that were deducted from your benefits earlier in the year. If you are itemizing your deductions, these amounts are reported on your Schedule A.

TurboTax automatically computes the taxable portion and the tax due on your Social Security benefits, if you enter the amount from your 1099-SSA on the screen shown in Figure 23.3.

FIGURE 23.3.

TurboTax prompts you to enter the relevant amounts from the 1099-SSA and automatically computes your tax liability.

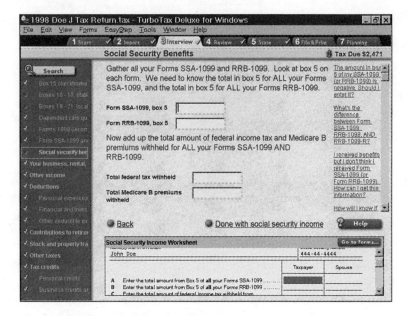

If your were computing your tax liability for Social Security benefits, the Internal Revenue Code prescribes a special two-tier tax calculation for doing so. The amount of your Social Security benefits that are taxable is the *lessor* of one-half of your Social Security benefits or the amount that you calculate using a the "first tier" calculation. The second tier is used to ensure that no more than 85% of your Social Security benefits are taxed.

The purpose of the first tier calculation is to find the *lessor* one-half of your Social Security benefits or the following calculated amount:

1. The sum of your adjusted gross income, one-half of your Social Security benefits, and tax exempt interest you received during the year.

2. Minus the "base amount" of $25,000 ($32,000 for married taxpayers filing jointly, or 0 if filing separately).

If you perform the first tier of the calculation and find that one-half of your Social Security benefits are less than the calculated amount, you do not need to perform the second tier of the calculation. Otherwise, if the calculated amount is more than one-half of your Social Security benefits, you need to perform the second tier calculation.

23

The second tier calculation is simply a matter of taking the *lessor* of (1) the first tier amount or (2) 85% of your total Social Security benefits.

The mechanics of the two-tier Social Security calculation are best illustrated by example. Assume that Tara received $10,000 of Social Security benefits in 1998. Assume further that Tara has an adjusted gross income of $25,000 and a tax-exempt interest income of $1,500. Tara has $3,250 of taxable Social Security benefits computed as follows:

Adjusted Gross Income	$25,000
Add: Tax Exempt Interest	$1,500
Add: $\frac{1}{2}$ Social Security	$5,000
Subtotal	$31,500
Less: Tier 1 Base Amount	($25,000)
Excess over Base Amount	$6,500
Multiplied by 50%	$3,250

The Tier 1 calculated amount ($3,250) is less than one-half of Tara's Social Security benefits and less than 85% of the total Social Security benefits pursuant to the Tier 2 calculation.

This complicated calculation is best avoided by using the EasyStep Interview.

Special Tips for Small Businesses

Small business owners have the opportunity to deduct many expenses that are unavailable to people who are employed. Most commonly, Schedule C filers avail themselves of home office deductions, automobile expenses, and so on. The next section shines a spotlight on some more sophisticated lesser known tax opportunities for small businesses.

Hiring Family Members

Nepotism results in definite tax advantages if you are a Schedule C filer and have children under the age of 18. You can hire your children to do any type of work that you pay others to do. You and your children are exempt from the requirement of withholding and paying Social Security tax. Moreover, there is no federal (and generally no state) income tax imposed upon the first $4,250 of their earnings.

The implications of this are that you can deduct $4,250 of payments that you make to your children as a business expense, and you do not have to withhold taxes. Neither do your children have to pay tax on their earnings. However, there are a few caveats.

First, the amounts that your children are paid for their services must be reasonable. The federal minimum wage is a defensible amount for this purpose. Second, the work itself must be reasonable. It must be—well, work. Cleaning, filing, and answering telephones are reasonable activities for which to compensate your child based upon their skill level.

If your children put $2,000 of their earnings in a Roth IRA, these amounts are permitted to grow tax-free until their retirement. Upon retirement, they can make tax-free withdrawals and thus *never* have to pay tax on their wages.

Self-Employed Health Insurance Deduction

If you are self-employed, you can opt to write off 40% of your health insurance costs as an adjustment (that is, a direct reduction) of your income. This is more advantageous than taking the premium cost as an itemized deduction on Schedule A because you don't have to meet the 7.5% floor, as discussed in Hour 13, "Non-Business Deductions."

If you have more than one Schedule C business, you must allocate your health insurance costs among them.

The Section 179 Expense Deduction

In 1998 you can elect to write off $18,500 of assets that you would normally be required to depreciate. Expensing the assets immediately is more advantageous than depreciating them, which entails deducting a portion of their original cost over a number of years. This type of deduction is called a Section 179 expense. It is also sometimes referred to as first year expensing. The amount that taxpayers may take is being increased each year and will reach $25,000 in the year 2003.

You may expense only the portion of the asset that is used for business purposes. For example, if your computer is used 80% for business and 20% for personal use, you may expense only 80% of the purchase price.

You cannot claim a Section 179 deduction for property that is with a business use percentage of less than 50%. You can only claim the deduction for tangible personal property. You cannot claim a Section 179 deduction for amounts in excess of the income generated from your Schedule C business.

Additionally, you must have paid for the item in cash rather than acquired it in an exchange for another asset. You also may not expense property purchased from a spouse, parent, or child.

The Section 179 deduction is a tremendous tax benefit, even if the rules do seem complicated. TurboTax Interview screens, such as the one shown in Figure 23.4, ensure that you do not inadvertently claim a deduction for property that is not eligible for the election.

FIGURE 23.4.

TurboTax guides you through the section 179 requirements and calculates the amount of the deduction.

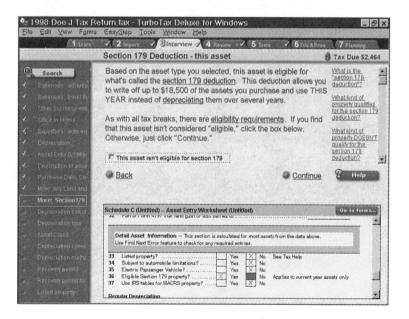

Consider a Subchapter S Corporation

If you file a Schedule C and have a substantial investment in a profitable business, you may be able to save some self-employment taxes by incorporating your business. Generally, small businesses of 75 or fewer shareholders form Subchapter S corporations.

Shareholder/owners of Subchapter S corporations may elect to receive a portion of the return from their businesses as dividends rather than salary. Dividends are subject to income taxes, but not the 15.3% self-employment tax.

If you do incorporate, you are required to file two income tax returns each year: one for the corporation and one for yourself. Additionally, IRS regulations and precedents require that you must pay yourself a reasonable salary. In other words, you cannot opt to pay yourself dividends that replace your salary entirely; you must pay yourself salary equal to the fair market value of your services. Any amount above and beyond the reasonable salary is appropriately characterized as a return on investment and may be treated as a dividend that is exempt from the self-employment tax.

Year-End Tax Planning Tips

In addition to making your estimated payments throughout the year, it is a good idea to take stock of your tax situation at year-end. Generally, most year-end tax planning strategies are based on the fundamental principle of deferring income into a later year and accelerating deductions to the current year. The following are just a few of the many last-minute planning strategies that can save you from having to write a larger than expected check on April 15:

- Pay two years of mortgage and real estate taxes in a single year. This is an especially effective strategy if you are a taxpayer whose deductions are just under the standard deduction amount but can be brought over by "bunching" two years worth of real estate and mortgage payments into one year. Pursuant to this strategy, it enables you to maybe itemize every other year (as opposed to not at all).

- Bill your customers for November and December services after January 1.

- Defer payment of any bonus to which you are entitled to next year.

- Buy some equipment eligible for the section 179 deduction before year-end.

- Prepay business travel, training, publications, and other expenses that you expect to incur just after the close of the taxable year.

- Make some last-minute charitable contributions.

- Prepay your state income taxes.

- Contribute to your 401(k), SEP, IRA, SIMPLE, or Keogh Account (see Hour 22, "IRAs, Pension Plans, and Annuities").

- Have a Christmas party for your employees.

Other tax planning strategies are appropriate at any time of the year. For example, you should be aware of opportunities for tax-free investing. Are you better off at tax time with a municipal bond with a lower rate of return than with a fully taxable mutual fund, despite a lower rate of return? Also, be sure to watch your capital gains holding periods, discussed in Hour 12, "Income from the Sale of Property." You may be able to save substantial taxes simply by waiting a few weeks or months to sell an asset.

In any event, you should consult the resources available to you. There is a wealth of publications and newspaper columns devoted to tax planning, and you can find seminars offered in most locales. Your accountant may even sponsor one.

Summary

This hour provided a discussion of some advanced tax planning topics that do not fit neatly into other categories. The medical savings account is a hybrid between the IRA and medical expense deduction. It provides an excellent opportunity to defer additional income taxes above and beyond what you are permitted to deduct using an IRA account. Social Security benefits may be taxable, but the test for determining their tax treatment is cumbersome and best left to TurboTax. Small businesses can derive special tax benefits by hiring family members, availing themselves of the Section 179 expense deduction, and taking health insurance premiums as adjustments rather than Schedule A itemized deductions. Finally, this hour concludes with a list of last-minute tax planning strategies that can benefit everyone.

23

Q&A

Q When hiring family members, there is an exemption from Social Security taxes for a minor child under the age of 18. Is there any type of corresponding exemption for a spouse?

A No, you must withhold Social Security payments from the wages of a spouse who is on your payroll. One strategy, however, that may be helpful if you both work for the business is to have one spouse not take a salary at all. You can then increase the salary of the other spouse. You do not need to withhold the 12.4% Social Security tax for any amounts over $68,400 that the employed spouse earns. (See Hour 10 for more information on the self-employment tax and Social Security wage base.)

Q Can I prepay unlimited amounts of business expenses in advance to accelerate the deduction for them into the current year?

A The prepayment strategy does not work well for expenses that extend beyond one year. These types of prepayments are considered assets that must be amortized (expensed) over their useful lives.

Hour 24

All About Audits

This hour explores an anxiety producing topic that is guaranteed to evoke a response from every taxpayer. Who doesn't silently curse an envelope that bears an IRS return address when they're *not* expecting a refund check?

Concern about being audited is entirely understandable, even if you have taken only the most defensible positions on your income tax return. Many audits are random, meaning they are not triggered by the information on the return. Other audits are precipitated by taxpayer error, omitted information, or items on the return that vary significantly from national averages. This hour, to some extent, assists you in minimizing the potential for having your return selected for audit.

Highlights of this hour include

- How the IRS is structured
- How returns are selected for audit
- The IRS screening process
- Using TurboTax to avoid audits
- The Taxpayer Bill of Rights
- Other tips for avoiding audits

Some Insights About How the IRS Is Set Up

The parts of the IRS with which taxpayers interact are known as service centers. There are several service centers located throughout the country. You file your tax returns with the center located closest to you. After your return arrives at the service center, it is initially checked for accuracy.

Incorrectly added numbers trigger, at the very least, a letter from the IRS. This is sometimes referred to as a correspondence audit, as discussed later this hour. You can attempt to call the IRS to resolve the matter if it is relatively simple. The correspondence generally provides a number for you to call. But before relying upon the telephone to resolve an issue with the IRS, you want to consider how the IRS service centers are set up.

The agency employs highly specialized people to deal with specific tax issues, such as home office deductions or automobile expenses. These people are experts on the issues in their area. But they are *not* the people that you reach by telephone. You speak with someone who has access to your file and is trained solely for answering telephone inquiries. In other words, the person on the telephone is someone who is trained to handle calls and not someone who is specialized in the area of tax that you are questioning them about. Surveys have shown an alarming number of incorrect answers by IRS personnel in response to seemingly simple taxpayer inquiries.

Do not rely upon the IRS for sophisticated telephone advice, or attempt to resolve complicated tax matters by phone. In fact, do not call the IRS for anything more complicated than a request for a specific form.

There is one exception to the general rule of not attempting to solve problems with the IRS by telephone. Under certain circumstances, you may find it helpful to contact the IRS Problems Resolution Staff. Problems Resolution personnel are stationed in local service centers and IRS offices all over the country are actually specialized in solving taxpayer problems. If you want the Problems Resolution division to take on your matter, it's best to have a good paper trail beforehand.

Try contacting the Problems Resolution personnel if you are the victim of a computer error of some sort, *and* more than one attempt to handle the matter by the correspondence has been unsuccessful.

How Returns Are Selected for Audit

In 1997, the IRS audited about 1% of all returns filed. Because about 155 million tax returns were filed, more than 2 million taxpayers and businesses had to provide documentation to back up the items claimed on their tax returns. And collectively, those selected paid something in the neighborhood of $28 billion in additional revenue. A return may be selected for audit up to three years after filing and remains available for audit for the full three years.

Who Is Most Likely to Be Audited?

Although there are no statistics, it is common knowledge that self-employed individuals are much more likely to be audited than persons who have all their income summarized on a W-2. Also, the higher the income, the greater the statistical likelihood of being targeted. A person with taxable income in excess of $100,000 has a three times greater chance of being audited than someone with income of less than $25,000.

The *type* of deductions that you take may also increase your audit odds. Certain deductions, such as a home office and automobile related expenses, are carefully scrutinized by the IRS, as discussed in Hour 10, "Taxation of a Business." It's to your advantage to maintain scrupulous documentation concerning these deductions if you take them.

Geography is another factor. A taxpayer in San Francisco is three times more likely to be audited than someone from Milwaukee, Wisconsin. Possibly because San Francisco has a much higher proportion of self-employed entrepreneurs.

Finally, sheer luck is a factor. The IRS randomly selects a certain proportion of returns each year for random audit. Random audits are not specifically based on the information that appears on the returns.

The IRS Screening Process

All returns are put through an initial screening process to determine whether they are selected for audit. Table 24.1 contains a partial list of factors that can heighten your chances of winning this unlucky lottery.

TABLE 24.1. TAXPAYER ERRORS THAT INCREASE AUDIT POTENTIAL.

Type of Error	What the IRS is Looking For
Incorrect Social Security Number; Failure to Sign Form	All returns are electronically screened for this purpose.
Missing Forms and Schedules	Your amounts may be correct, but the IRS wants to know how you arrived at them.

continues

TABLE 24.1. CONTINUED

Type of Error	What the IRS is Looking For
Math Errors	Small mathematical errors can prove costly! Statistically, a return that contains one or more mathematical errors is likely to contain other errors.
Incorrect Filing Status	The IRS wants to make sure that married people don't try to claim single filing status, that people who claim Head of Household status are entitled to it, and so on.

The IRS also uses a complicated statistical analysis of the information contained on the returns. The Discriminate Factor System (DIF) is used to compare the information on your return against various statistical norms. For example, according to these norms it may be anticipated that a single woman living in Wisconsin having a $60,000 a year income makes charitable contributions and has itemized deductions within a certain range. Variations from the statistical norm, and controversial deductions such as a home office, are assigned points under a DIF scoring system. The higher the DIF score, the more likely an audit. If this Wisconsin taxpayer in our example has a disproportionate amount of charitable contributions and other deductions in relation to her income, the return is given a high DIF "score" and possibly selected for audit.

Using TurboTax to Avoid Audits

TurboTax review features are discussed in detail in Hour 17, "TurboTax Review Features." Because TurboTax automatically handles the calculations that are required for your return, the program then virtually eliminates the possibility that your return is flagged for mathematical errors.

Two other review features that help you avoid audits are Audit Alert function and the U.S. Averages review feature. Hour 17 covers how to use these features. These features are accessed from the screen shown in Figure 24.1.

FIGURE 24.1.

Access all or selected TurboTax Review features by checking the ones you want to use on this screen.

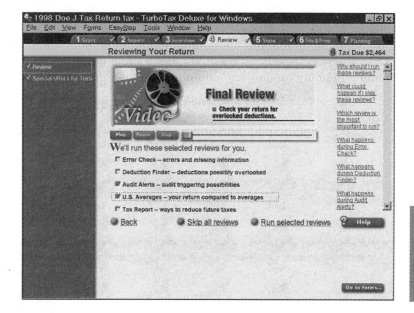

Types of Income Tax Audits

If you are singled out for audit, don't panic. The IRS, as discussed later in this hour, is required to tell you exactly which items they are questioning. And many audits do not result in "adjustments." If your return is selected, you can expect one of the following three types of audit procedures: correspondence audits, office audits, or field audits.

Correspondence Audits

A correspondence audit is the inquiry of choice for most of us, because it does not involve an intimidating face to face meeting with a live IRS agent. The IRS notifies you via correspondence of a mathematical error or missing documentation. You can either accept the adjusted amount and pay it, or submit an explanation as to why you feel the IRS is in error.

Office Audits

An office audit is a bit more intimidating. You are invited to come into the IRS office with your records and supporting documents to meet with an IRS agent.

You have the right to be accompanied to the IRS office by an accountant, attorney, or enrolled agent who is certified to represent clients in IRS matters. Your rights to representation are further discussed in the following section.

Field Audits

Field audits are commonly conducted when the target of the audit is a business with voluminous records. In the interests of convenience, the audit is held at the taxpayer's place of business.

> Conventional wisdom has it that you want to avoid field audits. It is a definite advantage to be able to carefully compile requested information than have to pull them out on the spot at the bidding of your "guests."

What to Do If You Are Audited

The IRS initially notifies you by letter if you are the subject of an audit. The audit letter tells you which tax year is being reviewed and which items are the focus of the examination. The letter also tells you the type of audit and, if necessary, which records to bring. There are a few issues to consider after you receive an audit letter, including whether you will have representation, which information you should provide, and what rights you have in the process.

Decide on Representation

A CPA, a lawyer, or an enrolled agent can represent you before the IRS. They can even show up for you if you authorize them to do so by power of attorney. IRS Form 2848 is used for this purpose. If the IRS agent poses any questions you are unsure of, your representative can generally arrange to get back to the agent later. This is a commonly accepted practice.

> It is a good idea to designate a representative to appear at the audit for you if you are nervous or the type of person that just can't seem to formulate a brief answer to a question.

> When hiring representation for an audit, do not hesitate to ask for a written fee arrangement up front. Ask whether an hourly rate or a flat fee is charged. If the rate is hourly, ask the total estimated fee under different scenarios. This helps avoid misunderstandings. You should not feel awkward asking these questions if your tax advisor does not bring them up first.

Marshall Your Documentation

Review the audit letter to determine the items under review and the documentation that you need to substantiate them. For example, if your entertainment expenses are under review, you want to make sure you have all your receipts.

Occasionally, deductions have been taken for expenses that obviously were incurred, but you don't have exact substantiation as to the amount. The IRS may still allow the deduction if it is based upon a reasonable approximation. For example, you can work with the IRS to approximate the travel expenses between two office locations as closely as possible.

Provide Only Required Information

The correspondence that you receive from the IRS puts you on notice as to the matters under investigation; the IRS can ask you only about these items. However, if you begin to volunteer all information and documents that are not requested, the IRS has the right to delve into those matters as well. It is best to confine the scope of the audit by making sure that your answers are concise, correct, and accurate.

24

Exercise Your Rights

The IRS has a staggering array of powers over the nation's taxpayers. During the course of an audit the agency is permitted to do the following:

- Examine any of your books, papers, account information, or other records that are relevant to the information on the return.
- Summon you to appear at its office and provide information under oath.
- Summon third parties (such as your accountant, banker, or stockbroker) to provide information about you and your financial transactions.

These powers are formidable, indeed. However, they are not unlimited. In addition, you, as a taxpayer, are not without legal protections in the form of the Taxpayer Bill of Rights and Freedom of Information Act.

Taxpayer Bill of Rights

Technically, IRS audits are undertaken to "verify" information on returns, not for increasing tax collected. The agency maintains that its employees are specially trained to explain and to protect taxpayers' rights. A new Taxpayer Bill of Rights introduced in 1997 attempts to ensure that taxpayers are afforded certain protections.

You can obtain a copy of the lengthy Taxpayer Bill of Rights directly from the IRS. Some of the highlights of this legislation are as follows:

- You are entitled to courteous treatment from the IRS.
- You have a right to know why the IRS is requesting information from you.
- The IRS is not permitted to share your information or records that you provide to them with other government agencies.
- You have the right to have someone else represent you in meetings and communications with the IRS (for example, an accountant or an attorney).
- You have a right to tape record any meetings or communications with the IRS.

These new protections are calculated to improve the public image of the IRS. You should not hesitate to avail yourself of them, particularly the requirement that you must be informed as to which items on your return are under scrutiny and why the IRS is asking you for specific information.

Other Protections for Taxpayers

In addition to the new Bill of Rights, taxpayers can invoke an old standby, the Freedom of Information Act. Under the act, you can request information directly from the IRS to help you prepare for an audit. For example, if you receive a notice that the IRS thinks you understated your royalty income, you can request copies of the 1099-Misc Forms that contain information about this item directly from the IRS.

If the IRS has already audited your return for one of the previous two years and found no discrepancies, you may request that the audit be abandoned. If you notify the IRS of the previous futile audit(s) that resulted in no changes, the agency likely considers it a waste of time to bark up the same tree.

Summary

This hour provided you with some tips on how to avoid the audit process and how to weather it if you're not successful in doing so. Always remember that missing 1099 Forms and schedules and disproportionately high deductions can make you a more likely audit target. Other factors such as occupation, geography, and luck can also play a part. The IRS conducts three types of audits: correspondence, office, and field audits. You are entitled to be represented by an attorney, accountant, or an enrolled agent regardless of the type of audit. Additionally, taxpayers have a number of relatively new legal protections in the audit process as a result of the Taxpayer Relief Act of 1997.

Q&A

Q How long should I retain the records that I use to prepare my tax return?

A Generally, you should retain your records for at least three years from the due date of your return, because this is the period of time during which your return may be selected for audit. However, if the IRS determines that you *intentionally* misrepresented information on your return, there are no statute of limitations for audit.

Q If I am selected for audit in one year, how does this effect my chances of being audited in subsequent years?

A If the audit was random and resulted in no adjustments, you should not have an increased chance of being audited in future years. If an audit was precipitated by items on your return that were substantially higher or lower than the national averages, there is a good chance your return may be flagged again for the same thing. However, if the previous audit resulted in no adjustments, you may be able to convince the IRS that a subsequent one would also be a waste of time. If a previous audit *did* result in adjustments, the prevailing wisdom is that you are a target for repeated audits because the IRS hopes to find similar taxpayer errors in future returns.

24

PART VII
Appendixes

APPENDIX A

Glossary

active income   Income that is earned from employment or a business activity in which the taxpayer materially participated. See *material participation*.

adjusted gross income   The total of all income less various expenses attributable to the production of income, contributions to qualified plans and IRAs, alimony, moving expenses, and other adjustments identified in Internal Revenue Code Section 62. Adjusted gross income is the starting point for computing deductions that are based on, or limited by, a percentage of adjusted gross income.

alimony   Periodic payments made as the result of the dissolution of a marriage that are not child support or made pursuant to a division of property.

appreciated property   Property that has a fair-market value that is greater than its original purchase price.

at risk   At-risk rules limit the amount that can be deducted from a business activity to the amount of cash or the adjusted basis of property that a taxpayer contributed to the activity.

Audit   The process by which the Internal Revenue Service verifies the accuracy of items reported on a tax return.

capital gain dividends   A distribution to a shareholder of a corporation that represents a portion of the revenue derived from the sale of corporate assets.

capital loss carry forward   Losses from a prior year that could not be deducted in full during that year, which have reported and are deducted in a subsequent year.

casualty   A type of loss that meets the criteria of being sudden, unexpected, and unusual in nature. Examples of deductible casualty losses include those arising from fire, storm, shipwreck, or theft.

child support   Payments made specifically for the purpose of providing for the needs of a natural or adopted child subsequent to divorce or legal separation. These payments are distinguished from alimony by virtue of the purpose for which they are made.

correspondence audits   A type of audit pursuant to which the Internal Revenue Service verifies an item on a tax return by sending correspondence to a taxpayer requesting additional information.

costs of goods sold   The cost of producing or storing manufactured goods. This amount is subtracted directly from revenue on a Schedule C, to arrive at gross profit and/or gross income for the business reported on the Schedule C.

credits   Amounts that directly reduce the amount of tax due. Credits have the same effect as a payment with respect to reducing the amount of tax due.

custodial parent   For tax purposes, a parent with whom a child resides for more than half of the tax year.

Dependent   A person who meets the legal requirements necessary to be claimed as an additional exemption amount on your tax return for supporting them.

Depreciation   A deduction allowed for use and obsolescence of property that is taken ratably over the useful life of the property.

Discrimination Factor System (DIF)   The statistical scoring system used by the Internal Revenue Service to select returns for audit.

dividend income   The portion of earnings and profits of a corporation distributed to its shareholders.

earned income credit   A special tax credit available to low-income taxpayers having at least one qualifying child. Unlike most other credits, the earned income credit may be taken even if a taxpayer does not have a tax liability that exceeds the amount of the credit. It is sometimes referred to as a refundable credit.

election   A choice between two different options for reporting a taxable event or attribute, for example, a taxpayer may elect to take certain foreign taxes paid as a credit *or* a deduction.

employees Persons who perform work under the direction and control of their employer. Withholding of income and other payroll taxes is required for workers legally classified as employees.

enrolled agent A person who meets certain requirements established by the Internal Revenue Service for representing taxpayers before the agency.

entertainment expenses Expenses attributable to entertaining clients, prospective customers, or business associates for the purpose of furthering business communications or interests.

estimated payments Payments made during the year intended to approximate the taxpayer's year-end liability. Such payments are required and failure to make them in a timely manner results in underpayment penalties, unless you meet the criteria for one of the exceptions.

exemptions A deduction amount allowed for a taxpayer, taxpayer's spouse, and qualified dependents. This amount may be reduced or eliminated for high income taxpayers.

FICA taxes Social Security taxes required to be withheld from an employee's paycheck and matched by corresponding contributions from the employer pursuant to the Federal Insurance Contributions Act.

field audit An audit conducted by the Internal Revenue Service at the taxpayer's place of business.

FIFO An inventory tracking and expensing system that matches the oldest inventory purchases with current revenues. This results in higher reported revenue in times of increasing inventory costs.

filing status The category used to determine the tax rate applicable to a particular taxpayer based upon certain personal characteristics of the taxpayer.

Freedom of Information Act Federal law that requires governing and affording U.S. citizens' access to public records.

FUTA The Federal Unemployment Tax Act imposes a tax on all employers with employees who worked more than 20 weeks during the current or preceding calendar year, or paid wages of more than $1,500 at the rate of 6.2%. A partial credit is allowed for state unemployment tax liability.

gross income Income from all sources, however derived.

head of household A filing status available to single or legally separated taxpayers having at least one qualifying dependent. See *filing status*.

A

holding period   The length of time that an asset is owned by a taxpayer.

independent contractors   A person who performs work, but is not subject to the direction and control of an employer in carrying out responsibilities. An independent contractor is not subject to withholding.

installment sale   A sale of property for which payments are received over more than one tax period, and the appropriate amounts attributable to the returns of the taxpayer's basis and taxable income are recognized as appropriate.

interest   Any type of payments made in exchange for the use of money.

inventory   Assets held for sale or use by a business.

itemized deductions   Deductions specifically listed and totaled on Schedule A, subject to any applicable limits.

LIFO   An inventory tracking and expensing system that matches the most recent inventory purchases with current revenues. This results in lower reported revenue in times of increasing inventory costs.

material participation   Generally refers to any business activity in which the taxpayer worked for 500 hours or more during the tax year. Material participation refers to the criteria used to determine whether income from a business venture is considered earned (active) or unearned (passive). See *active income* and *passive income*.

medical savings account   A type of account similar to an IRA to which a taxpayer may make deductible contributions. A medical savings account must be maintained in conjunction with a high-deductible insurance plan.

miscellaneous deduction   A type of deduction that, when aggregated with other miscellaneous deductions, must exceed 2% of the taxpayer's adjusted gross income before it can be subtracted from adjusted gross income.

multiple support agreement   An agreement that authorizes a taxpayer to claim another as a dependent even though other taxpayers may also be eligible to do so.

Nexus   The legal connection or relationship of an individual to a particular state that enables that state to impose income taxes on the taxpayer.

office audit   A type of audit pursuant to which the taxpayer is asked to come to the Internal Revenue Service office to verify information on the taxpayer's return.

original discount interest   The excess of a bond or note's stated redemption price over its issue (purchase) price. This amount is considered taxable income.

passive income   Income that is not earned from employment or material participation in a business activity. See *material participation*.

self-employment tax   A Social Security and Medicare tax imposed on self-employed individuals at the rate of 15.3%.

sole proprietorship   A business owned by one taxpayer that reports its income and deductions on Schedule C included with the Form 1040 filed by the taxpayer.

standard deduction   A set amount that may be deducted by a taxpayer in lieu of itemizing deductions.

Sub-Chapter S Corporation   A small business corporation that has 35 or fewer shareholders, meets other requirements, and is afforded special tax treatment.

Taxpayer Bill of Rights   Federal legislation introduced in 1998 that affords taxpayers certain rights with respect to contact with the Internal Revenue Service, including the right to be informed as to the scope of the examination and the right to be treated with courtesy by the agency.

underpayment penalties   A penalty imposed for failure to pay sufficient estimated tax during the year.

wage base   The amount of wages used for a specific calculation.

A

APPENDIX B

State Tax Agencies

Alabama Department of Revenue
Income Tax Forms
P.O. Box 327410
Montgomery, AL 36132-7410
(334) 242-1000
www.ador.state.al.us

Alaska Department of Revenue
State Office Building
P.O. Box 110420
Juneau, AK 99811-0420
(907) 465-2320
www.revenue.state.ak.us

Arizona Department of Revenue
P.O. Box 29002
Phoenix, AZ 85038-9002
(602) 542-4260
www.revenue.state.az.us

Arkansas Department of Finance and Administration
Revenue Division
P.O. Box 3628
Little Rock, AR 72203
(501) 682-1100
www.state.ar.us/revenue/

California Franchise Tax Board
Tax Forms Request
P.O. Box 942840
Sacramento, CA 94240-0040
(800) 852-5711
www.ftb.ca.gov

Colorado Department of Revenue
1375 Sherman Street
Denver, CO 80261
(303) 232-2416
www.state.co.us

Connecticut Department of Revenue
State Tax Department
25 Sigourney Street
Hartford, CT 06106-5032
(800) 382-9463
www.state.ct.us/drs

Delaware Department of Finance
Division of Revenue
Delaware State Building
820 North French Street
Wilmington, DE 19801
(302) 577-8200
www.state.de.us/revenue

**District of Columbia Department
of Finance and Revenue**
Room 1046
300 Indiana Avenue, N.W.
Washington, D.C. 20001
(202) 727-6170
www.dccfo.com

Florida Department of Revenue
104 Carlton Building
Tallahassee, FL 32399-0100
(850) 488-5050
www.fcn.state.fl.us/dor/

Georgia Department of Revenue
507 Trinity-Washington Building
Atlanta, GA 30334
(404) 656-4188
www2.state.ga.us/Departments/DOR/

Hawaii Department of Taxation
830 Punchbowl Street
P.O. Box 259
Honolulu, HI 96809-0259
(800) 222-3229
www.state.hi.us/tax/tax.html

Idaho State Tax Commission
800 Park Boulevard, Plaza IV
Boise, ID 83722
(800) 972-7660
www2.state.id.us/tax/forms.htm

Illinois Department of Revenue
Willard Ice Building
101 W. Jefferson
Springfield, IL 62702
(800) 732-8866
www.revenue.state.il.us

Indiana Department of Revenue
100 North Senate
Room N105
Indianapolis, IN 46204-2253
(317) 233-4018
www.state.in.us/dor/

**Iowa Department of Revenue and
Finance**
Hoover State Office Building
Des Moines, IA 50319
(800) 367-3388
www.state.ia.us/government/drf/

Kansas Department of Revenue
Docking State Office Building
915 S.W. Harrison
Topeka, KS 66612
(785) 296-3909
www.ink.org/public/kdor/

Kentucky Revenue Cabinet
200 Fair Oaks Lane
Frankfort, KY 40620
(502) 564-4581
www.state.ky.us/agencies/revenue/
revhome.htm

Louisiana Department of Revenue
8490 Picardy Avenue
Building 600
Baton Rouge, LA 70809-3684
(225) 925-4611
www.rev.state.la.us

Maine Bureau of Taxation
Income Tax Section
State Office Building
Station 24
Augusta, ME 04332
(207) 624-7894
janus.state.me.us/revenue

Maryland Comptroller of the Treasury
Revenue Administration Division
Annapolis, MD 21411-0001
(800) 638-2937
www.comp.state.md.us

Massachusetts Department of Revenue
Customer Service Bureau
P.O. Box 7010
Boston, MA 02204
(800) 392-6089
www.state.ma.us/dor/dorpg.htm

Michigan Department of the Treasury
Revenue Administration Services
The Treasury Building
430 West Allegan Street
Lansing, MI 48922
(800) 367-6263
www.treas.state.mi.us

Minnesota Department of Revenue
Mail Station 7704
10 River Park Plaza
St. Paul, MN 55146-7704
(800) 652-9094
www.state.mn.us/ebranch/mdor/

Mississippi Department of Revenue
State Tax Commission
P.O. Box 1033
Jackson, MS 39215-3338
(601) 923-7000
www.mstc.state.ms.us/revenue/

Missouri Department of Revenue
P.O. Box 3022
Jefferson City, MO 65105-3022
(800) 877-6881
dor.state.mo.us

Montana Department of Revenue
Income Tax Division
P.O. Box 5805
Helena, MT 59604-5805
(406) 444-3674
www.mt.gov/revenue/rev.htm

Nebraska Department of Revenue
Nebraska State Office Building
301 Centennial Mall South
P.O. Box 94818
Lincoln, NE 68509-4818
(800) 742-7474
www.nol.org/revenue

Nevada Department of Taxation
Capitol Complex
Carson City, NV 89710-0003
(702) 687-4892

B

**New Hampshire Department of
Revenue**
P.O. Box 457
Concord, NH 03302-0457
(603) 271-2191
www.state.nh.us/revenue/
revenue.htm

New Jersey Division of Taxation
P.O. Box 269
Trenton, NJ 08646-0269
(609) 588-2200
www.state.nj.us/treasury/taxation

**New Mexico Taxation and Revenue
Department**
P.O. Box 630
Santa Fe, NM 87504-0630
(505) 827-2206
www.state.nm.us/tax/trd_form.htm

**New York Department of Taxation
and Finance**
Taxpayer Service Bureau
West Averell Harriman Campus
Albany, NY 12227
(800) 462-8100
www.tax.state.ny.us

**North Carolina Department of
Revenue**
P.O. Box 25000
Raleigh, NC 27640
(919) 715-0397
www.dor.state.nc.us/DOR

North Dakota
Office of the State Tax Commissioner
State Capitol
600 East Boulevard Avenue
Bismark, ND 58505-0599
(701) 328-2770
www.state.nd.us/taxdpt

Ohio Department of Taxation
Income Tax Division
P.O. Box 530
Columbus, OH 43266-0030
(614) 433-7750
www.state.oh.us/tax/

Oklahoma Tax Commission
Income Tax Division
P.O. Box 26800
Oklahoma City, OK 73126-0800
(405) 521-3160
www.oktax.state.ok.us

Oregon Department of Revenue
955 Center St., N.E.
Salem, OR 97310
(503) 378-4988
www.dor.state.or.us

Pennsylvania Department of Revenue
711 Gibson Boulevard
Harrisburg, PA 17104-3200
(888) 728-2937
www.revenue.state.pa.us

Rhode Island Division of Taxation
One Capitol Hill
Providence, RI 02908-5800
(401) 222-1111
www.tax.state.ri.us

South Carolina Tax Commission
Individual Income Tax Division
301 Gervais Street
P.O. Box 125
Columbia, SC 29214
(800) 763-1295
www.dor.state.sc.us

South Dakota Department of Revenue
445 E. Capitol Avenue
Pierre, South Dakota 57501
(800) 829-9188
www.state.sd.us/state/executive/
revenue/revenue.html

Tennessee Department of Revenue
Andrew Jackson State Office Building
500 Deaderick Street
Nashville, TN 37242
(615) 741-4465
www.state.tn.us/revenue

Texas
Comptroller of Public Accounts
111 East 17th Street
Austin, TX 78774
(512) 463-4600
www.window.texas.gov

Utah State Tax Commission
210 North 1950 West
Salt Lake City, UT 84134
(800) 662-4335
www.tax.ex.state.ut.us

Vermont Department of Taxes
109 State Street
Montpelier, VT 05609-1401
(802) 828-2865
www.state.vt.us/tax

Virginia Department of Taxation
Taxpayers Assistance
P.O. Box 1115
Richmond, VA 23218-1115
(804) 367-8031
www.state.va.us/tax/tax.html

Washington Department of Revenue
General Administration Building
P.O. Box 47478
Olympia, WA 98504-7478
(800) 647-7706
www.wa.gov/DOR/wador.htm

West Virginia State Tax Department
Taxpayer Service Division
P.O. Box 3784
Charleston, WV 25337-3784
(304) 558-3333
www.state.wv.us/taxrev

Wisconsin Department of Revenue
P.O. Box 8933
Madison, WI 53708-8933
(608) 266-1961
www.dor.state.wi.us

Wyoming Revenue Department
Herschler Building, 2nd Floor West
122 West 25th Street
Cheyenne, WY 82002-0110
(307) 777-7961
www.state.wy.us

B

APPENDIX C

Sample Mileage Log

Date	Beginning Odometer Reading	Ending Odometer Reading	Destination

Date	Beginning Odometer Reading	Ending Odometer Reading	Destination

INDEX

Symbols

X-Z